COMMUNITY TRANSLATION

Community translation or public service translation is on a global scale often unregulated and dependent on individual awareness, good will and even charity work. The social impact and mission of community translation, the key role of the translator's psycho-sociocultural awareness and its role depending on local and global changes in human migration and linguistic diversity make community translation a constantly evolving and yet under-investigated activity and profession. This book covers key practical and theoretical approaches towards community translation, providing insights into the current state of the field and the latest research, trends, guidelines, initiatives and gaps.

Combining knowledge in the area of translator ethics, pedagogy, legal and social and health-related settings, this volume covers community translation in a wide range of countries and regions. *Community Translation: Research and Practice* is an essential guide both for those studying and working in this area worldwide. This volume is a springboard for further studies and research in this emerging field.

Erika Gonzalez is a Senior Lecturer in Translating and Interpreting Studies at Royal Melbourne Institute of Technology (RMIT University), Australia, and a senior fellow of the Higher Education Academy (SFHEA) in the UK. She has served in the Executive of the Australian Institute of Interpreters and Translators (AUSIT) for several years and was the national president from 2019–2022. Erika is a practising conference interpreter and translator, as well.

Katarzyna Stachowiak-Szymczak is an adjunct professor at the University of Warsaw, Poland. She is also a practising translator and interpreter, as well as the co-founder of the Polish Association of Conference Interpreters.

Despina Amanatidou is a certified interpreter and translator (English > Greek) who works full time as a medical interpreter. She is also the Vice President of Events and Professional Development for the Australian Institute Interpreters and Translators (AUSIT).

COMMUNITY TRANSLATION

Research and Practice

Edited by Erika Gonzalez, Katarzyna Stachowiak-Szymczak and Despina Amanatidou

LONDON AND NEW YORK

Designed cover image: Getty Images | ajijchan

First published 2023
by Routledge
4 Park Square, Milton Park, Abingdon, Oxon OX14 4RN

and by Routledge
605 Third Avenue, New York, NY 10158

Routledge is an imprint of the Taylor & Francis Group, an informa business

© 2023 selection and editorial matter, Erika Gonzalez, Katarzyna Stachowiak-Szymczak and Despina Amanatidou; individual chapters, the contributors

The right of Erika Gonzalez, Katarzyna Stachowiak-Szymczak and Despina Amanatidou to be identified as the authors of the editorial material, and of the authors for their individual chapters, has been asserted in accordance with sections 77 and 78 of the Copyright, Designs and Patents Act 1988.

With the exception of Chapter 10, no part of this book may be reprinted or reproduced or utilised in any form or by any electronic, mechanical, or other means, now known or hereafter invented, including photocopying and recording, or in any information storage or retrieval system, without permission in writing from the publishers.

Chapter 10 of this book is available for free in PDF format as Open Access from the individual product page at www.routledge.com. It has been made available under a Creative Commons Attribution-Non Commercial-No Derivatives 4.0 license.

Trademark notice: Product or corporate names may be trademarks or registered trademarks, and are used only for identification and explanation without intent to infringe.

British Library Cataloguing-in-Publication Data
A catalogue record for this book is available from the British Library

ISBN: 978-1-032-16167-9 (hbk)
ISBN: 978-1-032-16162-4 (pbk)
ISBN: 978-1-003-24733-3 (ebk)

DOI: 10.4324/9781003247333

Typeset in Times New Roman
by Apex CoVantage, LLC

CONTENTS

List of Contributors   vii
Foreword   x
Acknowledgements   xii

Introduction   1

1 Challenges in Community Translation Service Provision: The Australian Perspective   5
Erika Gonzalez and Despina Amanatidou

2 The Battle to Intervene: Constrained Advocacy for Community Translators   23
David Katan and Cinzia Spinzi

3 Translators' Ethics in Community Translation: A Case Study of English–Japanese Translators in the Australian System   42
Maho Fukuno

4 You Don't See What I See: Assessing Contextual Meanings in Translated Health Care Texts in New Zealand   68
Wei Teng

5 Speak My Language! The Important Role of Community Translation in the Promotion of Health Literacy   101
Ineke Crezee and Hoy Neng Wong Soon

6 Community Translation for Oncological and Palliative Care   142
  Katarzyna Stachowiak-Szymczak and Karolina Stachowiak

7 Challenges and Constraints in the Translation of
  Wiretapping in Spain   167
  Mohamed El-Madkouri Maataoui and Beatriz Soto Aranda

8 Life Stories in Translation: Community Translators as
  Cultural Mediators   181
  Marija Todorova

9 The Voices of Migrant Families: (Auto)biography,
  Testimonio, Service-Learning, and Community Translation   194
  Alicia Rueda-Acedo

10 The Multilingual Community Translation Classroom:
   Challenges and Strategies to Train Profession-Ready
   Graduates   212
   Miranda Lai and Erika Gonzalez

Index   *230*

CONTRIBUTORS

Despina Amanatidou is a certified interpreter and translator (English > Greek) who works full time as medical interpreter and has more than 11 years of experience. Despina has been a member of the Australian Institute Interpreters and Translators (AUSIT) since 2016. She currently serves in the AUSIT's executive board as vice-president for events and professional development.

Ineke Crezee is well known for her work on health interpreter/translator education. She is Aotearoa New Zealand's first full professor of translation and interpreting, and in 2020 was made an Officer of the New Zealand Order of Merit for her services to interpreter and translator education.

Mohamed El-Madkouri Maataoui holds two doctorates from Universidad Autónoma de Madrid and from Universidad Complutense de Madrid. He is a full professor attached to the Department of Linguistics at Universidad Autónoma de Madrid. He has more than 80 publications. His areas of research interest include linguistics applied to translation, traductology and critical discourse.

Maho Fukuno is a PhD candidate in translation studies at the School of Literature, Languages and Linguistics, Australian National University. Her project explores how translators negotiate their subjectivity and ethical roles by examining translators' narratives on English–Japanese community translation. She is also an English > Japanese translator certified by the National Accreditation Authority for Translators and Interpreters (NAATI).

Erika Gonzalez is an associate professor in translating and interpreting studies at the Royal Melbourne Institute of Technology (RMIT University) in Australia. She was the national president of the Australian Institute of Interpreters and Translators (AUSIT) from 2019–2022. Her research interests focus on the professionalisation of community interpreting and translation, pedagogy and work-integrated learning. Erika is also a senior fellow of the Higher Education Academy (SFHEA). Her major publications lie in the fields of intercultural mediation, translation, corpus linguistics and public service interpreting.

David Katan is a professor of English and translation at the University of Salento (Lecce), specialising in intercultural communication. Publications include *Translating Cultures* (third edition), contributions for the Routledge encyclopaedias of translation and conflict, and translation and globalisation, and for the Benjamins *Handbook of Translation Studies*.

Miranda Lai is a senior lecturer in interpreting and translating studies at the Royal Melbourne Institute of Technology (RMIT University) in Australia. Her research interests include translating and interpreting pedagogy, police interpreting, ethics for interpreters and translators, and interpreters' vicarious trauma and self-care.

Alicia Rueda-Acedo is an associate professor at the University of Texas at Arlington (UTA). She has extensive publications in transatlantic and feminist literature and literary journalism. She is the director of the Spanish Translation and Interpreting programme at UTA, a programme oriented towards community translation and service-learning.

Beatriz Soto Aranda earned her PhD degree in linguistics (2003) from Universidad Autónoma de Madrid (2003) and her PhD in translation and interpreting (2017) from Universidad Jaume I (UJI Thesis Award). She is currently an associate professor of Arabic-Spanish translation at Rey Juan Carlos University, where she has been the director of the Master's in Legal Translation and Court Interpreting and Coordinator of the Bachelor's in Translation and Interpreting. Her research interests include postcolonial, legal and Children and Young Adults (CYA) literature translation.

Cinzia Spinzi is an associate professor at the University of Bergamo. She holds a PhD in *English for Specific Purposes*, a Master's in translation studies from the University of Birmingham and a research fellowship from City University of London.

Karolina Stachowiak, MD, graduated from the Poznań University of Medical Sciences and completed her medical internship at the Hospital of the Ministry of the Interior and Administration in Poznań. Her interests include psychiatry and research in improving the physician-patient relationship and cooperation.

Katarzyna Stachowiak-Szymczak, PhD, MSc, works as an adjunct professor at the University of Warsaw. Her research interests revolve around the cognitive aspects of interpreting and standards in the conference and the work of community interpreters and translators. As a teacher, she focuses on introducing new tools and methods for students at the master's level, at the same time being engaged in teaching simultaneous and consecutive interpreting, as well as medical and technical translation. She is also is a practising translator and interpreter, with experience in remote and distance work, as well as the co-founder of the Polish Association of Conference Interpreters and a member of the Polish Committee for Standardization.

Wei Teng, a NAATI-certified interpreter, is a lecturer of translation/interpreting studies and Chinese language at the University of Canterbury in New Zealand. His research focuses primarily on the area of community translation/interpreting, with particular interest in pragmatic equivalence, pragmalinguistic failures and contrastive analysis within the framework of systemic functional linguistics.

Marija Todorova is a research assistant professor at the Department of Translation, Interpreting and Intercultural Studies at Hong Kong Baptist University. She has authored *Translation of Violence in Children's Literature* (Routledge 2022) and co-edited *Interpreting Conflict* (Springer 2021). She is editor of *New Voices in Translation Studies*.

Hoy Neng Wong Soon is of Samoan and Chinese descent. She was born, raised and educated in Samoa before moving to Aotearoa New Zealand for tertiary education at the Auckland University of Technology. Hoy Neng is a qualified interpreter and translator (health and legal). She has been working as an interpreter for many organisations, in a variety of settings including forensic psychiatry and other mental health settings. She is one of the youngest Samoan translators and a reviewer of many translated texts in Aotearoa New Zealand and abroad.

FOREWORD

It is pleasing to note that there is a growing interest in community translation, as this edited volume and other recent publications demonstrate. This area of translation studies and translation practice has not received sufficient attention in the past – at least not as much attention as required by its social role and its contribution to social justice and cohesion. *Community Translation: Research and Practice* is therefore a welcome addition to the growing body of literature.

The special nature and social significance of community translation require interdisciplinary research into a number of areas including, most importantly, the role, training and socialisation of translators, quality assurance and professional standards, dissemination media for translated contents and the impact of community translation on different aspects of society, especially key areas such as health care literacy and civic engagement. I am pleased to note that the chapters in this volume address a number of these issues. David Katan and Cinzia Spinzi (Chapter 2), as well as Maho Fukuno (Chapter 3), for example, deal with the role of community translators. Miranda Lai and Erika Gonzalez (Chapter 10) examine translator training. Chapter 5 by Ineke Crezee and Hoy Neng Wong Soon, as well as Chapter 4 by Wei Teng, address health care translations and their role in the promotion of health literacy. Marija Todorova's Chapter 8 takes us away from the typical view of community translation as the translation of public service texts to the translation of asylum seekers' narratives as an interaction with their new sociocultural context and a pathway towards their social integration and intercultural connectiveness. Thus, groups whose members are usually thought of as translation users become text producers, which reminds us of the bidirectionality of community translation.

To highlight just a couple of contributions in this volume, David Katan's point about the advocacy and agency of community translators throws us into the ongoing controversy about detachment and agency, but in a context (community translation) where agency should be less problematic. Community translators often find themselves torn between the expectations of public services and professional bodies, on the one hand, and the requirements of community translation as a special area of practice and the expectations of end users, on the other hand. It is interesting to note that Katan calls for "constrained advocacy". It is also worth remarking that he calls on community translators to develop emotional competencies, which would equip them to embark upon "the battle to intervene" as intercultural mediators or transcreators. Closely related to this is Ineke Crezee and Hoy Neng Wong Soon's contribution about community translation and health literacy. It is well known that language barriers create other barriers in multilingual societies where community languages do not have the same status. Health care is one of the most important areas in which community translation can make a difference by breaking language barriers and facilitating access to information and health literacy. It is an area in which language is expected to be scientific, neutral and precise, but at the same time, translations are expected to be meaningful, culturally appropriate and accessible to community end users. The authors take us through the challenges associated with such communicative situations, and do so with innovative dissemination methods, focusing on a language (Samoan) that is not often covered in community translation literature.

Once again, this edited volume is a welcome addition to the developing body of scholarly publications on community translation. I hope that work on the volume and the exchanges that usually take place as part of the editing process will further strengthen international links between the authors. International and interdisciplinary collaboration is sorely needed to advance research, education and professional practice in this area.

Sydney, 4 July 2022
Associate Professor Mustapha Taibi
Western Sydney University

ACKNOWLEDGEMENTS

First and foremost, we would like to express our sincere gratitude to the colleagues who have entrusted us with their chapters. We thank them for their hard work and their patience, and for promptly responding to our various requests for revisions.

A great deal of appreciation is reserved to the many reviewers of this volume for their time and effort. We are much obliged for the thoughtful comments and insights they provided to the authors. This endeavour would not have been the same without the expert suggestions and feedback of Uldis Ozolins (Royal Melbourne Institute of Technology, Australia), Anne Beichnet (Université de Moncton, Canada), Jim Hlavac (Monash University, Australia), Catherine Way (Universidad de Granada, Spain), Simo Maatta (University of Helsinki, Finland), Elisabet Tiselius (Stockholm University, Sweden), Andrew Revolta (University of Westminster, United Kingdom), Brooke Townsley (Middlesex University, United Kingdom), Michael Carl (Kent State University, United States), Olga García-Caro (Royal Melbourne Institute of Technology, Australia), Anna Jelec (Adam Mickiewicz University, Poland) and Agnieszka Biernacka (University of Warsaw, Poland). Finally, we would like to acknowledge our research assistant Pearl Amadieu for her excellent work with the edition and proofreading of the volume.

Finally, we would like to recognise the publishers at Routledge for the opportunity to work on this project, and in particular, our editorial assistant Talitha Duncan-Todd for her assistance and guidance.

INTRODUCTION

The publication of this book has its roots in the 2nd International Conference on Community Translation hosted at RMIT University, Melbourne in December 2019. The conference was organised by the International Community Translation Research Group (ICTRG) and the Australian Institute of Interpreters and Translators (AUSIT). This volume represents a compilation of some of the papers presented at the conference. It also includes chapters that were not initially presented at the conference but offer additional insight into the current state of community translation.

Community translation starts with a text published by a "social agent" (Taibi, 2011) that needs to be accessed by the members of a language minority in a given country or region. These may be official documents and informative materials produced by local and national authorities, hospitals, courts, ethnic leaders, etc., to reach a multilingual community (Taibi, 2011). Community translation grants speakers of minority languages the right to access public information and ensures efficient communication among the members of a community (Taibi, 2011). In some countries, community translation is officially offered to citizens, immigrants, visitors, and refugees at a local and/or national level. However, in many other countries, it remains unregulated and dependent on individual awareness, good will and even charity work. Community translation responds to the linguistic diversity prompted by local and global changes in human migration, and it plays an increasingly important role in culturally and linguistically diverse societies. Yet, community translation remains an under-researched activity and profession.

Despite being an established subdiscipline of translation studies, research on community translation continues to be neglected. Kelly (2014) referred to community translation as "the poor sister of a poor sister" (as cited in Taibi & Ozolins, 2016, p. 17), the latter being community interpreting, illustrating the only partially successful attempts of service providers to establish community translation as a profession. As a research area, community translation could be described in a similar way, since there is still a paucity of studies and training material, despite a relatively rapid growth in demand for this type of translation.

This demand has further increased in recent years. A few months after the 2nd International Conference on Community Translation, the world faced a global-scale pandemic that saw national borders shut and millions of people confined to their homes. Governments were faced with unprecedented public health challenges, and in many multilingual societies, the diffusion of public health information related to the COVID-19 pandemic became a key issue. In this context, community translation fulfilled a strategic role and brought to light the importance of multilingual communication policies.

However, community translation has not only been in the spotlight because of its essential contribution to health literacy but often because of translation or dissemination errors. The importance of this is crucial, as there are country-dependent differences in community translation status. While Australia pioneers in the professionalisation of community translation – having introduced a five-level certification system administered by the National Accreditation Authority for Translators and Interpreters (NAATI) – standards are only selectively implemented in other countries, and in many cases, community translation remains unregulated. In some parts of the world, translation exists in community settings without being properly recognised as community translation or as a profession. For this reason, there is a strong need to both standardise and study community translation.

The volume starts with Chapter 1 by Erika Gonzalez and Despina Amanatidou, who present the way in which community translation was rendered by public and private language service providers (LSPs) in Australia amidst the COVID-19 pandemic. Having conducted a survey among LSPs, they discuss and find possible areas for improvement in translator recruitment, project organisation, managing high-demand languages and scaling budgets and expectations towards the final product. The authors formulate clear recommendations on how to tackle the four main gaps they identify. To borrow an example from González and Amanatidou, remuneration should mirror translator education and certification level, which promotes training and upskilling. This chapter constitutes an accurate update of the state of community translation in Australia and can also be used as a guide for LSPs and related institutions, as well as private parties and local authorities worldwide.

In Chapter 2, the role of the translator as an advocate is discussed by David Katan and Cinzia Spinzi, who present community translation as intercultural mediation. The authors portray translation as a form of reader-dependent intervention on the source text and propose that translators should be skilled in what they refer to as "constrained advocacy". This chapter also comments on extralinguistic skills translators should possess, such as empathy and assertiveness.

In Chapter 3, Maho Fukuno takes a slightly different approach, discussing the community translator's role and ethics, albeit from the translator's perspective. The author collected questionnaire responses from Australian NAATI-certified translators on perceived responsibility for the target text, impartiality, and advocative role, among other topics. These were compared with responses from translators who were trained in Japan and not NAATI-certified. The chapter ends with comments on how to implement the results both in Australia and abroad, which constitutes a valuable source of information and inspiration for countries and communities with less advanced certification systems than Australia.

In Chapter 4, Wei Teng focuses on objective methods of evaluating the quality of community translations. The rationale behind his discussion lies in different perceptions of what is considered a high-quality translation by translators and end-readers. Wei Teng proposes an innovative model of assessing translation alongside four quality dimensions, thus introducing new ways of looking at the translation product, with implications for teaching and practice. At the same time, this chapter shows that the reader's perception plays a valuable role in identifying what is considered a high-quality translation.

Chapter 5 by Ineke Crezee and Hoy Neng Wong Soon explores the role of linguistic diversity and community translation in the promotion of health literacy. The authors analyse common misunderstandings of medical language and other challenges in community translation for health care. Crezee also reports on interesting solutions to ensure multilingual communication with patients, such as the use of patient navigators or talking cards. This chapter constitutes an extremely valuable input into bridging the gap between community translation and health literacy.

The topic of community translation for health care is continued by Katarzyna Stachowiak-Szymczak and Karolina Stachowiak in Chapter 6. Having discussed community translation policies and quality assurance, the authors delve into community translation for oncological and palliative care. The chapter also reports on two studies that point to potential challenges in community translation for health care, as well as the importance of briefing community translators who work in health care settings.

Chapter 7 delves into guarantee and quality of translated wiretap materials. Mohamed El-Madkouri Maataoui and Beatriz Soto Aranda analyse the wiretapping translation market and legal framework in Spain, as well as professional requirements for translators in this field. The chapter starts with a picture of community translation as an unregulated profession in Spain. The authors comment on threats to translation quality which are rooted in translation outsourcing and the selection of translators with inadequate credentials. They continue by describing the working conditions of translators and the related psychological burden. Chapter 7 points out the importance of ensuring both quality translation and translator wellbeing.

In Chapter 8, Marija Todorova discusses the role of community translators as cultural mediators who communicate the narratives of refugees and asylum seekers to a wider audience, and their role as advocates for these storytellers. This chapter shows the important role translation plays in shaping and understanding the cultural and ethnic landscape of a given community.

Chapter 9 by Alicia Rueda-Acedo gives insight into the symbiotic relationship between academic and local communities in the process of community translation. The author reports on a student service-learning project centred on translating the stories of migrant families from Spanish into English. By participating in the translation of a story collection, students gain real-life experience prior to graduation. Translating the collection benefited both the academic faculty and the local community by making it accessible in English and therefore to a larger readership. By examining the process of translation and collaboration between parties, Alicia Rueda-Acedo shows possible market-oriented teaching solutions and ways to increase awareness about both community translation and socially important subjects.

In the closing Chapter 10, Miranda Lai and Erika Gonzalez discuss and provide constructive criticism on community translation training methods and strategies developed at RMIT University in Melbourne, Australia. The authors present the solutions developed, and potential gaps to fill, in training curricula designed in a highly multilingual society with established and emerging languages. The chapter offers guidance on developing pedagogical materials and is beneficial to both teachers and programme designers.

This volume constitutes an up-to-date collection of studies, essays, discussions, reflections and guidelines (both tentative and official) for community translation worldwide. At the same time, it displays the latest developments in a discipline that is still evolving. The book combines knowledge in three main areas of interest: legal, social and health. It can be useful for multiple users in the era of global changes, massive migration triggering linguistic diversity in many regions and global events such as pandemics and environmental disasters. Importantly, the book covers issues, rules, conditions and the status of community translation in many different countries and geographical regions, benefitting a global audience.

References

Taibi, M. (2011). Public service translation. In K. Malmkjær & K. Windle (Eds.), *The Oxford handbook of translation studies* (pp. 214–227). Oxford University Press. https://doi.org/10.1093/oxfordhb/9780199239306.013.0016

Taibi, M., & Ozolins, U. (2016). *Community translation*. Bloomsbury Academic.

1
CHALLENGES IN COMMUNITY TRANSLATION SERVICE PROVISION

The Australian Perspective

Erika Gonzalez and Despina Amanatidou

1 Introduction

Highly diverse nations such as Australia depend heavily on efficient translation services to communicate with their multilingual population (see Chapter 10 for statistical data). Grey and Severin (2022) warn of the risks of not including everyone in public message diffusion and explain that "linguistic exclusion from government communications can create real dangers to individuals and communities and push people towards misinformation and it is a fundamental problem for societies founded on principles of equality, responsible government, and equal civic participation" (p. 25). As the COVID-19 pandemic exemplified, language barriers in multilingual societies contribute to inequality and sociopolitical fragmentation:

> In times of crises there is an opportunity for new insight and knowledge to emerge, but crises also make communication gaps and voids of social meaning painfully visible. Covid-19 is foregrounding the consequences of what it means (not) to have access to knowledge, safety, justice, and voice – and lack of access is often aggravated, if not produced, by language barriers.
> *(Piekkari et al., 2021, p. 590)*

As Smith and Judd (2020) rightly anticipated, vulnerable populations such as the elderly, persons with disabilities, those living with chronic ailments, Indigenous communities, those in prison, and culturally and linguistically diverse (CALD) communities have been the hardest hit by the pandemic. Taibi (2018) provides a plausible explanation for this situation:

> Because the end users are often disempowered people who speak minority languages, and also as a result of budgetary constraints in public services, it

is often the case that *ad hoc* measures are adopted, if at all, to cater for the communication needs of these community members.

(Taibi, 2018, p. 8)

In an interview regarding crisis communication, Professor Ingrid Piller notes that not having access to quality and trusted information that has been delivered in a timely manner accentuates vulnerability (Skelly, 2020). Moreover, as Devakumar et al. (2020) explain, "health protection relies not only on a well-functioning health system with universal coverage, but also on social inclusion, justice and solidarity" (p. 1194). Reliable, targeted, and accurate translations are indispensable in ensuring social inclusion, justice, and health equality among CALD communities.

2   Community Translation and the Communication of Public Messages

In global health crises, translation plays a vital role and it becomes "the basic means of intercultural communication" (Cappuzzo, 2021, p. 40). Community translation enables the empowerment of "disempowered social groups" (Taibi, 2018, p. 8) by providing them with equal access to information produced by public services and government departments and agencies. Therefore, it can be posited that community translation plays a pivotal role in enabling social inclusion, participation, and access to information in highly diverse and multilingual societies. Lesch (2018) views community translation as "a means to an end; providing communities with the means to inform and skill themselves and putting their needs on the agenda, making effective communication with the reader the only valid measure of its success" (p. 69). According to this perspective, community translation becomes a question of appropriateness and accessibility. Community translation is produced for a broad range of communities and their members within a country (Ko, 2018), and it is "an activity that facilitates written communication between components of the same society, where some member groups do not have a good command of the dominant language" (Taibi & Ozolins, 2016, p. 53).

Australia is a leader in the field of community translation and interpreting (see Taibi et al., 2021; Hlavac, 2021, for a review of translation and interpreting in Australia). It has one of the most comprehensive certification systems in the world, administered by the National Accreditation Authority for Translators and Interpreters (NAATI); a robust national professional association known as the Australian Institute of Interpreters and Translators (AUSIT); a union that represents translators and interpreters (Translators and Interpreters Australia [TIA]); and a variety of universities and technical and further education (TAFE) vocational colleges, as well as registered training organisations (RTOs), that deliver high-quality education in a broad spectrum of languages. Yet the pandemic revealed that there are still issues in terms of quality, consistency, and adequacy when it comes to public communications for those who are not fluent in English. The translation and communication issues identified throughout the pandemic ranged from target texts with poor grammar and syntax, inadequate register, and formatting errors, to mistranslations and mixture of languages (Dalzell, 2020a, 2020b; Yosufzai, 2020). These problems generate a lack of trust and severe negative effects such as the disengagement of the most vulnerable communities.

According to Dut (2021), a doctor based in Melbourne and a member of the South Sudanese community, "trust between communities and authorities is arguably the most important tenet for the pandemic response" (p. 427). Therefore, collaboration – or what we refer to as a *co-design approach* – between those generating the source messages and the communities which will be consuming them, becomes vital for the successful communication of public messages. Section 2.1 will illustrate how this co-design approach fits with functionalist translation theories, as well as recent quality assurance frameworks developed for community translation.

2.1 Quality: A Matter of Shared Responsibility

In the translation process, there are a variety of agents and participants who play equal roles in ensuring the quality of the final product or translation. The theme of the 2007 Critical Link Conference, held in Sydney, clearly stated that quality is a shared responsibility (Hale et al., 2009). The conference and subsequent publication were focused on community interpreting, but it can be argued that the collaboration and active engagement of all the participating agents is equally important in community translation to ensure quality outcomes. For this reason, we believe that functionalist translation theories are particularly relevant to community translation.

Functionalist translation theories emerged at the end of the 1970s and paid special attention to the purpose of the text, the recipients of translated texts, and the cultural context in which such texts are consumed and framed (Vermeer, 1978; Hönig & Kussmaul, 1982; Holz-Mänttäri, 1984; Reiss & Vermeer, 1984/2014; Nord, 1997). Holz-Mänttäri's *Translatorial Action* (1984) is of particular importance for community translation. Her model, an extension of Vermeer's (1978) skopos theory, considers the translation process as a goal-driven and outcome-oriented human interaction (Munday, 2016; Madayenzadeh, 2019). Holz-Mänttäri (1984) identified six key participants in the translation process:

1   The initiator: the organisation or client who requires the translation
2   The commissioner: the intermediary (usually an agency or individual) who contacts the translator
3   The source text producer: writers who produce the source text and who are not necessarily involved in the target text
4   The target text producer: the translator(s)
5   The target text user: the person or audience who uses the target text
6   The target text receiver: the final consumer or audience of the target text

In a nutshell, Holz-Mänttäri's theory aims to "analyze the roles of the participants and situational conditions in which translational activities take place. She emphasises the special function of translation in communicating across cultures"

(Yi, 2013, p. 76). The quality, acceptability, and readability of the final product depends on the level of cooperation and engagement of all the participants in the translation process. Although this is applicable to any translation genre, it acquires special importance in the field of community translation since target texts contain public information that can be vital to the wellbeing and safety of the target population and readers (e.g., public health and environmental crisis messaging).

Taibi (2018) clearly states that "quality assurance in community translation is multi-faceted and, as in other fields, involves a number of stages, actors, and actions (adequate training, appropriate recruitment processes, assessment and processing of source texts, production process, consultation with target communities, etc.)" (p. 8). He proposes a multidimensional framework which includes four stages (1. the societal level, 2. the inter-professional level, 3. the translation stage, 4. the post-translation stage) and involves multiple agents including policy makers, trainers and educators, language service providers (LSPs), translators, public service staff, and the community (Taibi, 2018, p. 13). A study conducted in Australia during the pandemic demonstrated that a partnership between CALD leaders, communities, and government is critical for effective health communication. In their recommendations, the authors emphasised that translations alone will not promote changes in attitude or compliance if information is not framed within an appropriate contextual environment:

> The process of language translation must also consider the audience's frame of reference, and the context in which the translated material will be used, which can be done by partnering with community leaders to understand the barriers to understanding and adopting the information.
>
> *(Wild et al., 2021, p. 4)*

A recent study on participatory research collaboration conducted by Polaron, a Melbourne-based LSP, showed that challenges with quality assurance can arise from the present system's inability to effectively consider the target audience and the contexts in which the translated texts will be consumed (Polaron Language Services, 2021). After hosting a collaborative CALD interactive online forum with a variety of stakeholders, Polaron drafted a report with recommendations on how to engage communities in the communication process. It is important to highlight here that co-design or the participation of the community applies to both pre- and post-translational processes and activities. The following points aim to explain how community co-design processes can be implemented by industry stakeholders to better support multicultural communities and help organisations share their message:

1. Involve CALD communities from the start . . .
2. Allocate a budget and time for worthwhile translations . . .
3. Work with NAATI-certified Australian translators and interpreters . . .
4. Training [staff of organisations that work with multicultural communities] . . .

5   Share information with CALD communities through multiple platforms . . .
6   Identify sub-groups of a community and understand their specific needs
7   Timely and quality translations
8   Use technology intelligently

(Polaron Language Services, 2021, pp. 8–9)

Despite a lack of structure and the issues with multilingual communications at the inception of the pandemic, Australian state and federal government departments were quick to develop task forces, initiatives, and advisory committees to address these communication gaps by engaging a variety of stakeholders including community leaders, health experts, and AUSIT. For example, the Culturally and Linguistically Diverse Communities COVID-19 Health Advisory Group was established by the Department of Health to provide "advice on the experience of culturally, ethnically and linguistically diverse people and communities in relation to the COVID-19 pandemic" (Department of Health, 2022, "Role" section). Another similar example is the Victorian Government's CALD Communities Taskforce, which works with "community organisations, local governments and the Victorian Multicultural Commission to develop community specific, locally delivered solutions that will help slow the spread of coronavirus (COVID-19)" (Victorian Government, 2021). These efforts are commendable and show a level of engagement that is vital to promoting a collaborative approach that will ensure the appropriate drafting, translation, diffusion, and consumption of multilingual materials.

Given the interest and level of engagement shown by several authorities, we considered it important to identify issues in the commissioning of multicultural communications that may generate undesirable results. The identification of problematic themes will allow us to propose remedial actions to improve the quality of messages produced for multilingual communities. With this in mind, we surveyed one of the key stakeholders in the multilingual communication process: the commissioner or intermediary (i.e., LSPs). This party sits in the middle of the communication process by liaising with clients, translators, and even the target readers on some occasions. Given the pivotal role they fulfil, LSPs are witnesses of the challenges, opportunities, and potential remedies that can be put in place to improve multilingual communication processes.

2.2   Language Service Providers: The Glue That Binds It All Together

Community translations in Australia involve multiple languages (over 60 in some cases), and the direct engagement of translators would be a nearly impossible task. Therefore, all government departments work with public or private LSPs. These companies are selected through tender processes and their selection is usually in the hands of procurement teams that deal with the purchase of all kinds of goods and services, on top of translations. As the commissioners or intermediaries, LSPs are responsible for engaging the translator team and have first-hand information on the challenges and issues involved in the translation process. They also play a pivotal role in the production of the final message that is distributed to communities. As Ozolins (2007) states, LSPs are crucial in determining the "industrial, ethical and professional environment" (p. 121) in which translators and interpreters work. Considering their strategic role in the multilingual communication process, we surveyed leading Australian LSPs to gather internal information regarding community translation projects.

3 The Survey

The survey was distributed to 64 LSPs in July 2021. Of these, 59 were private enterprises and five were public companies or part of the language service department of a major hospital or were a non-governmental organisation (NGO) with its own translation service. The survey was distributed via email from Erika Gonzalez's university email account. The email contained an invitation message, a participant information sheet with the relevant ethics clearance reference number, and the link to the survey.

The tool employed for the survey was a questionnaire designed and administered via Qualtrics, a web-based software. The questionnaire was comprised of 20 questions, with a combination of closed and open questions. It was divided into four sections with the aim to gather information regarding: a) the profile of the company; b) recruitment of translators and the translation process; c) challenges; and d) future directions. Respondents were also provided with the opportunity to add comments on the last question.

A total of 22 initial responses were collected (34% response rate). However, from question five onwards, only 18 of those 22 continued with the survey (28.12%). The four companies that abandoned the survey were all small companies – three of the companies had 0–10 employees and one company had between 10 and 50 employees. Their responses have been invalidated and removed from the statistics to avoid a skewed interpretation of the results. Out of the 18 which continued with the survey, four (22.22%) provided translation services at the national level, six (33.33%) at the state level, and eight (44.44%) at both national and state levels. Table 1.1 shows the size of the companies in terms of the number of employees.

The next question asked about the volume of community translation projects completed in the previous 12 months, as shown in Table 1.2.

TABLE 1.1 Size of the Company

Number of Employees	Percentage (%)	Count
0–10	55%	10
10–50	5%	1
50–100	11%	2
100+	27%	5

TABLE 1.2 Volume of Work in the Last Year

Number of Community Translation Projects in the Last 12 Months	Percentage (%)	Count
0–10	0%	0
10–50	5%	1
50–100	33%	6
100–300	22%	4
300–500	16%	3
500+	22%	4

TABLE 1.3 Most Relevant Translator Attributes

Attribute	Minimum	Maximum	Mean	Standard Deviation	Variance
Availability	4.00	5.00	4.40	0.49	0.24
Highest NAATI credentials	3.00	5.00	4.17	0.90	0.81
Interpersonal and intrapersonal skills	2.00	3.00	2.50	0.50	0.25
NAATI credentials and relevant education qualifications in translation	1.00	4.00	2.33	1.25	1.56
Experience	1.00	3.00	2.00	1.00	1.00

Of the 18 respondents that addressed the question about translator recruitment practices, the highest and most valued attribute at the time of engaging a translator was availability, followed by the highest NAATI credentials, and third by interpersonal and intrapersonal skills (e.g., easy to deal with, responsive translators, etc.). The combination of both the highest NAATI credentials and education was valued as the fourth attribute, followed by experience in last place. Table 1.3 shows the statistical values for each of the qualities mentioned.

When asked if these preferences are applied in practice, 17 respondents out of 18 (94.4%) said "yes" and one respondent said "no," arguing that it depends on the "availability and urgency of the demand."

Regarding the translation review process and quality control mechanisms, eight respondents (44.44%) stated that translations are "sometimes" reviewed by a second NAATI-certified translator, while six respondents (33.33%) said that they are "always" reviewed by a second NAATI-certified translator. Three respondents (16.67%) mentioned that their translations are revised by both certified translators and community readers or checkers. None of the respondents chose the answer "no, never" or "sometimes, by community checkers." When asked why the revision only eventuates sometimes, one out of five respondents (20%) mentioned budgetary constraints, and the other four respondents adduced the following "other reasons":

- "It is the client's discretion. A few organisations prefer to get the translations checked in-house by community workers."
- "Some of the work is simple or very short or the clients does [sic] not have funds to do it."
- "The translation checks are not always requested by the client, [the agency] has promoted peer review and clients are now requesting this more and more."
- "We do it on request (if the document is for publication)."

The next question asked if the LSPs encouraged the use of computer-assisted translation (CAT) tools for community translation projects. Ten respondents (55.56%) stated that they do not, while eight respondents (44.44%) stated that they do. The responses provided to justify the non-use of CAT tools were as follows:

- "It is not accurate."
- "We are impartial to the use of CATs in that I do not encourage it but neither do I discourage it. I have translators who do use them and those who don't."
- "The method of translation is chosen by the assigned translator, it is accepted that some use CAT tools, where relevant and practical for the source document provided."
- "No resources to promote or test its utility in our context."
- "We allow each translator to work as they feel comfortable."

Those who responded "yes" to the previous question, were asked if they face difficulties when developing projects with CAT tools. Six respondents (66.67%) stated that they do not face any issues, while three (33.33%) mentioned that they do. The following open comments were provided to justify their response:

- "Not all translators are on board with them, especially in new and emerging languages and the older (and therefore more linguistically experienced) cohort."
- "The lack tech-savyy [sic] linguists."
- "Not all the translators use the same CAT tools with the same specs."

The questionnaire also enquired about the use of machine translation (MT) for community translation projects. Two respondents (11.11%) mentioned using it, while 16 respondents (88.89%) said they do not use MT. Both companies that use MT said that they perform post-editing in their projects.

In the section regarding challenges, the questionnaire asked about the main challenge LSPs face at the time of delivering multilingual community translation

Challenges in Community Translation Service Provision **13**

projects. This question was addressed by 16 respondents. Table 1.4 reflects their responses.

The next question asked about the five languages in highest demand. This question was completed by 11 respondents (61.11%), as shown in Table 1.5.

The next question asked about the most challenging languages. This question was also completed by 11 respondents (see Table 1.6).

TABLE 1.4 Challenges in Community Translation Projects

Challenges	Percentage (%)	Count
Difficulties sticking to the budget	6.25%	1
Engaging properly certified and/ or qualified translators in certain languages	43.75%	7
Layout and design issues in multilingual materials	50%	8
Other	0%	0

TABLE 1.5 Languages in Most Demand

Top Languages	Number of Responses
Arabic (and Juba Arabic)	11
Chinese (Simplified and Traditional)	11
Vietnamese	7
Italian	4
Greek	3
Dari, Hindi, Kurdish (Kumanji and Sorani), Nepali, Persian, Spanish	2

TABLE 1.6 Most Challenging Languages

Language	Number of Responses
Arabic	4
Assyrian, Farsi, Punjabi	3
Dinka	3
Amharic, Dari, Karen, Tamil, Tigrinya, Tongan	2
Burmese, Chaldean, Chinese, Chin Hakha, Fijian, Hebrew, Hindi, Juba Arabic, Khmer, Kurmanji Kurdish, Nepali, Nuer, Oromo, Rohingya, Samoan, Sinhalese, Somali, Sorani Kurdish, Tibetan	1

The questionnaire also included a specific question about the volume of work during the COVID-19 pandemic. Of the 16 respondents (88.88%) who answered this question, 12 (75%) agreed that the pandemic influenced the volume of translations produced, while according to the other four respondents (25%), it did not. The respondents who agreed were asked to further comment on the matter and the main themes that transpired from these comments were: the increased volume of community translations, the faster turnaround times required, lack of client willingness to follow the LSP's advice, challenges with non–NAATI-certified languages, and unrealistic expectations on what rare and emerging language translators can produce within given time frames and complexity. One respondent commented that the established quality assurance processes were "cumbersome," arguing that once numerous projects were completed and delivered, there was an increased frequency of clients requesting changes, additions, and amendments based on feedback and/or suggestions given by community members at various focus groups and workshops.

The next question was an open question that asked about the factors that could improve the delivery of multilingual community translation projects. The open answers provided were varied:

- "Longer lead times."
- "More NAATI credentialing in 'rare and emerging' languages."
- "Greater cohesion between source document author, graphic designer (if any), the translator (either through an agency or direct) and the typesetter (whether that is the same translator, agency worker, or the graphic designer again)."
- "Most constraints are due to the English-speaking service providers not understanding the level of complexity of what is required, and not really caring about it."
- "More awareness amongst translators of the importance of taking a communicative approach as opposed to placing so much emphasis on being linguistically accurate. The need for translators to take a more collaborative approach, ask questions and engage in conversations about cultural appropriateness of concepts, wordings and approaches of the English text prior to translation. Translators are not often given the opportunity to express concerns on the appropriateness of the English and therefore they don't speak up when they know a translation might not work for their community."
- "Suitable professional training of linguists."
- "Purchasers [government departments] generally are not aware of limitations of non-NAATI languages and especially what a RPT [recognised practising translator] can and cannot manage in terms of timeframes and complexity."
- "Further education in the community about the roles of NAATI Certified Translators versus community proof-readers – roles and intents are different and are widely misunderstood."
- "Processes that can better align the target audience needs with the translators' professional constraints."

- "Sufficient budget and prior planning to developing multilingual resources. Organisations and public service agencies need to identify the needs of their CALD communities and allocate proper budgeting so translation is provided as a must service rather than an added on."
- "If the clients provide Word documents of the ST [source text] to be translated."
- "Ensuring the English source is accurate before sending to translate, holding meeting [sic] with community groups before coming up with the English wording, explaining the meaning of acronyms."

The last question was allocated for free comments. The responses for this section were also varied:

- "It is essential that we foster collaboration between community project leaders and translators and/or agencies. However, this is not so easy to implement due to limitations in resources i.e. time, human resources."
- "In some languages, e.g., Arabic, there appears to [be] a lot of disagreements between different translators. This is probably due to the many different versions of Arabic, but also, I suspect, as a result of an uneven standard of proficiency amongst certified translators. In smaller languages, e.g. Nepali, there are so few translators that it becomes objectively difficult to ascertain standards of translation."
- "We provide the NAATI Certified translation and assume the customer will organise another company to proof check which they often don't, publishing a translation and never checking if someone has changed the layout and formatting, never consulting with the community or end users as to the relevance and if understandable, many customers often use an unqualified staff member to translate or get a machine translation . . . . Then, we are asked to proof check and the mistakes are incredible and large parts need to be re-translated."

4 Discussion of Survey Results

The response rate for the questionnaire was 28%. According to Chung (2021), any response rate above 25% is deemed satisfactory for obtaining statistically significant data. Moreover, it can be deduced that the 18 LSPs that responded to the survey are most likely similar to the non-respondents in terms of volume, geographical location, and type of work they do, since all the surveyed companies operate within the same market, geographical location (Australia), and share the same workforce given that freelance translators work for several LSPs at the same time. LSPs are an understudied subject in translation studies (Ozolins, 2007), and therefore, even data emerging from a small-scale survey such as this will add to the literature and body of knowledge in this area.

The profile data shows that the respondents are mainly small enterprises with a limited number of employees. These employees are usually the project managers and administrative staff, while the rest of the workforce consists of contractors or freelancers who are hired on a project-by-project basis. Although we explained that for the purpose of this survey, contractors should be excluded from the employee list, the data shows that many respondents included contractors. TIA has been fighting for the inclusion of contractors as employees and that is why some LSPs show such high staffing volumes (in theory, there is only one company in Australia which has over 100 employees).

Most of the surveyed respondents work on community translation projects on a continuous basis, as shown by the volume of projects completed a year. This proves the observation made by other scholars that most translators and interpreters in Australia work in community settings (Hlavac, 2021; Taibi et al., 2021), and this is especially the case for those who work from English into languages other than English (LOTE). In terms of the most valued attributes of this workforce, it was surprising to find that a combination of the highest NAATI credentials and an education in the field of translation were not the most sought-after qualities. The highest valued attribute was availability. If we correlate this response with the results obtained for the question related to challenges – tight deadlines and quick turnaround times were themes that emerged in most of the responses – the value placed on availability is consequently understandable. However, this raises concerns about quality and the lower value placed on translator education and experience. Experience was the least valued attribute. One of the hypotheses for such a result can be drawn from the fact that experienced translators may charge higher fees due to their training and expertise. As pricing plays a pivotal role in procurement processes and government tenders, LSPs are perhaps not willing to engage the most experienced professionals in the sector or are not in a position to do so. One of the respondents also stated that some of the most experienced translators are not "tech-savvy," which may justify the preference for other attributes over professional experience. These data also show a need for clients (in this case, those who commission the translations) to work in a more collaborative manner with LSPs to allow for the incorporation of quality enhancement mechanisms in the translation process. Unrealistic expectations regarding deadlines will undoubtedly compromise quality outcomes.

Regarding the translation process, according to most of the respondents, the revision of the materials does not always or automatically happen. Instead, this seems to depend on the client's requirements, as well as their budget. We believe that the revision of translations should be part of the deliverables produced by the LSP, and therefore, the revision process and associated costs should be integrated into tenders. It is also important to highlight that translation revisers (certified translators who review the translation completed by the initial translator) do not fulfil the same role as community readers or checkers, and therefore, these two roles should not be conflated, as was done by some of the respondents. Community readers or checkers cannot substitute the work done by translation revisors. We consider that having community readers or checkers would be the cherry on top of the cake – a beneficial addition to the translation process and an important way to involve communities in the diffusion of multicultural messaging. However, if translations are of poor quality, the onus risks falling on the target readers (in this case, the community), which defies the purpose of their inclusion in the translation process. To avoid such situations, there should be clear guidelines and a well-defined structure in which each participating agent takes responsibility for their part in the overall communication process.

The open comments provided by the LSPs also show a lack of agreement and standards regarding interactions with the clients and translators themselves: "Translators are not often given the opportunity to express concerns on the appropriateness of the English and therefore they don't speak up when they know a translation might not work for their community." This specific comment indicates problematic behaviour, as translators should be able to provide their opinion. On the other hand, LSPs should ask their translators to consider the appropriateness of the source text so the client may be notified of any inaccuracies that will affect the final message.

Another surprising result of the survey was the non-use of CAT tools in community translation projects. If we take COVID-19 translations as an example, the use of CAT tools would ensure terminological coherence and also faster completion of the projects. Two of the respondents adduced lack of reliability as a reason for non-use, which may indicate that they confused CAT tools with MT. For most of the respondents, the lack of "tech-savvy translators" also seemed to be problematic, and this issue was more accentuated in the case of translators from new and emerging languages, as well as some of the most experienced translators. The use of MT was not widespread among the respondents, and those who used it mentioned putting the relevant post-editing processes in place. These data show the need to upskill a significant percentage of the translator workforce.

In terms of the most in-demand languages for community translation projects, the results of the survey coincide with the most represented languages at the national level: Mandarin, followed by Arabic, Vietnamese, Cantonese, and Punjabi (Australian Bureau of Statistics, 2022). These languages vary slightly depending on each state and territory.

Translation demands also depend on new arrivals and migration flows, as newly arrived communities require more information and support. For example, among the 24,926 Syrian and Iraqi refugees who migrated to Australia between 1 July 2005 and 31 December 2017, 18,324 had no English competence whatsoever and 5,241 had a poor level of English (Collins et al., 2018). These statistics illustrate how conflicts around the globe have a significant impact on local translation demands. In this case, the new arrivals increased the demand for well-established languages such as Arabic, but also for a new and emerging language such as Kurdish and its different dialects. The five most in-demand languages identified by the LSPs are well catered to in terms of tertiary education options and certification.

In the case of the most challenging languages, it was surprising to see well-established languages such as Arabic and Farsi on the list. As the survey responses reflected, this could be due to the challenges posed by different alphabets and scripts in the layout of the published materials (which is beyond the scope of translation). During the pandemic, there was an instance in which Arabic and Farsi languages were mixed up in an informative brochure (Dalzell, 2020a). This reaffirms the need to incorporate solid revision processes before translations reach communities. This type of final revision could be conducted by community checkers or readers. As Taibi (2018) mentions, community feedback is crucial given the impact community translation has in terms of "social inclusion, equity, participation and change" (p. 22). Broad differences in the geographical backgrounds of the translators, as well as differences in their discipline-specific educational backgrounds, were highlighted by one respondent as factors which could add to the challenges of Arabic. The introduction and use of style guides, as well as glossaries, in project workflows would assist translators in languages such as Arabic, Spanish, and French, among many others, given that the communities and translators themselves come from a vast range of countries and regions. At the time of drafting the present chapter, AUSIT was working on the development of style guides for Arabic, Chinese, and Spanish thanks to a grant received by the Federation of Ethnic Communities of Australia (FECCA) and the Department of Health.

In the case of other challenging languages, difficulties arise from the lack of training and certification opportunities. For example, of the 63 languages identified as priorities for the translation of public health information by the Department of Health, 52.4% (33) have NAATI certification testing available at the level of certified translator. According to the NAATI translation directory (NAATI, 2022), 9.5% (6) have no practising translators with formal credentials whatsoever. These languages are Hakha Chin, Malayalam, Karen, Rohingya, Southern Kurdish, and Tibetan. Malayalam, for example, is one of the most represented LOTE in the Northern Territory. Translator education and training in new and emerging languages remains a challenge, as explained by Lai and González in Chapter 10.

Another important theme that emerged from the survey is the need for greater communication and collaboration between the authors of English materials, LSPs, and translators. This would have a positive impact on the translation quality assurance process. Responses to the survey demonstrate a general lack of consensus in relation to the negotiation and implementation of various aspects of quality assurance, especially regarding the stakeholder responsible for translation checking and community feedback. LSPs should instigate communication and dialogue between the different parties they liaise with – an important step in the collaborative approach that will ensure quality standards are met by all parties engaged in the process.

5 Conclusions

The pandemic highlighted communication issues at the time of delivering messages for CALD communities. As Grey (2020) points out, it is paramount to foster greater transparency regarding how communication policies are implemented at the time of collaborating with CALD communities. Community translation protocols could assist in bridging some of the issues addressed here, as they would allow each party – and especially those who commission the translations – to have a clear overview of the translation process and the responsibilities of each stakeholder involved. AUSIT, as part of the project supported by FECCA and the

Department of Health, was drafting community translation protocols at the time this chapter was being written.

Based on the results of this survey and the literature review, the following recommendations could assist all agents involved in the translation process to address gaps in community translation service provision.

1. Implementation of rigorous quality control mechanisms: LSPs should have an internal system to ensure quality at all stages of the translation process, including a translation revision step for every translation project. LSPs should also keep a record of translation issues, client complaints, and community feedback about translations; conduct regular internal reviews of the identified issues; and build feedback into further professional development (PD) for translators and other relevant staff. In order to be implemented, these steps will have to be considered in the tenders so that the cost of the translation revision is reflected in the pricing.
2. Recruitment: LSPs should ensure highly qualified NAATI-certified translators are recruited for work relating to public health messaging. Job and/or project allocation systems should be developed in a manner that gives priority to translators with the highest qualifications and level of NAATI certification, as well as relevant expertise and experience in the specific field of translation. For high-demand languages, LSPs should, ideally, consider establishing permanent panels of in-house translators. Such panels can also be used to revise translations and offer training and support for less experienced colleagues.
3. Support and capacity building: LSPs should offer regular PD to their workforce including, but not limited to, the use of CAT tools, MT post-editing, translation revision, translation theories, etc. LSPs need to have a long-term vision and support capacity building in those areas and languages for which there is a shortage of qualified translators. LSPs also need to have a mentoring system in place for newer translators, whether they are in-house translators or contractors. Tandem translations should be considered for languages where there is a lack of capacity, or for translators working into languages of new and emerging communities in Australia.
4. Alteration to pay-scaling: Remunerate professionals according to their level of certification and education. The higher the NAATI credential and education level, the better the pay. This will incentivise individuals to upskill.

In terms of the commissioning organisations, we recommend that:

1. Reasonable expectations are set regarding deadlines and budgets.
2. An increased focus is placed on the pre-planning and provision of translation briefings.
3. Content should be drafted and designed based on the target reader profile and needs, which requires community consultation whenever possible and when the circumstances allow it.

4   Source texts are edited in plain English. This would not only make the translation process easier, but also improve the comprehension of crucial messages.
5   Training initiatives for translators are supported and funded, especially for languages of new and emerging communities. It is essential that government bodies support training projects to increase the number of qualified and certified translators. This should be seen as vital in improving both the quantity and quality of translated materials. The ongoing engagement, education, and training of a greater number of translators in these languages should be seen as a key focus for all stakeholders involved in the translation industry. This can be achieved by offering grants and scholarships to complete tertiary translation education and by funding PD opportunities, mentoring, and certification.

Translators, on the other hand, should keep up with language maintenance and PD. They should develop negotiation skills and assertiveness, as well as understanding the full cycle of project management.

These recommendations illustrate the important role that all agents play in community translation. Functionalist translation theories fit with the calls from community advocacy groups to foster co-design approaches that include the end-users in the translation and multilingual communication processes. Quality is indeed a shared responsibility, and a lack of engagement on the part of some players in the process will undoubtedly affect the work others do. LSPs, as a strategic agent in the communication process, have the responsibility to educate clients, but also to encourage and foster capacity building and upskilling for community translators – especially those who work with new and emerging languages.

References

Australian Bureau of Statistics. (2022). *2021 census*. www.abs.gov.au/census

Cappuzzo, B. (2021). The importance of multilingual information and plain English in response to the COVID-19 pandemic. *European Scientific Journal*, *17*(30), 37–52. https://doi.org/10.19044/esj.2021.v17n30p37

Chung, L. (2021, December 8). What is a good survey response rate for customer surveys? *Delighted*. https://delighted.com/blog/average-survey-response-rate#:%7E:text=The%20response%20rates%20are%20usually,range%20of%205%25%20to%2030%25

Collins, J., Reid, C., Groutsis, D., Watson, K., & Ozkul, D. (2018, March). *Syrian and Iraqi refugee settlement in Australia* (Working paper no. 1). www.uts.edu.au/sites/default/files/article/downloads/Collins.Reid_.Groutsis.Australia.Syrian-Conflict%20Refugee%20Settlement%20in%20Australia.pdf

Dalzell, S. (2020a, August 13). Government coronavirus messages left "nonsensical" after being translated into other languages. *ABC News*. www.abc.net.au/news/2020-08-13/coronavirus-messages-translated-to-nonsense-in-other-languages/12550520

Dalzell, S. (2020b, November 19). Federal government used Google Translate for COVID-19 messaging aimed at multicultural communities. *ABC News*. www.abc.net.au/news/2020-11-19/government-used-google-translate-for-nonsensical-COVID-19-tweet/12897200

Department of Health. (2022, February 6). *Culturally and linguistically diverse communities COVID-19 health advisory group*. Australian Government. www.health.gov.au/

committees-and-groups/culturally-and-linguistically-diverse-communities-COVID-19-health-advisory-group#role

Devakumar, D., Shannon, G., Bhopal, S., & Abubakar, I. (2020). Racism and discrimination in COVID-19 responses. *The Lancet, 395*(10231), 1194. https://doi.org/10.1016/S0140-6736(20)30792-3

Dut, G. M. (2021). The experience of South Sudanese migrant families during the COVID-19 pandemic in Melbourne. *Australian and New Zealand Journal of Public Health, 45*(5), 427–429. https://doi.org/10.1111/1753-6405.13134

Grey, A. (2020, June 29). Australia's multilingual communities are missing out on vital coronavirus information. *ABC News*. https://www.abc.net.au/news/2020-06-29/coronavirus-multilingual-australia-missing-out-covid-19-info/12403510

Grey, A., & Severin, A. A. (2022). Building towards best practice for governments' public communications in languages other than English: A case study of New South Wales, Australia. *Griffith Law Review, 31*(1), 25–56. https://doi.org/10.1080/10383441.2022.2031526

Hale, S., Ozolins, U., & Stern, L. (Eds.). (2009). *The critical link 5: Quality in interpreting – a shared responsibility*. John Benjamins Publishing Company.

Hlavac, J. (2021). The development of community translation and interpreting in Australia: A critical overview. In J. Wakabayashi & M. O'Hagan (Eds.), *Translating and interpreting in Australia and New Zealand* (pp. 65–85). Routledge. https://doi.org/10.4324/9781003150770

Holz-Mänttäri, J. (1984). *Translatorisches Handeln. Theorie und Methode* [Translational action: Theory and method]. Suomalainen Tiedeakatemia.

Hönig, H. G., & Kussmaul, P. (1982). *Strategie der Übersetzung. Ein Lehr- und Arbeitsbuch* [Translation strategy: A learn-and-work book]. Narr.

Ko, L. (2018). Community translation in the Australian context. In M. Taibi (Ed.), *Translating for the community* (pp. 138–155). Multilingual Matters. https://doi.org/10.21832/TAIBI9139

Lesch, H. (2018). From practice to theory: Societal factors as a norm governing principle for community translation. In M. Taibi (Ed.), *Translating for the community* (pp. 69–97). Multilingual Matters. https://doi.org/10.21832/TAIBI9139

Madayenzadeh, M. (2019). *An investigation of Holz-Mänttäri's translatorial action: A sociocultural model?* ResearchGate. www.researchgate.net/publication/333728799_An_Investigation_of_Holz-Manttari%27s_Translatorial_Action_A_Sociocultural_Model

Munday, J. (2016). *Introducing translation studies: Theories and applications* (4th ed.). Routledge.

National Accreditation Authority for Translators and Interpreters (NAATI). (2022). Online directory. https://www.naati.com.au/online-directory/?require=translator&for=[29,613,1367]

Nord, C. (1997). *Translating as a purposeful activity. Functionalist approaches explained*. St Jerome.

Ozolins, U. (2007). The interpreter's "third client": Interpreters, professionalism and interpreting agencies. In C. Wadensjo, B. E. Dimitrova, & A. Nilsson (Eds.), *The critical link 4: Professionalisation of interpreting in the community. Selected papers from the 4th international conference on interpreting in legal, health and social service settings, Stockholm, Sweden, 20–23 May 2004* (pp. 121–131). John Benjamins Publishing Company.

Piekkari, R., Tietze, S., Angouri, J., Meyer, R., & Vaara, E. (2021). Can you speak Covid-19? Languages and social inequality in management studies. *Journal of Management Studies, 58*(2), 587–591. https://doi.org/10.1111/joms.12657

Polaron Language Services. (2021). *CALD Co-design impact report*. www.polaron.com.au/wp-content/uploads/2021/09/Final-Co-Design-Impact-Report-PDF.pdf

Reiss, K., & Vermeer, H. J. (2014). *Towards a general theory of translational action: Skopos theory explained* (C. Nord, Trans.). Routledge (Original work published 1984).

Skelly, S. (2020, October 13). Lost in translation: COVID-19 leaves migrants behind. *The Lighthouse*. https://lighthouse.mq.edu.au/article/october-2020/lost-in-translation-COVID-19-leaves-migrants-behind

Smith, J. A., & Judd, J. (2020). COVID-19: Vulnerability and the power of privilege in a pandemic. *Health Promotion Journal of Australia*, *31*(2), 158–160. https://doi.org/10.1002/hpja.333

Taibi, M. (2018). Quality assurance in community translation. In M. Taibi (Ed.), *Translating for the community* (pp. 7–25). Multilingual Matters. https://doi.org/10.21832/TAIBI9139

Taibi, M., & Ozolins, U. (2016). *Community translation*. Bloomsbury Academic.

Taibi, M., Ozolins, U., & Maximous, A. (2021). Interpreter education in Australia: Community settings, generic skills. In J. Wakabayashi & M. O'Hagan (Eds.), *Translating and interpreting in Australia and New Zealand* (pp. 86–104). Routledge. https://doi.org/10.4324/9781003150770

Vermeer, H. (1978). Ein Rahmen für eine allgemeine Translationstheorie. *Lebende Sprachen*, 99–102.

Victorian Government. (2021, June 7) *Supporting multicultural communities through coronavirus (COVID-19)*. www.vic.gov.au/supporting-multicultural-communities-through-coronavirus-COVID-19

Wild, A., Kunstler, B., Goodwin, D., Onyala, S., Zhang, L., Kufi, M., Salim, W., Musse, F., Mohideen, M., Asthana, M., Al-Khafaji, M., Geronimo, M. A., Coase, D., Chew, E., Micallef, E., & Skouteris, H. (2021). Communicating COVID-19 health information to culturally and linguistically diverse communities: Insights from a participatory research collaboration. *Public Health Research & Practice*, *31*(1), Article e3112105. https://doi.org/10.17061/phrp3112105

Yi, Z. (2013). Communicative purposes in translational activities: A functional study on target prefaces and postscripts. *Intercultural Communication Studies*, *22*(2), 75–90. https://web.uri.edu/iaics/files/Zhang-Yi.pdf

Yosufzai, R. (2020, September 30). The Australian community translators fighting coronavirus one word at a time. *SBS News*. www.sbs.com.au/news/the-australian-community-translators-fighting-coronavirus-one-word-at-a-time/19448378-4630–465f-a1f8-a6cffd9e74c4

2

THE BATTLE TO INTERVENE

Constrained Advocacy for Community Translators

David Katan and Cinzia Spinzi[1]

1 Setting the Scene

1.1 Who Is a Community Translator?

Our aim in this chapter is to show where we believe this profession can transform to meet academic ideals, and what the main obstacles are to effectuating this change. Academically, there has always been a clear divide between two ideals: the text-centred, faithful – or "*latere*" – approach and the more reader-oriented, free, or "*creare*" approach (Katan, 2018). While translation practice had been characterised by a "subservient" (Simeoni, 1998) faithfulness to the source text rather than to the target text reader, functionalist theories by the turn of the century had changed the focus towards translator agency and the needs of the readership (Gentzler, 2001).

Community translation (also known as public service translation) was conceived in the wake of this reader-oriented turn (Lesch, 1999), though it has since encountered definitional problems and a lack of autonomy (see Taibi, 2011). In fact, community translation was originally discussed within the wider realm of public service interpreting and translation, although by interpreters rather than by translators themselves. It emerged as a practice to cope with the numerous waves of migration and the basic needs of new non-nationals for immediate oral rather than written mediation to access public services (see Valero-Garcés, 2014). It was only as of 2014, following two specific conferences[2] that community translation started to be considered as a distinct subfield within translation studies.

The question, then, is: to what extent do community translators in practice embody the enabling, social mission profile suggested by scholars? To answer this question, the present chapter looks at a global online translator/interpreter (T&I) survey conducted by Katan (in press), which had the aim of investigating the T&I perceived habitus. The methodology of the survey replicated a previous study by

DOI: 10.4324/9781003247333-3

Katan (2011) focused on translators' and interpreters' perceptions of their working world. Given the fragmented nature of the translation profession globally, the respondents were found through mailing lists, beginning with a group of known professional freelance translators and translation academics who also translate. Of the 661 replies collected, 64% described their "main role" as "translators", while 21% saw themselves primarily as "interpreters", often adding terms such as "court" or "audiovisual". The 15% who "also translate" described themselves principally as "teachers/lecturers", "project managers", "localisers", and so on.

The survey included both closed and open questions regarding role and field of work. Determining which of the respondents were, or could be, community translators was not straightforward (cf. Valero-Garcés, 2019). For example, 50 respondents ticked "legal/court" or "medical/health" translation. As Taibi (2018a) explains, the focus of community translators is necessarily on the "socio-economic gap between the dominant social group and minority groups needing community translations" (p. 1), along with a social mission or an empowering approach (Valero-Garcés, 2014; Taibi & Ozolins, 2016). Clearly, neither legal nor medical translations to be read by peers (such as legal or medical practitioners) represent the typical readership of community translations. In general, the target reader will be a defendant or a patient, and there will also be significant "linguistic and terminological gap[s]" between the writer and end user (Taibi, 2018a, p. 1).

On the other hand, the 29 respondents who ticked "translation in immigration" and/or "other public services" as their main role could be counted as "community translators", though over a third (38%) of this group also ticked "also interpret" as a main role, underlining the lack of differentiation between written and oral roles (see Luque, 2017). Furthermore, four respondents in this group called themselves "community interpreters", and in the open question, "What do you call yourself?", none mentioned "community translator". These findings support Townsley's (2018) observation that interpreters who also translate for the community do not regard themselves as "community translators per se" (p. 114). Nevertheless, this group working as translators in immigration and/or other public services provides us with a small but homogenous group who we suggest should qualify uncontroversially as "pure community translators".

Respondents were thus divided into two groups. Those who did not answer other specific questions were eliminated, leaving 25 pure community translators and a control group of 632 non-community translators. The first question asked, "if the job is considered to be a 'good linguistic transfer of the original', to what extent is the translator concerned with reader reaction?" This question was actually divided into two parts. First, the respondents were asked about their ethos, or how they would translate in theory, under "ideal" circumstances. They were then asked about their practice – that is, how they translate "in reality". In response to the first part of the question about ethos, there was no difference between the pure community translators and the control group;[3] neither group showed any particular inclination to go beyond the text (see Figure 2.1). However, in response to the second part of the question about practice, the pure community translators were less constrained than the control group, given that 20% believed that they could "in reality" be concerned with reader reaction (compared to the 14% of the control group; see Figure 2.1). This could suggest that community translation work is less restrictive than other fields of translation work, but that pure community translators are no more concerned about supporting their reader than any non-community translator. It should, however, be stressed that due to its small sample size, the results of the survey are not statistically significant.

The following question in the survey asked respondents whether their prime loyalty was with "the source text", "the reader", "the commissioner (or translation brief)", or "it depends" (explained as, "meaning yourself, i.e., your own translation choices, which may oscillate between all the above at any given moment"). The latter would indicate a translator's own more interventionist and proactive approach. Figure 2.2 illustrates respondents' answers; the 0–4 axis represents

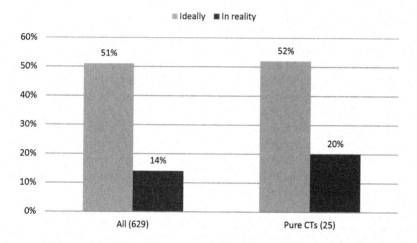

FIGURE 2.1 Concern for the reader

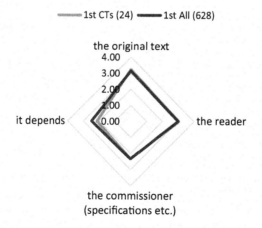

FIGURE 2.2 Loyalty

the value given to the loyalty, with the maximum (4) representing a universally agreed first choice. As shown in Figure 2.2, the answers given by the two groups were once again almost indistinguishable.

Though the reader does come a close second, loyalty to the original text combined with lack of belief in the translator's own decision-making ability, suggests that the pure community translators were even less proactive than the control group. This result supports Yu's (2014) experience in proofreading the translation of community brochures: "most translators tend to take a very cautious approach.... They believe that the safest way is to do a literal translation, which, however, often results in an awkward and sometimes incomprehensible target text" (as cited in Taibi & Ozolins, 2016, p. 69). Both Townsley (2018) and Taibi (2018b) point to poor training as an important factor, to which we will now turn.

1.2 The Translation Trainee

This cautionary approach had already been highlighted with Simeoni's (1998) "willing subservience" as a trait affecting the profession as a whole, but what we can see here is that it already dominates at the training stage. Sewell (2004) noticed similar conservatism with her students. She notes that translation classes were always more popular than the conversation classes and concluded that this was because students felt more comfortable when working with a text than having to create their own conversation. As she explains, conversation is more open-ended than translation, "which can be measured against a visible yardstick, the ST [source text]" (Sewell, 2004, p. 158). This text-centric approach, according to Sewell, satisfies the following needs:

1   The need for confidence and self-esteem
2   The need not to lose face
3   The need to be rewarded
4   The need for certainty, for closure, for autonomy
5   The needs arising from any introversion in our personalities

(Sewell, 2004, p. 153)

In a similar vein, Pym (2008) observes that when making decisions, translators either take the safe alternative or transfer the responsibility for the translation decision to a higher authority, particularly when the reward is low. This observation is also exemplified in a translation project which was organised for students at the University of Salento. The project was part of an international student translation programme (Campbell & Katan, 2022) in which three students in the Spanish language stream had the opportunity to transcreate a public health brochure for the Spanish-speaking community in the United States before embarking on the translation course itself. Their task was to translate a cancer advice brochure from English to Spanish, and the brief made it clear that their task was to adapt the brochure for the Spanish-speaking immigrant community in the United States. Though they had not yet started the course, they were given material on transcreation and were encouraged to produce avatars (personas) of the new

Spanish-speaking readership, and to change the photographs where appropriate so that the images accompanying the text fit the physical features and traits of the target readership. The American commissioners, college students of a technical writing course, were given a brief on how to produce the brochure in English and were told that it also needed to be translated into Spanish. They were not told about transcreation. The students followed the *latere* instructions given by the student-commissioners, "producing a close translation to the original English version, rather than offering alternative visuals or images that were better suited for the Spanish user group" (Campbell & Katan, 2022, p. 448), though with a simplification of one or two medical terms.

When asked why they had intervened so little, they were genuinely surprised that challenging the commissioner might have been an option. The same student reaction has been reported by Morón (in press) regarding her project to train translators in transcreation: "The transcreator's intervention and the need to negotiate with the client were viewed with astonishment by many of the participants who revealed that they felt more confident with translational modalities in which the translator could remain invisible" (p. 8). Her solution was to add more autonomous and creative problem-solving exercises whereby, for example, the students simulated their own transcreation briefs and offered alternative translations that they could justify (Morón, in press). However, these exercises do not directly move the trainees out of their cautionary, safe solutions or towards fulfilling their enabling, social mission as *constrained advocates*.

2   Defining Constrained Advocacy

First, we will outline how we believe the term *advocacy* fits the social mission of the community translator. In general, professional interpreting organisations discuss advocacy as an ethical dilemma, or simply as unprofessional (Kalina, 2015; Katan, 2016; Phelan et al., 2019). Regarding translators, the American National Association of Judiciary Interpreters and Translators (NAJIT, 2017) clearly states that "advocacy [is] forbidden" on the job because "translators must not let their own biases interfere with the transfer of meaning" (p. 3). However, we believe this is a particular understanding of advocacy that does not fit the social mission of community translation.

In politics, advocacy *is* about bias, and about influencing through lobbying to intervene and achieve a specific goal (e.g., De Rango, 2020). In translation, following a functionalist approach, advocacy is about intervening to enable effective communication. Reiss and Vermeer (1984/2014), in particular, talk of operative texts (such as administrative forms) that require an adaptive approach to reach "maximum effectiveness" (p. 52). This means that the community translator should encourage the writer to communicate so that the reader has access to intended meaning in a way that is "coherent with the receivers' situation" (Nord, 2018, p. 31). If the writer uses opaque bureaucratese, a noninterventionist translation will not facilitate effective communication. The same is true for the asylum seeker who may use a culturally specific oral account that does not necessarily fit with the hosting culture's narrative discourse norms. A transcribed or translated verbatim report will unnecessarily reduce the asylum seeker's chances of a fair evaluation. As Barsky (1996) observes, renditions containing "hesitations, grammatical errors and various infelicities – inevitably jeopardizes the claimant's chances of obtaining refugee status, irrespective of the validity of the claim" (p. 52). So, the form of advocacy proposed here is that used by social care organisations, such as the UK-based Social Care Institute for Excellence (SCIE, 2020): "Advocacy promotes equality, social justice, social inclusion and human rights. It aims to make things happen in the most direct and empowering ways possible. It recognises that self-advocacy . . . is the ultimate aim" ("Principles" section). Crucially, regarding the translator's possible bias interfering with the transfer of meaning, the British mental health charity Mind (2018) states that its advocates will not "give you their personal opinion", "solve problems and make decisions for you", or "make judgements about you" (para. 6).

2.1 The Community Translator as Advocate

We suggest that the advocacy of community translators should be similar, and that their aim should be to provide a translation that will "support people to self-advocate as far as they are able to" (SCIE, 2020, "Self-advocacy" section). Blackledge and Creese (2021) offer a perfect example: Li Na, a "*de facto* interpreter/translator" working at a community centre in the UK, recontextualised a Chinese woman's benefits claim – given orally in Mandarin – into a written statement in English (p. 7). As the authors state:

> It is this intermeshing of translation and recontextualisation that enables Li Na to reshape her client's narrative. In the practice of Li Na this process is about advocacy, and working for what she believes to be the best interests of her client. [Li Na explains how she transcribed the client's account] "I am just letting them know the truth, the answers you gave them are not up to what [your] mum has been describing" . . . . Li Na has done all she can to translate and recontextualise the narrative in a way that gives her client the best possible chance of being granted the benefits for which she has applied.
> *(Blackledge & Creese, 2021, p. 7)*

This telling example illustrates how the interpreter/translator's expertise in reformulating the oral story into more acceptable and convincing bureaucratic language results in an effective communication. However, what makes this case particularly pertinent is that the de facto T&I is employed as an "advice and advocacy worker", and that she was offered the job because she is "good with people" (Blackledge & Creese, 2021, p. 6). In other words, for her interpersonal – rather than linguistic – skills.

Clearly this form of advocacy may be seen as a form of activism on two fronts. First, there is the issue of intervention on linguistically defective or opaque STs that translators (in all fields) are often faced with (e.g., Molnár, 2013). Second, these texts – even without linguistic flaws – tend to be designed only to be effective for fluent insiders, thereby excluding outsiders. For example, a study conducted by Geldenhuys (2019) shows that the forms written by governmental officials for the Water and Sanitation Department in Cape Town (South Africa) are created without the collaboration of any language, communication, or design teams. She continues by saying that "throughout the research I was made aware that the municipality and customer are frequently locked in an unequal power relationship struggle" (2019, p. 108). For example,

> the sequencing of marital status and the use of unusual acronyms or abbreviations are even more confusing. I regard myself as form literate and it took me a while to understand what is meant by the abbreviations MOCP and MICP ["married out of community of property" and "in community of property"]. Not even the search engine Google could provide me with an explanation for these abbreviations.
>
> *(Geldenhuys, 2019, pp. 76–77)*

Not understanding which marital status box to tick certainly reduces the applicant's ability to access municipal services, but what is even more alienating is the South African police procedure ostensibly designed to communicate detainees' rights. The rights are read out to detainees by a member of the police force, though Carney's study (2021) suggests that only those between graduate and postgraduate level will understand the text. For example, the rights form includes the following opaque legalese: "as a person arrested for the alleged commission of an offence, you have the following rights" (Carney, 2021, p. 2).

Ruiz-Cortés (in press) provides another clinical study of municipal application forms, this time in Spain, which once again illustrates the asymmetries between the authorities producing the forms and the end users. What these studies highlight is the initial hurdle that a community translator is often faced with: the ST written by an institution or a professional with little understanding of who they are trying to reach or what an effective communication strategy might entail. This marks a crucial break with public service interpreting, which is not concerned with the ST and its effectiveness given its *verba volant* temporary nature. On the other hand, the community translator as a critical reader is in a prime position to comment on the ST, which (*scripta manent*) is destined to remain and will continue to be used in the community.

So, the focus of the community translator's on-the-job tasks must necessarily extend from the text itself to involvement with the institution (i.e., the commissioner or client representing the institution). This involvement will usually be in terms of collaboration, first and foremost regarding the brief and the feasibility of the skopos, but also regarding more general communication issues. Ruiz-Cortés (in press), for example, suggests that translators test the ST for communicability. She adopts Hill-Madsen's term of "diaphasic interlingual translation . . . in which the translator intervenes to adapt a [source text] to the textual and linguistic abilities of the [target text] audience by clarifying the complex and specialised texts for the non-expert readers" (p. 4). This is clearly not "translation proper" (Jakobson, 1959), but is – as exemplified by plain language research (Cupido & Lesch, 2020) – a case of intratextual translation. If we accept that the community translator's role is to give "voice and access to information, services and participation" (Taibi, 2018b, p. 8), regardless of language, or of whether the text is "source" or "target", then intervening on the source text is certainly part of a community translator's remit. Examples of this form of "translation *plus*" can be found in *Cultus* (Katan & Spinzi, 2021). At this point, we do accept that community translation must include a form of activism, similar to political lobbying, as the following "Guide to Policy Advocacy" states:

> the ultimate target of any advocacy effort is to influence those who hold decision-making power. In some cases, advocates can speak directly to these people in their advocacy efforts; in other cases, they need to put pressure on these people by addressing secondary audiences (for example, their advisors, the media, the public).
> *(Young & Quinn, 2012, p. 26)*

According to the editors of *The Routledge Handbook of Translation and Activism* (Gould & Tahmasebian, 2020), the core distinction of activism fits perfectly with that of advocacy:

> We consider a translation to be activist whenever and however it stirs readers and audiences to action. The goal of provoking the reader may stand in tension with – and even contradict – a literal rendering of words on the page.
> *(p. 4)*

They take activism one step further, stating that translation is "irrevocably political" (Gould & Tahmasebian, 2020, p. 4). We instead suggest that advocacy is irrevocably diplomatic, with the community translator managing the translation project in terms of collaboration.

2.2 Constraints on Advocacy

It is at this point that the *constrained* element comes into play. Following Darwish (2003), "constraints are inhibitive. They restrict the choices and block the alternatives and on a higher plane cause confliction between that which is desired and that which is achievable" (p. 122). The choices and (lack of) alternatives will be determined by the requirement to produce a text based on some form of previous text and will be constrained by the potentiality of that previous text (i.e., what could or might have been expressed or meant as evidenced by cues in the text itself). The "higher plane", as Darwish (2003) explains, includes the translator's brief and the other actors involved, who will generally have the desire – if not the authority – to reduce intervention to a minimum. Community translators will always be constrained by their role as mediators, which means that they will always be seeking what is achievable, rather than what is desirable. This means that they will consider the context(s) and the present power structure to make pragmatic judgements based on diplomacy and the interests of all concerned rather than on political activism. Clearly, though, any ability to take on constrained advocacy must start with a re-examination of what competences we expect our translators to possess.

3 Soft Skills in Translation Competence

We now turn to what we see as the major barrier to transforming this idealised profession into reality: the core competences necessary to motivate translators to start acting as constrained advocates. In translation studies, the idea of translation competence – including a set of linguistic and extra-linguistic skills – was introduced with the PACTE project (Process in the Acquisition of Translation Competence and Evaluation, 2003) and was consolidated with the work of scholars such as Kelly (2005), Katan (2008), Göpferich (2008), and the EMT group (European Master's in Translation Expert Group, 2009, European Master's in Translation, 2017). The skills required refer explicitly to textual and contextual aspects of translation. The skills required for collaboration and constrained advocacy also began to appear, for example in Kelly's (2005) framework where they were subsumed under the category of interpersonal competence. More recently, in her contribution on community translator competences, Kelly (2018) focusses on the particularities of the intended readership (e.g., asylum seekers, refugees, migrants, etc.) whose vulnerability – sometimes coupled with low levels of literacy – require particular interpersonal skills. We also begin to observe the competences necessary for the translator's battle to intervene. In Kelly's (2005) words, those non-cognitive skills refer to the "ability to work with other professionals involved in [the] translation process (translators, revisers, documentary researchers, terminologists, project managers, layout specialists), and other actors (clients, initiators, authors, users, subject area experts). Teamwork. Negotiation skills. Leadership skills" (p. 33).

These interpersonal skills have increasingly become included as a competence for translators, to "manage communication with various agents in the commissioning process" (Tomozeiu & Kumpulainen, 2016, p. 269). The EU-funded project Promoting Intercultural Competence in Translators (PICT, 2012), has also incorporated a set of interpersonal sub-components for translators, which includes empathy, curiosity, proactiveness, and a high level of awareness in social positioning. Obviously, these skills are critical to any communicative event, but the PICT project deserves credit for highlighting how the translator's work requires interactive abilities at all stages of the translation process, consequently bringing into question what "on the job" should entail.

What we notice is an almost Kuhnian shift in understanding. As we have seen, there is an idea within the academic community, at least, that the community translator's role should include intervention outside of the translation itself and should involve looking for solutions in collaboration with authors, commissioners, and clients. As certain members of the PICT project have noted, a "shift from the skill to the human component of that skill is essential to defining new trends in translators' training and pedagogical theory" (Tomozeiu et al., 2016, p. 255).

The European Master's in Translation (EMT, 2017) now also includes personal and interpersonal competences which encompass "all the generic skills, often referred to as 'soft skills'", such as the ability to work in a team, planning and management tasks, and engagement in the process of personal development (EMT, 2017, p. 10). Finally, as Hubscher-Davidson (2013) aptly puts it, the ability "to recognize what a client, author or reader feels or requires, and finding ways to handle and transfer their perspectives is necessary for successful translation/interpreting performance and part of what psychologists call emotional intelligence" (p. 333).

We suggest that non-cognitive emotional competences are not simply add-on components but are the motivational key to the community translator identity, without which the translator will remain ineffective. Consequently, these competences are of a different order. This idea is clearly explained by the Theory of Logical Levels which posits that there is a logical, hierarchical order of types or orders, each facilitating or motivating the next (Katan & Taibi, 2021). These ideas were first discussed by Bertrand Russell with his theory of Logical Types (Whitehead & Russell, 1910), which was subsequently developed by Gregory Bateson (1972): "the theory asserts that no class can, in formal logical or mathematical discourse, be a member of itself; that a class of classes cannot be one of the classes which are its members" (p. 280). This leads to the modelling of competences in the form of a hierarchy.

Following the Iceberg model, what the translator does – and the quality of the translation itself – are part of the tip of the iceberg or the set of visible competences. These competences are influenced by invisible competences that lie underneath and that cover the "know-how" of the translator (meta-competencies). These will, in turn, be fostered or blocked by an even more hidden and deeper level, which is represented by the class of emotional competencies. Emotional competencies will only be effectively realised once translators actively identify themselves with the idealised mission. However, believing in the mission is not enough. If the emotional competencies are not fostered, then the full realisation of a community translator's role will be compromised.

The competences at the tip of the iceberg are more easily attainable through technical learning and instruction, whereas those at the deepest, hidden levels of the iceberg are influenced by the translator's own innate disposition towards that particular competence. That said, as Kautz et al.'s (2014) intergovernmental report on fostering non-cognitive skills concludes: "What used to be regarded as traits fixed at conception are now understood to be skills that can be augmented through guidance and instruction" (p. 11), and there are now many resources dedicated to training emotional intelligence (EI) (e.g., Patra & Shetgovekar, 2020).

Though there is not the space here to discuss the training possibilities, we can map out the main competencies that should be taught, and how they operate at the base of the Logical Levels model. There are a number of terms and distinctions already in use to describe this hidden Logical Level, and its associated competencies, and we will refer to them interchangeably, as the authors do. Figure 2.3 outlines the Logical Levels organisation of the competencies.

Enlarging the more simplistic two-level (visible-hidden) Iceberg model, Hall's Triad of Culture (Hall, 1959/1990; Hall & Trager, 1953) added a third order of culture which lies partially hidden, just below the tip of the iceberg. The Logical

The Battle to Intervene 33

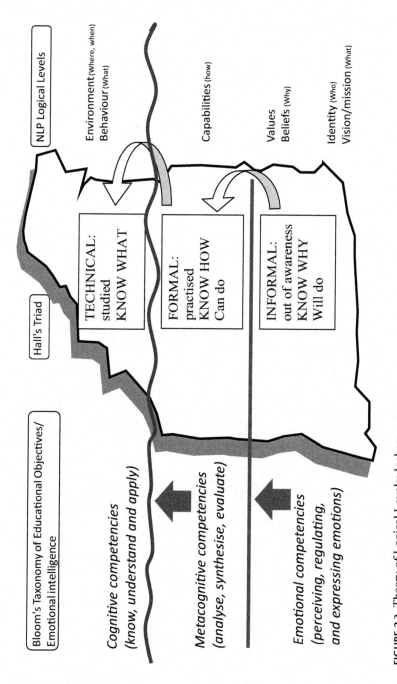

FIGURE 2.3 Theory of Logical Levels: Iceberg

Source: adapted from Katan & Taibi, (2021), p. 51

Levels model has been blended into this model, adding subdivisions within each level. Figure 2.3 also includes Bloom et al.'s (1956) popular learning taxonomies. The cognitive and metacognitive cover the first two, visible and partially submerged, levels. Hall (1959/1990) explains that visible learnings are "technical", as they are generally learned through instruction. Bloom et al. (1956; as cited in Anderson et al., 2001) list these competencies in terms of conscious intellectual effort, such as knowing and understanding about languages and cultures. Just below the tip of the iceberg are those competences that are not studied in a classroom or through a book, but are generally learned "formally" through inculcation, through diligent practice, and over time. These are the meta-competencies: the abilities to analyse, synthesise, and evaluate when and how to use the learned technical competencies. In general, university training ends here, with the community translator able to analyse and evaluate on-the-job translation options.

However, these abilities remain theoretical rather than actually practiced. Similarly, Hymes (1974) theorised the differentiation between communicative competence and actual communicative performance, pointing out that language learners might formally be able to speak the language but, in reality, lack the (social and cultural) competences to actually perform. To actualise the community translator mission and foster constrained advocacy, university training should focus on what Hall (1959/1990) calls the most hidden "informal" level, in which learning is usually "out-of-awareness". This is the level of the non-cognitive skills which interact with core beliefs about what we can do, about who we are, and about our vision or mission in the world. In everyday life, these competencies are rarely either the object of study or are formally learned (Hall, 1959/1990). They are generally the product of nature and nurture, whereby family, peers, schooling, and society at large provide unconscious and out-of-awareness models regarding how to interact with others and with the givens of reality (Hall & Trager, 1953, pp. 24–25).

Çoban (2019) stresses that soft skills are so important in communication that a successful communicative performance may result from individuals with a low level of intelligence quotient (IQ) but with a high level of non-cognitive skills. This represents a tangible example of how the Logical Levels model works. Good soft skills relate to innate and attitudinal traits that form part of core values and beliefs, as well as identity. These motivate – and can even compensate for – the lack of the more visible cognitive competences (e.g., IQ, general knowledge, and language fluency).

Emotional traits, EI, and EQ (emotional quotient) have been discussed in translation, though mainly to analyse and recreate style in literary translation (Hubscher-Davidson, 2007; Munday, 2008) and in creative (re)writing (Loffredo & Perteghella, 2006). However, as Hubscher-Davidson (2013) explains, these studies focus exclusively on EI and on-the-job translating, while the focus here is on EI and the need for constrained advocacy to produce effective translations.

Salovey and Mayer (1990) defined EI as "the ability to monitor one's own and others' feelings and emotions, to discriminate among them and to use this information to guide one's thinking and activity" (p. 189). This definition was based on the theoretical premises of Gardner's model of multiple intelligences

(1983/2004). A product of these studies is the conceptualisation of EI as a personality trait or "a constellation of emotion-related dispositions located at the lower levels of personality hierarchies" (Mavroveli et al., 2009, p. 259), which add the ability to relieve stress, communicate effectively, empathise with others, overcome challenges, and defuse conflict.

4 Transforming the Profession

What we suggest here is to begin focusing training on these non-cognitive competencies and to extend the understanding of the on-the-job givens, as well as offering alternative models of response on how to interact with others, such as developing the ability to empathise, handle uncertainty, and be assertive without losing control. It is the development of these competences that will open the door to the actualisation of the community translator's social mission.

To achieve these aims, it will be necessary to foster the trainee's identification with the community translator's mission. However, as we have seen, most translation trainees are attracted to the text (rather than to people), preferring to remain within their comfort zones and avoid risk, as well as embracing subservience rather than asserting themselves or their ideas – so incorporating the development of these competences should be a *sine qua non* for translator training. In what follows, we propose a brief outline of areas to be developed.

4.1 Uncertainty Avoidance

The first emotional competence that needs to be developed is the ability for the community translator to tolerate that "zone of uncertainty" (Inghilleri, 2005) that comes with changing the status quo. For the social mission to take place, the community translator will clearly need to be proactive and flout the norms regarding both translator behaviour and translation approach. As we have noted, the community translator is rarely expected to do more than carry out their brief in silence. So, before the silence can be broken the community translator will need to envisage, as Pym (2021) suggests, "that risk taking can be justified, pleasurable and socially rewarded" (p. 455). This tendency to accept – if not enjoy – the uncertainty that comes with pushing to expand the traditional habitus is also influenced by cultural background (Hofstede, 1991; Katan & Taibi, 2021, pp. 271–272).

4.2 Empathy

Metaphorically conceptualised as "our social radar", empathy means "sensing what others feel without their saying" (Goleman, 1998, p. 134), and can only be developed once uncertainty avoidance is mastered (Merlini, 2015). Health care specialists have already begun to see empathy as a tool to help and enhance diagnosis, and as a communicative skill that can be taught and trained (see Merlini & Gatti, 2015), including to public service interpreters and translators (Valero-Garcés, 2021), so community translators need to empathise both with the institutions – as well as with their ideal readers. What empathy particularly relates to here is the ability to maintain relationships and collaborate with institutions to effectuate constrained advocacy.

4.3 Assertiveness

Once empathy and full (non-political) respect for both parties is established, the work of constrained advocacy can begin. Interestingly, Leanza (2005) specifically points to this void in (interpreter) training: "interpreters are not trained to be assertive in the face of institutional authority. For example, the Advocate role was not addressed in their training" (p. 186). Clearly, the assertiveness required to intervene can only be entertained once the community translator is comfortable, or at least ready, to accept the uncertainty of facing up to the institutional authority. Assertiveness refers to "the ability to communicate clearly, specifically, and unambiguously, while at the same time being sensitive to the needs of others and their responses in a particular encounter" (Stein & Book, 2006, p. 75). In a similar vein, Dutt (2012) describes assertiveness as standing up for oneself without offending the rights of others and achieving what one needs using reasonable means.

As we have underlined, norms governing translation practice globally are those of the subservient translator, reactive rather than proactive: the translator accepts a commission and then translates according to pre-set guidelines. Autonomy is usually limited to the organisation of the text at the level of the sentence. Any other variations are regarded as flouting the official or unwritten norms. As previously argued in this chapter, constrained advocacy means that the community translator will be asserting the need to make changes, as any consultant would, consonant with the constraints of the original intent of the message and the empowerment needs of the recipient.

5 Conclusion

Globalisation and mass movements have seen the academic community envisage new profiles for community interpreters and translators, though often treated indistinctly. Their *raison d'être* is social and to empower. The reality, as we know – for the community translator, at least – is very different. There are few recognised professional community translators, and those translators working in the community are no different to their *latere* colleagues, having little idea of any enabling social function or mission. Hence, community translation has little visibility or cognisance of itself, and it is struggling to make headway in what is already a poor family of translators.

So, if any intervention is to take place to create texts that communicate and enable, the status quo must be questioned on at least two levels. First, community translators urgently need to extend their ideas of what on-the-job entails and begin to work with (rather than for) the institution to provide a service. Second, training needs to focus on developing the soft, non-cognitive competences related to the community translator mission.

Taking the Logical Levels/Iceberg model as a useful metaphor, we can see that trainees need to take on board at an early stage the identity, vision, and mission of a community translator, but also to acquire the EI to motivate the metacognitive and the cognitive competencies. This will allow the traditionally risk-averse translator to tolerate – and even appreciate – the uncertainty of moving from silent subservience at the end of the production chain towards gaining a collaborative status, able to mediate between the institution and the more vulnerable client. Once a relationship has been established, constrained advocacy can begin, allowing both the weaker client and the more powerful institution to engage in a way that public services may act in the public interest, while always remembering that the advocacy will be constrained and that community translators will need to choose their battles.

Notes

1 David Katan is responsible for Sections 1–2; Cinzia Spinzi is responsible for Sections 3–5.
2 The first conference, "Translating Cultures: Translation as a Tool for Inclusion/Exclusion in a Multicultural Society" was organised at the University of Westminster, London, UK, in June 2014; the following conference on "Community Translation" was organized at the University of Western Sydney, Australia, in September 2014.
3 Not all the respondents replied to all the questions.

References

Anderson, L. W. (Ed.), Krathwohl, D. R., (Ed.), Airasian, P. W., Cruikshank, K. A., Mayer, R. E., Pintrich, P. R., Raths, J., & Wittrock, M. C. (2001). *A taxonomy for learning, teaching, and assessing: A revision of Bloom's taxonomy of educational objectives* (Complete ed.). Longman.
Barsky, R. F. (1996). The interpreter as intercultural agent in convention refugee hearings. *The Translator, 2*(1), 45–63. https://doi.org/10.1080/13556509.1996.10798963
Bateson, G. (1972). *Steps to an ecology of mind*. Ballantine Books.
Blackledge, A., & Creese, A. (2021). Recontextualisation and advocacy in the translation zone. *Text & Talk, 41*(1), 1–21. https://doi.org/10.1515/text-2019-0123
Bloom, B. S. (Ed.), Engelhart, M. D., Furst, E. J., Hill, W. H., & Krathwohl, D. R. (1956). *Taxonomy of educational objectives: The classification of educational goals. Handbook 1: Cognitive domain*. David McKay.
Campbell, J. L., & Katan, D. (2022). User-centered design (UCD) and transcreation of non-profit communications in a technical communication classroom. 2022 *IEEE International Professional Communication Conference (ProComm) Proceedings*, pp. 444–450. https://doi.org/10.1109/ProComm53155.2022.00087.
Carney, T. R. (2021). Understanding one's rights when arrested and detained: An assessment of language barriers that affect comprehension. *South African Journal of Criminal Justice, 34*(1), 1–30. https://journals.co.za/doi/pdf/10.47348/SACJ/v34/i1a1
Çoban, F. (2019). The relationship between professional translators' emotional intelligence and their translator satisfaction. *International Journal of Comparative Literature & Translation Studies, 7*(3), 50–64. https://doi.org/10.7575/aiac.ijclts.v.7n.3p.50
Cupido, A., & Lesch, H. (2020). Gemeenskapsvertaalpraktyk: Gewone taal vir die hervertaling van'n bankteks [Community translation. Plain language for the retranslation of a banking text]. *Litnet Akademies, 17*(1), 138–170. https://journals.co.za/doi/epdf/10.10520/EJC-1d8d24d2da

Darwish, A. (2003). *The transfer factor: Selected essays on translation and cross-cultural communication*. Writescope Publishers.

De Rango, E. (2020). Lobbying and advocacy: Start here. *The Commons Social Change Library*. https://commonslibrary.org/lobbying-and-advocacy-start-here/

Dutt, R. (2012). *And the lion smiled at the rabbit: Manage emotions to win*. Wisdom Tree Publishers.

European Master's in Translation. (2017). *European master's in translation: Competence framework 2017*. European Commission. https://ec.europa.eu/info/sites/default/files/emt_competence_fwk_2017_en_web.pdf

European Master's in Translation Expert Group. (2009). *Competences for professional translators, experts in multilingual and multimedia communication*. European Commission. https://ec.europa.eu/info/sites/default/files/emt_competences_translators_en.pdf

Gardner, H. (2004). *Frames of mind. The theory of multiple intelligences* (20th anniversary ed.). Basic Books (Original work published 1983).

Geldenhuys, N. (2019). *The language of forms: A discourse analysis of municipal application forms*. [Master's thesis, University of Western Cape]. UWC Electronic Theses and Dissertations Repository. http://etd.uwc.ac.za/xmlui/handle/11394/6952

Gentzler, E. (2001). *Contemporary translation theories* (Rev. 2nd ed.). Multilingual Matters.

Goleman, D. (1998). *Working with emotional intelligence*. Bantam Books.

Gould, R., & Tahmasebian, K. (2020). Introduction: Translation and activism in the time of the now. In R. Gould & K. Tahmasebian (Eds.), *The Routledge handbook of translation and activism* (pp. 1–9). Routledge.

Göpferich, S. (2008). *Translationsprozessforschung. Stand – Methoden – Perspektiven* [Translation and interpreting process research: State of affairs, methods, perspectives]. Gunter Narr.

Hall, E. T. (1990). *The silent language*. Doubleday (Original work published 1959).

Hall, E. T., & Trager, G. L. (1953). *The analysis of culture*. American Council of Learned Societies.

Hofstede, G. (1991). *Cultures and organizations: Software of the mind*. McGraw-Hill.

Hubscher-Davidson, S. (2007). *An empirical investigation into the effects of personality on the performance of French to English student translators* [Unpublished doctoral dissertation]. University of Bath.

Hubscher-Davidson, S. (2013). Emotional intelligence and translation studies: A new bridge. *Meta*, *58*(2), 324–346. https://doi.org/10.7202/1024177ar

Hymes, D. (1974). *Foundations in sociolinguistics: An ethnographic approach*. University of Pennsylvania Press.

Inghilleri, M. (2005). Mediating zones of uncertainty: Interpreter agency, the interpreting habitus and political asylum adjudication. *The Translator*, *11*(1), 69–85. https://doi.org/10.1080/13556509.2005.10799190

Jakobson, R. (1959). On linguistic aspects of translation. In R. A. Brower (Ed.), *On translation* (pp. 232–239). Harvard University Press. https://doi.org/10.4159/harvard.9780674731615.c18

Kalina, S. (2015). Ethical challenges in different interpreting settings. *MonTI. Monographs in Translation and Interpreting*, Special Issue 2, 63–86. https://doi.org/10.6035/MonTI.2015.ne2.2

Katan, D. (2008). University training, competencies and the death of the translator: Problems in professionalizing translation and in the Translation Profession. In M. T. Musacchio & G. H. Sostero (Eds.), *Tradurre: Formazione e professione* (pp. 113–140). CLEUP.

Katan, D. (2011). Occupation or Profession: A survey of the translators' world. In R. Sela-Sheffy & M. Shlesinger (Eds.), *Identity and status in the translational professions* (pp. 65–88). John Benjamins Publishing Company.

Katan, D. (2016). Translation at the cross-roads: Time for the transcreational turn? *Perspectives, 24*(3), 365–381. https://doi.org/10.1080/0907676X.2015.1016049

Katan, D. (2018). Trans*latere* or trans*creare*: In theory and in practice, and by whom? In C. Spinzi, A. Rizzo, & M. L. Zummo (Eds.), *Translation or transcreation? Discourses, texts, and visuals* (pp. 15–38). Cambridge Scholars Publishing.

Katan, D (in press). Specialist translator wanted. A survey of the translator's world. In G. Palumbo, K. Peruzzo & G. Pontrandolfo (Eds.), *A life in specialized translation: In honour of federica scarpa*. Peter Lang.

Katan, D., & Spinzi, C. (Eds.). (2021). Translation *plus*: The added value of the translator [Special issue]. *Cultus: The Journal of Intercultural Mediation and Communication, 14*. www.cultusjournal.com/index.php/archive/27-issue-2021-v-14-translation-plus-the-added-value-of-the-translator

Katan, D., & Taibi, M. (2021). *Translating cultures: An introduction for translators, interpreters and mediators* (3rd ed.). Routledge.

Kautz, T., Heckman, J. J., Diris, R., ter Weel, B., & Borghans, L. (2014). Fostering and measuring skills: Improving cognitive and non-cognitive skills to promote lifetime success. *OECD*. www.oecd.org/education/ceri/Fostering-and-Measuring-Skills-Improving-Cognitive-and-Non-Cognitive-Skills-to-Promote-Lifetime-Success.pdf

Kelly, D. (2005). *A handbook for translator trainers*. St. Jerome.

Kelly, D. (2018). Education for community translation: Thirteen key ideas. In M. Taibi (Ed.), *Translating for the community* (pp. 26–41). Multilingual Matters. https://doi.org/10.21832/TAIBI9139

Leanza, Y. (2005). Roles of community interpreters in pediatrics as seen by interpreters, physicians and researchers. *Interpreting, 7*(2), 167–192. https://doi.org/10.1075/intp.7.2.03lea

Lesch, H. (1999). Community translation: Right or privilege. In M. Erasmus (Ed.), *Liaison interpreting in the community* (pp. 90–98). Van Schaik.

Loffredo, E., & Perteghella, M. (Eds.). (2006). *Translation and creativity: Perspectives on creative writing and translation studies*. Continuum.

Luque, F. G. (2017). Sworn translators in the legal context: A field of confluence between translation and interpreting. *International Journal of Legal Discourse, 2*(2), 209–224. https://doi.org/10.1515/ijld-2017-0012

Mavroveli, S., Petrides, K. V., Sangareau, Y., & Furnham, A. (2009). Exploring the relationships between trait emotional intelligence and objective socio-emotional outcomes in childhood. *British Journal of Educational Psychology, 79*(2), 259–272. https://doi.org/10.1348/000709908X368848

Merlini, R. (2015). Empathy: A "zone of uncertainty" in mediated healthcare practice. *Cultus, 8*, 27–49.

Merlini, R., & Gatti, M. (2015). Empathy in healthcare interpreting: Going beyond the notion of role. *The Interpreters' Newsletter, 20*, 139–160. http://hdl.handle.net/10077/11857

Mind (2018, March). *Advocacy in mental health*. www.mind.org.uk/information-support/guides-to-support-and-services/advocacy/what-is-advocacy/

Molnár, O. (2013). Source text quality in the translation process. In J. Zehnalová, O. Molnár, & M. Kubánek (Eds.), *Tradition and trends in trans-language communication*, (pp. 59–86). Palacký University Olomouc.

Morón, M. (in press). Creativity as an added value in translators' training: Learning through transcreation. In G. Massey, E. Huertas Barros, & D. Katan (Eds.), *The human translator in the 2020s*. Routledge.

Munday, J. (2008). *Style and ideology in translation: Latin American writing in English*. Routledge.
National Association of Judiciary Interpreters & Translators Advocacy Committee (2017). *Advocacy 101 for interpreters and translators*. National Association of Judiciary Interpreters & Translators. https://najit.org/wp-content/uploads/2016/09/Advocacy-101-for-Interpreters-and-Translators-NAJIT-4.2017.pdf
Nord, C. (2018). *Translating as a purposeful activity: Functionalist approaches explained* (2nd ed.). Routledge.
Patra, S., & Shetgovekar, S. (2020). Unit 5: Emotions, self-control and assertiveness. *eGyanKosh*. http://egyankosh.ac.in//handle/123456789/69793
Phelan, M., Rudvin, M., Skaaden, H., & Kermit, P. S. (2019). *Ethics in public service interpreting*. Routledge. https://doi.org/10.4324/9781315715056
Process in the Acquisition of Translation Competence and Evaluation (PACTE group [Beeby, A., Fernández Rodríguez, M., Fox, O., Hurtado Albir, A., Neunzig, W., Orozco, M., Presas, M., Rodríguez, P., & Romero, I. N.]) (2003). Building a translation competence model. In F. Alves (Ed.) *Triangulating translation: Perspectives in process oriented research* (pp. 43–66). John Benjamins Publishing Company.
Promoting Intercultural Communication in Translators. (2012). *Intercultural competence curriculum framework*. www.pictllp.eu/en/curriculum-framework
Pym, A. (2008). On omission in simultaneous interpreting: Risk analysis of a hidden effort. In G. Hansen, A. Chesterman, & H. Gerzymisch-Arbogast (Eds.), *Efforts and models in interpreting and translation research: A tribute to Daniel Gile* (pp. 83–105). John Benjamins Publishing Company.
Pym, A. (2021). Translation, risk management and cognition. In F. Alves & A. L. Jakobsen (Eds.), *The Routledge handbook of translation and cognition* (pp. 445–458). Routledge.
Reiss, K., & Vermeer, H. J. (2014). *Towards a general theory of translational action: Skopos theory explained* (C. Nord, Trans.). Routledge (Original Work published 1984).
Ruiz-Cortés, E. (in press). The translator as a plain text designer for the Public Administration: A necessary role? In G. Massey, E. Huertas Barros, & D. Katan (Eds.), *The Human Translator in the 2020s*. Routledge.
Salovey, P., & Mayer, J. (1990). Emotional intelligence. *Imagination, Cognition and Personality*, 9(3), 185–211. https://doi.org/10.2190/DUGG-P24E-52WK-6CDG
Social Care Institute for Excellence (2020, October). *Advocacy: Inclusion, empowerment and human rights*. www.scie.org.uk/advocacy/commissioning/inclusion#:~:text=production%20workshop%20participant-,Principles,behalf%20 – %20is%20the%20ultimate%20aim
Simeoni, D. (1998). The pivotal status of the translator's habitus. *Target*, 10(1), 1–39. https://doi.org/10.1075/target.10.1.02sim
Sewell, P. (2004). Students buzz round the translation class like bees round the honey pot: Why? In K. Malmkjær (Ed.), *Translation in undergraduate degree programmes* (pp. 151–162). John Benjamins Publishing Company.
Stein, S. J., & Book, H. E. (2006). *The EQ edge: Emotional intelligence and your success*. Jossey-Bass.
Taibi, M. (2011). Public service translation. In K. Malmkjær & K. Windle (Eds.), *The Oxford handbook of translation studies* (pp. 214–227). Oxford University Press. https://doi.org/10.1093/oxfordhb/9780199239306.013.0016
Taibi, M. (2018a). Introduction. In M. Taibi (Ed.), *Translating for the Community* (pp. 1–5). Multilingual Matters. https://doi.org/10.21832/TAIBI9139
Taibi, M. (2018b). Quality assurance in community translation. In M. Taibi (Ed.), *Translating for the Community* (pp. 7–25). Multilingual Matters. https://doi.org/10.21832/TAIBI9139

Taibi, M., & Ozolins, U. (2016). *Community translation*. Bloomsbury Academic.

Tomozeiu, D., Koskinen, K., & D'Arcangelo, A. (2016). Introduction: Teaching intercultural competence in translator training. *The Interpreter and Translator Trainer*, *10*(3), 251–267. https://doi.org/10.1080/1750399X.2016.1236557

Tomozeiu, D., & Kumpulainen, M. (2016). Operationalising intercultural competence for translation pedagogy. *The Interpreter and Translator Trainer*, *10*(3), 268–284. https://doi.org/10.1080/1750399X.2016.1236558

Townsley, B. (2018). Community translation in the UK: An enquiry into practice. In M. Taibi (Ed.), *Translating for the community* (pp. 110–120). Multilingual Matters. https://doi.org/10.21832/TAIBI9139

Valero-Garcés, C. (2014). Introduction. Translation and interpreting in the public services: Crossing the threshold into adulthood. *FITISPos International Journal*, *1*, 1–8.

Valero-Garcés, C. (2019). Training public service interpreters and translators: Facing challenges. *Journal of Language and Law*, *71*, 88–105. https://doi.org/10.2436/rld.i71.2019.3262

Valero-Garcés, C. (2021). Interpreting and intercultural communication: Crossing domains in the era of globalization, technological advances and social networks. *Journal of Translation Studies*, *1*(2), 23–38. https://doi.org/10.3726/JTS022021.2

Whitehead, A. N., & Russell, B. (1910). *Principia mathematica* (2nd ed.). Cambridge University Press.

Young, E., & Quinn, L. (2012). *Making research evidence matter: A guide to policy advocacy in transition countries*. International Centre for Policy Advocacy. https://advocacyguide.icpolicyadvocacy.org/21-defining-policy-advocacy

3

TRANSLATORS' ETHICS IN COMMUNITY TRANSLATION

A Case Study of English–Japanese Translators in the Australian System

Maho Fukuno

1 Introduction

As an essential service for social justice in multicultural societies, community translation is inseparable from the ethics of society, institutions, and individuals. However, the ethical roles of translators in community settings, and more generally, is contested across academia and professional fields.

Several studies have brought to light the possibility of translators assuming an advocative role based on the teleological foundations of community translation (Fraser, 1993; Lesch, 1999, 2017; Taibi, 2017; Taibi & Ozolins, 2016). Lesch's (1999) argument for a reader-oriented approach to community translation is representative of this view:

> [Community translation] is an attempt to balance the power relationship between the sender and the receiver by prioritising the needs of the community. Effective, empowering communication between the author and the reader via the translated text implies that the translator needs to be on the side of the powerless, that is the reader (in this case).
>
> *(p. 93)*

Taibi and Ozolins (2016) have similarly defined community translation as "an empowering exercise for minority groups who lack a good command of the mainstream language(s)" (p. 74), describing the role of the translator as that of "advocate for the powerless" (p. 74).

In contrast with the advocative role image, an impartial and neutral role image is widely shared in the translation profession. In Australia, where community translation and interpreting are considered relatively well developed (Taibi & Ozolins, 2016; Valero-Garcés, 2014), the professional Code of Ethics maintained by the national professional association, the Australian Institute for Interpreters and Translators (AUSIT), includes impartiality as a key ethical principle:

DOI: 10.4324/9781003247333-4

Impartiality

Interpreters and translators observe impartiality in all professional contacts. Interpreters remain unbiased throughout the communication exchanged between the participants in any interpreted encounter. Translators do not show bias towards either the author of the source text or the intended readers of their translation.

Explanation: Interpreters and translators play an important role in facilitating parties who do not share a common language to communicate effectively with each other. They aim to ensure that the full intent of the communication is conveyed. Interpreters and translators are not responsible for what the parties communicate, only for complete and accurate transfer of the message. They do not allow bias to influence their performance; likewise they do not soften, strengthen or alter the messages being conveyed.

(AUSIT, 2012, p. 5)

The AUSIT Code of Ethics and its key principles are assimilated by translators and trainees through education, professional training, and professional development. Furthermore, knowledge and application of the Code of Ethics is tested as a prerequisite for the certification examination administered by the National Accreditation Authority for Translators and Interpreters (NAATI). These ethical principles are thus firmly consolidated in the professional discourse of translation within Australia.

The impartial role image of translators, enforced by external structures such as the professional norms and expectations (Kurger & Crots, 2014) described, tends to overlook the personal dimensions of translator ethics – that is, translators' personal beliefs and moral viewpoints (Kurger & Crots, 2014). However, the empowering and advocative role, mainly discussed in academia, reveals these personal dimensions by inviting translators' interpretations of power relationships, and the exercise of empathy and moral judgement, on a situational basis.

As Lambert (2018, 2021) has noted, previous work on professional translator ethics has paid insufficient attention to its personal dimensions. Moreover, while several studies have critiqued the impartial role image of translators as illusory (Abdallah, 2011; Baker, 2006; Kruger & Crots, 2014; Lambert, 2018; Tack, 2001; Tymoczko, 2007), they have not considered the context of community translation. In view of this gap in translation studies literature, this chapter presents an empirical, mixed methods study of translators' personal and external ethics in the field of community translation in Australia.

The study addresses the following questions: How do nationally certified translators perceive their role as a translator? How do they negotiate personal and external ethics? Section 2 will survey prevailing scholarly discourses on translators' roles, which will be covered again in Section 3 when outlining the research design and design process of an online questionnaire. Section 4 will quantitatively analyse the online questionnaire data. Section 5 will present the results of the qualitative analysis of the open responses from the questionnaire, followed by a discussion and a presentation of the study's implications for community translation.

2 Discourses on Translators' Roles

Previous literature on translators and interpreters (e.g., Angelelli, 2004; Nord, 1991; Taibi & Ozolins, 2016; Venuti, 1995) suggests that translators' ethical roles and role images can be analysed according to a range of interrelated axes, including impartiality–advocacy, visibility–invisibility, and the orientation of loyalty. Among these, the impartiality–advocacy axis was optimal for initiating the study because neutrality and impartiality are value-attached beliefs widely shared by translators and interpreters and constitute what Angelelli (2004) has called a "professional ideology" (pp. 19–22).

The impartial role image and its discourse, widespread within and beyond Australia, are enforced by the codes of ethics of various professional associations (e.g., Asociación Argentina de Traductores e Intérpretes [AATI], 2018; American Translators Association [ATA], 2010; AUSIT, 2012; see Baixauli-Olmos, 2021), and by translator and interpreter training worldwide (Angelelli, 2004). The impartial role image characterises the translator as neutral in relation to all parties involved in the translation context, including the source text (ST) author and the target text (TT) reader. This impartial image requires and is sustained by the translator's professional detachment (AUSIT, 2012). According to this image, translators only focus on accurately transferring the meaning of the ST to the target language (TL) without distortions, omissions, or insertions, and are therefore not responsible for the contents or intentions of the ST or TT, nor for the style of the written text. Judgements, decisions, and negotiations resulting from the accurate transfer of meaning are concerns for ST producers and TT readers. This view has been criticised for reducing the role of the translator to that of a mere "language modem" (Angelelli, 2004, p. 20).

This impartial role image is often associated with the translator's subservience to norms that idealise invisibility in translated communication, as critiqued by Angelelli (2004), Prunč (2007), Simeoni (1998), and Venuti (1995). Professional discourse and training also uphold the invisible image of translators, constructed as being committed to transferring accurate and neutral meanings between two languages (Angelelli, 2004). The invisible translator, following the norms expected by other parties in the translation process, translates accurately and "impartially" from the source language (SL) into the TL and produces natural translations that read as if they had been written in the TL from the start (Venuti, 1995). In these translations, the translator is invisible for TT readers. Contrastively, the visible translator produces, with their creative interventions, a translation that may read markedly as a translation from another language. A translator could become visible for various ideological, moral, or cultural reasons, such as foregrounding the ideational and aesthetic voice of the ST, especially when the SL is considered as being marginalised by English as the dominant language (Venuti, 1995).

However, as apparent in the following two cases, translator invisibility may not always accord with impartiality as described previously. First, when translators are subserviently responding to other parties' expectations of translator invisibility – whether they are the TT reader, the ST author, the client, the translation agency or all of them – the translators are not placing themselves in the exactly neutral position detached from the other parties. Second, in cases when translators who idealise invisibility work to produce meaningful and natural translations for TT readership as if the text had been originally written in the TL, they are not only committing themselves to the accurate transfer of meaning from the ST to the TT but also to mediating between two cultural communities and to considering the needs of the TT readership in terms of the goals they expect to achieve with the translation. Therefore, the concept of invisibility in this case can be construed as being reflected in professional responsibility enacted by translators when delivering a TT suitable for TT readership and the translation context. More broadly, this kind of invisibility may require, in practice, translators to have multidirectional loyalty – to the ST, the ST author, the client, and the end user (Nord, 1991), rather than being impartial in a detached manner. Hence, whether the invisibility is interpreted as being subservient or professionally responsible, functionally invisible translators may not exactly align with the impartial role image in the limited sense described previously but instead be positioned between this image and that at the other end of the axis: the advocative role image.

According to an extreme view of the advocative role image, translators are positioned to be supportive of and to advocate for the needs of a particular party in the translation context. Such advocacy essentially aligns with the fundamental purposes of community translation. Previous studies of community translation (Fraser, 1993; Lesch, 1999, 2004; Taibi, 2011, 2017; Taibi & Ozolins, 2016) have observed that, in the unequal relationship between ST producers and TT readers, translators tend to work for the disempowered party (i.e., the TT readers). Advocative translators assume responsibility not only for accurate linguistic transfer from the ST to TT, but also for the accessibility and effectiveness of the translation for TT readers. Therefore, the advocative role embraces both cultural mediation and interpersonal support geared specifically towards helping the disadvantaged party achieve their communicative goals.

Translators may, however, also advocate for the clients who are paying them, regardless of the clients' power and status in the communicative situation. This variant of the advocative role image is common among translators and interpreters working in the business domain (Takimoto, 2006).

3 Method

This research presents a case study of professional English–Japanese translators mainly working in Australia. The data were collected between 8 May 2019 and 26 July 2019 using an online questionnaire. The questionnaire was designed to survey translators' perceptions of their role and the interplay between personal and external ethics. The question items were derived from the discourses on role images previously discussed in this chapter. Ultimately, 71 translators completed the questionnaire. An explanatory mixed methods design (Creswell et al., 2003) was deployed with two analytical stages. In the first analytical stage, descriptive and inferential statistics were used to assess the closed-ended response data via IBM SPSS Statistics (Version 27). In the second stage, thematic analysis was employed to examine the translators' responses to an open-ended question via NVivo 12 Pro (QSR International, 2018).

This study is part of my current doctoral research project, the broader scope of which is to explore the effects of translator ethics and ideology on translation practice. It should be noted that, while this chapter specifically focuses on the analytical findings of the online questionnaire, the complete research design included both the questionnaire analysis and two subsequent community translation tasks, as well as follow-up interviews which examined translators' immediate retrospections.

3.1 Questionnaire Design

The questionnaire was administered using the online survey tool Qualtrics. The question-and-answer items were written in Japanese and were divided into four sections. This chapter, however, only focuses on the findings of the first three sections. The first section obtained demographic data on the participants, including age, gender, country of residence, and cultural identity. The second section focused on the participants' professional backgrounds, including their types of certification and training, duration of professional experience, and field(s) of translation work. The third section asked how often participants referenced a code of ethics and which code, the level of importance they gave to each of the nine key ethical principles included in the AUSIT Code of Ethics, and, finally, their perceptions of translator roles, measured as the level of agreement with six statements (listed in Table 3.1).

To facilitate the comparison of the responses in terms of their differences and similarities, most questions were multiple choice, multiple response, or closed-ended, requiring participants to provide one-word responses. In the third section of the questionnaire, responses were given according to a 5-point Likert scale, followed by an open-ended request: "翻訳者の役割について、ご自身の考えをご記入ください。 [Please write your thoughts about translators' roles]".

A dimension analysis (Angelelli, 2004; Hox, 1997) of the literature on translator roles and their associated discourses was initially conducted to identify constructs for observation. Based on this analysis, translator role image and three associated sub-constructs were identified: translators' perceptions about their positionality in relation to other parties in translation contexts (i.e., completely neutral or advocating for one or more parties), translators' perceptions about their responsibilities (i.e., what they are responsible for as translators), and translators' perceptions about their professional expectations (i.e., what they should do as translators). The Interpreter's Interpersonal Role Inventory (IPRI) developed by Angelelli (2004) was used as a point of departure to measure participants' perceptions of translator roles. Angelelli (2004) designed the inventory to observe interpreters' perceptions of, and attitudes towards, the (in)visibility of the interpersonal role (see Table 3.1).

3.2 Recruiting Participants

The primary study participants were English–Japanese translators working with a NAATI certification and knowledge of the AUSIT Code of Ethics. However, to compare translators certified in the Australian system with non-certified

TABLE 3.1 List of Statements About Translators' Roles

S1	翻訳者は、翻訳テキストの内容とスタイルに責任がある。 [Translators are responsible for the content and style of the TT.]
S2	翻訳者の役割は、原文の意味を原文作成者が表現した通りに翻訳することだ。 [The translator's role is to translate the meaning of the ST as the ST author expressed.]
S3	翻訳者は、その翻訳の背景状況の中で最も弱い立場に置かれている者を思いやって、翻訳のプロセスに向き合うべきだ。 [Translators should be empathetic to the weakest party in the translation context.]
S4	翻訳者は、文化的に不適切な言葉や表現を翻訳で調節するべきだ。 [Translators should adjust culturally inappropriate words and expressions in their TT.]
S5	翻訳者は、翻訳料金を支払っている依頼者の目的や利益を優先するべきだ。 [Translators should prioritise the aims and benefits of the client paying the translation fee.]
S6	翻訳者の役割は、翻訳を通して翻訳読者の生活を助けることだ。 [The translator's role is to help {improve} the lives of TT readers through translation.]

translators, translators based in Japan were also approached. The online questionnaire was delivered through multiple mailing lists and public notifications, thereby relying on availability sampling and snowball sampling techniques. These delivery methods included NAATI official mail-outs to certified translators and interpreters registered for the English–Japanese language pair, the mailing list of the Japan Association for Interpreting and Translation Studies, the forum and job noticeboard of the Japan Association of Translators (JAT), and the mailing lists and noticeboards of several international communications associations in Japanese cities with significant populations of non-L1 Japanese language users. Additionally, I directly contacted individual translators introduced to me by recruited participants.

4 Quantitative Analysis of the Online Questionnaire

4.1 Professional and Demographic Background

All 71 participants worked as English–Japanese translators, the majority of whom had substantial translation experience (see Appendix A). Almost half of the participants had more than 10 years of translation experience ($n = 33$, 46.5%), whereas others had 5–10 years of experience ($n = 21$, 29.6%). A majority of the participants ($n = 55$, 77.5%) had a NAATI certification in translation, interpreting, or both; 51 (72%) of whom held NAATI-certified translator credentials. Since 55 questionnaire respondents were English–Japanese translators and were NAATI-certified in either translation or interpreting, they were assumed to be well versed in the AUSIT Code of Ethics and were accordingly considered NAATI-certified translators. The most common field of translation, for both NAATI-certified and non-certified groups, was business and marketing (certified group: n = 45, 81.8%; non-certified group: n = 8, 50%). This was followed by community and public services translation (see Appendix B), although more NAATI-certified translators worked in this field (n = 27, 49.1%) than non-certified translators (n = 5, 31.3%).

Most of the translators (n = 49, 69%) had completed formal translation training (40 hours or more) and held a master's degree, a bachelor's degree, or an advanced diploma. Of those who had completed translation training, more than half had undertaken NAATI-endorsed training in Australia (n = 38, 53.5%), whereas relatively few had trained in Japan at private vocational training schools (n = 7, 9.9%). More than half of the translators referenced the AUSIT Code of Ethics in their professional practice (n = 40, 56.3%), however, they did so relatively infrequently (M = 2.11, with responses ranging from 1 = *not at all* to 5 = *always*). These data suggest that, at the time of the study, more than half of the participants had interacted with certification and training institutions as well as ethical codes, each of which externally enforces professional ethical values and norms in Australia.

Comparison revealed that both NAATI-certified (n = 55) and non-certified (n = 16) translators were more often female (see Appendix C). The mean age did not substantially differ between the certified (M = 46.67) and non-certified (M = 46.63) groups. Those in the certified group primarily resided in Australia (n = 42, 76.4%), but some divided their time between Japan and Australia (n = 2, 3.6%) or resided in New Zealand (n = 1, 1.8%), where NAATI certification will be adopted in community interpreting as of 2024 (Ministry of Business, Innovation and Employment, 2021). In the non-certified group, the majority also lived in Australia (n = 10, 62.5%); however, the proportion of translators based in Japan (n = 6, 37.5%) was larger than that of the certified group. In both groups, most participants identified as "Japanese" (certified group: n = 36, 65.5%; non-certified group: n = 14, 87.5%); however, a few certified translators identified as "Australian Japanese" (n = 3, 5.5%) or "Japanese Australian" (n = 3, 5.5%). These cultural identity and residence data indicate that some certified translators may have a stronger sense of intercultural identity and pursue an intercultural life more generally.

4.2 Perceptions of Translators' Roles

The analysis here focuses on participants' responses to the six statements about translator roles (see Table 3.1). Responses were given on a 5-point Likert scale, in which 1 = *strongly disagree*; 2 = *disagree*; 3 = *neither agree nor disagree*; 4 = *agree*; 5 = *strongly agree* (see Appendix D). In this section, the analysis will focus on attitudinal tendencies at the whole-sample level, while the next section will compare these tendencies between sample groups categorised by certification and professional background.

First, the internal consistency of the data was measured to assess how the responses to the statements were correlated with each other and, therefore, how consistently each of the response sets represented the participants' perceptions of translator roles. To accurately measure internal consistency, responses to statements that represented opposite attitudes towards the same construct had to be reversed (e.g., on a 5-point Likert scale, score 1 had to be reversed to score 5; score 2 to score 4; score 4 to score 2; score 5 to score 1). For example, on the one hand, Statement 2 (S2)[1] was derived from the impartial role image discussed in Section 2. On the other hand, the other statements were constructed to reflect variations of the advocative role image that assumed active responsibilities; for example, being responsible for the TT content and style, adjusting appropriate words and expressions in the TT, advocating for the benefit of clients, considering the weaker party involved in the translation process, and helping improve the lives of TT readers. Because the impartial and advocative role images can be perceived as two extremes of a role spectrum, it could be argued that the responses to S2 had to be reversed. However, after considering the potential multidirectionality within the advocative role image (i.e., a translator being supportive of various parties) and its varied relationships with the impartial role image, I decided not to treat S2 as representing attitudes opposite to those of the other statements and thus did not reverse the responses to S2. The internal consistency value (Cronbach's α) was consequently calculated without reversing the score of S2; the resulting consistency value (0.379) was considered unacceptably low,[2] but removing the responses to S2 did not improve the consistency value.

The lack of internal consistency within the statement set confirms that the statements that were written to describe the advocative role image vis-à-vis the impartial role image were not interpreted by the participants as consistently representing a single image of translators. Further, the statement that was intended to reflect the impartial role image was not necessarily interpreted as a position contrary to that expressed in other statement items concerning the advocative role image. This outcome suggests that a binary view of translator roles does not capture the complex dimensions of translators' consciousness about their roles and responsibilities towards different people and texts involved in the translation process, implying that such consciousness may not exclusively correspond with either the impartial or the advocative role image as defined in ethical codes or scholarly work.

Upon confirming that these six statements were not interpreted as representing a unitary role image, principal component analysis (PCA) was performed to observe multiple dimensions coexisting within the six statement items. The outcome identified two main dimensions: tentatively called Dimension 1, which includes S3, S4, and S6, and Dimension 2, which includes S1 and S2.

To further identify the themes of Dimensions 1 and 2, two analyses were conducted. First, the responses to S1 and S2 in Dimension 2 were compared with each statement in Dimension 1. That most participants agreed with S1 and S2 but were undecided about S3, S4, and S6 is especially noteworthy (see Figure 3.1 as an example). Further, several participants who agreed with S1 and S2 disagreed with S3, S4, and S6. These stark contrasts between the responses to Dimension 1

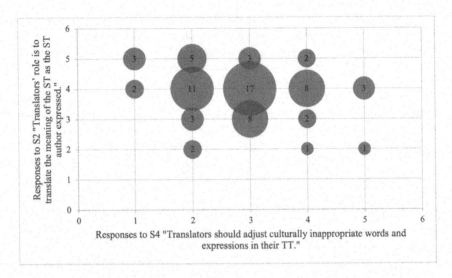

FIGURE 3.1 Comparison of response distributions of S2 and S4

and Dimension 2 indicate that the themes represented by these dimensions – namely, advocacy and impartiality – may be contrasting as well, even though their definitions may be unaligned with the view that their relation is one of binary opposition.

To explore this possibility, a correlation analysis[3] was run between a) the scores calculated for Dimension 1 and Dimension 2 (score 1 and score 2), and b) how much the translators valued key ethical notions: namely, impartiality, accuracy, and clarity of role boundaries. The latter set of variables were measured according to a 5-point Likert scale (5 = *very important* and 1 = *not important at all*; see Appendix E). The results showed weak, negative correlations between score 1 and the importance of impartiality ($r_s = -0.32, p < 0.01$) and between score 1 and the importance of accuracy ($r_s = -0.28, p < 0.05$). These results suggest that participants who placed more importance on the notions of impartiality and accuracy tended to be less supportive of the notions represented by Dimension 1. Namely, participants who highly valued the importance of impartiality and accuracy as professional ethical notions were more likely to disagree that translators should be empathetic in the translation context, should adjust expressions to make them more culturally appropriate, and should improve the lives of TT readers. These negative correlational relationships between Dimension 1 and ethical notions provided evidence for the two contrasting attitudinal themes previously proposed. Specifically, Dimension 1 seems to reflect an attitude closer to the advocative role image but also to coexist with Dimension 2, which appears to reflect an attitude closer to the impartial role image.

These identified characteristics yield insights into translators' perceptions of their roles in relation to prevailing discourses, as summarised in Section 2. First, despite academic observations of the advocative possibility and power of community translators' roles (Fraser, 1993; Lesch, 1999, 2004, 2017; Taibi, 2017; Taibi & Ozolins, 2016), the survey results revealed that translators overall seemed to agree more with the impartial role image and to respect the ethical roles of impartiality and accuracy. Second, the impartiality theme in the survey results suggests that translators who value faithfulness to, and the accurate transfer of, meanings from ST authors' writing tend to simultaneously claim responsibility for the content and style of the TT. The AUSIT Code of Ethics (2012) stipulates, under the principle of impartiality, that translators are not responsible for what the parties communicate but only for completely and accurately transferring their messages. This stipulation might seem to contradict the participants' claim of responsibility for TT content and style. However, considering the importance they placed on the ethical notions of impartiality and accuracy, assuming responsibility for TT content and style could be interpreted as a responsibility for achieving accuracy of content and style when being transferred from the ST to the TT, rather than the consequent use and effect of the TT. From this perspective, the co-presence of faithfulness to the ST, respect for the principle of impartiality, and responsibility for TT content and style, appears plausible. Such co-presence thus demonstrates a nuanced understanding of the impartial role image, one in which a translator is neither a responsibility-free language modem, nor merely subservient to invisibility norms or expectations of other parties involved in the translation process, as critiqued by scholarly work (e.g., Angelelli, 2004; Prunč, 2007; Simeoni, 1998; Venuti, 1995). The overall survey results thus show that impartial translators seem to maintain their own sense of responsibility and agency and do so in ways that are distinguishable from – but not necessarily exclusive of – an advocative role.

4.3 *Relationships Between Professional Backgrounds and Role Perceptions*

This section explores the effects of various external factors that enforce professional ethics on translators' perceptions of their ethical roles. To do so, the significance of differences in attitudes towards the impartial and advocative roles, as noted previously in relation to translators' professional backgrounds, was tested. I considered the following four contexts to have key impacts on translators' understandings and perceptions of external, professional ethics, particularly in the Australian system: undertaking NAATI-endorsed training, obtaining and maintaining NAATI certification, working as a professional translator, and referring to the AUSIT Code of Ethics during professional practice. Therefore, I compared the mean averages of the previously mentioned scores 1 and 2 (hereafter, advocacy score and impartiality score, respectively) among the groups divided by translation training types (NAATI-endorsed training, training in Japan, none, other), NAATI certification status (yes/no), the duration of professional experience (divided into seven categories, as shown in Appendix A), and the frequency of references to the AUSIT Code of Ethics (ranging from 1 = *not at all* to 5 = *always*).

An analysis of variance revealed no significant differences in the mean averages of the advocacy and impartiality scores in relation to translation training types, duration of professional experience, or frequency of references to the AUSIT Code of Ethics. The results for duration of professional experience differed from those of Kruger and Crots (2014), who found that translators with more professional experience tend to adhere to the external ethics of faithfulness. In contrast, in the present study, no significant effect of duration of professional experience was found.

However, a t-test highlighted notable differences in the impartiality scores between the NAATI-certified and non-certified groups ($p = 0.07$). As seen in the boxplot (see Figure 3.2; lines inside the boxes indicate median values and crosses indicate mean averages), the 55 NAATI-certified participants had a wider diversity of attitudes towards the impartial role (range = 4.50) than the 16 non-certified participants (range = 2.57). The mean average of the NAATI-certified group ($M = -0.12$) was slightly lower than that of the non-certified group ($M = 0.40$), but the NAATI-certified group included a range of lower scores (min. = -2.55) compared with the non-certified group (min. = -0.77). This indicates that the NAATI-certified translators agreed less than the non-certified translators with the impartial role.

In contrast, the t-test results ($p = 0.84$) indicated that the attitudes of the NAATI-certified translators towards advocacy ($M = -0.01$) varied to a similar extent as those of the non-certified translators ($M = 0.04$; see Figure 3.3).

In sum, the NAATI-certified translators in the current study tended to have more diverse attitudes than the non-certified translators towards impartiality, whereas both groups held similarly diverse attitudes towards advocacy. It should

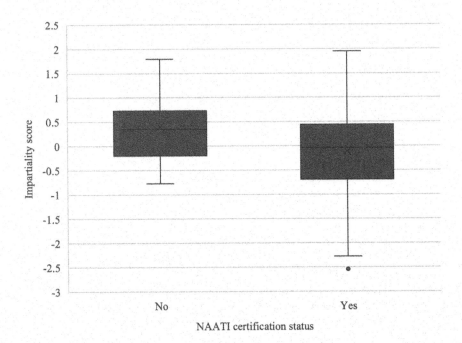

FIGURE 3.2 Comparison of impartiality scores by NAATI certification status

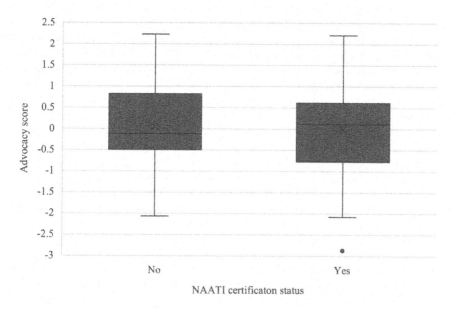

FIGURE 3.3 Comparison of advocacy scores by NAATI certification status

be noted that Takimoto (2006) demonstrated that interpreters in the Australian business interpreting context found it difficult to adhere to the AUSIT principle of impartiality in practice and that a majority of participants in this study worked in the business-related field of translation. Therefore, their experience may have influenced their attitudes towards impartiality. However, it is noteworthy that these results contradict the assumption that the NAATI certification system exerts a strong, unifying power over translator ethics in Australia, especially its external dimension.

5   Qualitative Analysis of Open-Ended Responses

The quantitative results of the questionnaire suggested certain tendencies in certified translators' perceptions of impartiality and advocacy that are insufficiently captured by a binary ideology of translators' roles. The findings also revealed the potential tendency for certified translators to have more diverse attitudes towards impartiality than assumed by the external dimension of ethics and seemed to disagree more with impartiality than those without certification and training. Viewing these results as possible manifestations of interactions between the personal and external dimensions of professional ethics, I conducted a thematic analysis of responses by NAATI-certified translators to the open-ended questions about translators' roles. Of these 55 translators, 50 provided written responses: 48 in Japanese and two in English. The themes that emerged from the analysis are presented in what follows, accompanied by excerpts from the translators' responses. The translators' IDs are provided in the format "T" + ID number.

The overarching themes were the aims and responsibilities of translators, which may have been influenced by the focus of the perception questions preceding this open question. In the aim-focused themes, several translators viewed the aim of translation as aiding communication between the ST author and TT readers, including describing their roles as: "コミュニケーションの仲介役" ["intermediary role of communication"] (T43); "橋を架けて、コミュニケーションの支えになること" ["to support communication by building a bridge"] (T3); "異なる言語を話す者たちの間に立ち、それぞれが伝えたいメッセージのエッセンスを...伝えること" ["standing between speakers of different languages and conveying ... the essence of the messages each of them wants to convey"] (T46); and "言語の障壁を取り除く" ["removing the linguistic barriers"] (T8).

This type of aim was, in some comments, associated with the values of translation accuracy, readability, and impartiality, as exemplified by the following comments: "読みやすく正確な翻訳を提供すること。翻訳調で読みにくくならないように心がけ、思い込みなどにより偏った訳出にならないように常に気を付けること" ["To provide easy-to-read and accurate translations. To make sure that {the translation} does not become hard-to-read translationese, and to always be careful not to make biased translations due to assumptions, etc."] (T64); "To faithfully communicate the message, without bias and with the best output possible" (T48). These comments highlight the interrelationship between the value given by translators to accuracy and self-control over their own bias, implying the translators' ethical standing based on the values of accuracy and impartiality, which in turn reflect the external dimension of professional ethics and codes.

In contrast, some translators who similarly viewed the aim of translation as successful communication focused on TT readers made the following comments: "翻訳者とは、その言語が読めない人のため...の役割である" ["A translator is a role ... for those who cannot read the [target] language"] (T71); and "読者が読んですっと頭に入るような、負担をかけない分かりやすい翻訳を心掛ける" ["to aim for easy-to-understand translations that can be easily read and understood by the readers and do not put a burden on them"] (T49). These comments reveal the translators' consideration for – and supportive attitudes towards – TT readers.

In the other aim-focused theme, some translators identified aims of translation beyond accurate and impartial meaning transfer, communication between the ST author and TT readers, or the understandings of TT readers. This view is represented by the following comments:

> 正確に翻訳することに加え、筆者、読者、翻訳費用の負担者のいずれかに必ず偏って翻訳を行うのではなく、使用目的に合わせて翻訳を行うべきだと思う。 [In addition to translating accurately, I think translators should translate according to the purpose of use, rather than always being partial to one party among the author, the reader and the person who bears the translation cost.]
>
> *(T4)*

> 言語の違いによる知識ギャップを進め、遠回りでも少しずつ言葉の違いに関係なく様々な知識や考え方に皆がアクセスできるよ

うになること。 [To advance {filling} the knowledge gap between languages, and for everyone to become, even in an indirect way, gradually able to access various knowledge and ways of thinking regardless of the differences of languages.]

(T19)

翻訳者の役割は原本の執筆者、翻訳の依頼者、読者ターゲット等すべての関係者の要求を酌みつつ、最も適切な翻訳をアウトプットすることだと思っています。 [I think that the role of translators is to output the most appropriate translation while taking into consideration the demands of all parties concerned, such as the original text author, the client of the translation and the target reader.]

(T32)

も含めて何がベストか提案できること。 [Being able to propose what is best, including {the use of} MT.]

(T56)

翻訳が必要とされる背景や目的をできるだけ正確に把握し、翻訳を依頼主目線で行うべきか、読み手目線で行うべきかを判断し、意図に沿う形で翻訳をしていく必要があると思います。 [I think it is necessary to grasp as accurately as possible the background and purpose for which the translation is required, determine whether the translation should be done from the perspective of the client or the reader, and translate in a way that is in line with the aim.]

(T70)

These responses concern not only the ST author and TT readers, but all the parties involved in the translation process, including the clients who request translations and the organisations for which they work. The scope of the vision reflected in the comment by T19 can be interpreted as the world beyond specific translation situations. These translators also view their aims as providing the best solution or translation output for each situation based on their interpretations and understandings of translation contexts and purposes. The purpose-based drive of their translation practice is crystallised by the comment "翻訳者は目的に合わせて翻訳すべきです" ["Translators should translate in accordance with the purpose {of the translation}"] (T51). This work of translators implies interpretive and active roles that transcend the impartiality and accuracy-based roles previously described.

These interpretive roles seem related to the other overarching theme, which focused on translators' responsibilities. T70 commented that translators are not responsible for the wording of the ST but have some responsibility for their translation output. Accordingly, they must make judgements based on their own ethical values to decide whether to accept a translation assignment, which highlights a personal dimension of ethics exercised in a professional capacity:

翻訳者は原文の文責を有している訳ではありませんが、翻訳を通じて、訳出した文章に対しては（一定の）責任を有すると考えている為、依頼内容が自分の倫理感に極端に相反する場合. . . 、その案件を引き受けるべきではないと考えており、もし自分にそのような依

頼が来た場合には、どれだけ応酬が魅力的であったとしても受けることはしません。[The translator does not have the responsibility for the wording of the original text, but since I think that the translator has (certain) responsibility for the text they produced through translation, I think [I] should not accept the assignment if the content of the [translation] request is extremely contrary to [my] own sense of ethics . . . and if that kind of request comes to me, I will not accept it no matter how attractive the remuneration may be.]

(T70)

T4 discussed the shared notions of accuracy and readability – these, T4 claimed, had relative value depending on the genre, which, they argued, the translator is responsible for discerning. They also claimed that translators were responsible for stylistic decisions:

例えば、学術論文とマーケティング素材の場合、正確性と読みやすさの優先順位はそれぞれ異なるので、それを見分けた上で作業する必要がある。また、日本語では動詞の活用により文章の印象が全く異なるので、どの語形を使うかの判断はほとんどの場合、翻訳者が行うことになる。[For example, academic papers and marketing materials have different priorities for accuracy and readability, so it is necessary to discern that before working. Also, in Japanese, the impressions of sentences are completely different depending on the conjugations of verbs, so in most cases, the judgement as to which word form to use is done by the translator.]

(T4)

On the other hand, comments such as "言語の翻訳をすること。それ以上でも以下でもない" ["to translate the language. Nothing more or less than that"] (T61) and "テキストの内容は作者が書いている通りのことを伝えているので、翻訳者に内容の責任はないと考えている" ["In terms of the content of the text, {the translator is} conveying exactly what the author has written, so I think the translator is not responsible for the content"] (T8) reflect another version of translators' perceived responsibilities, one that is closer to the ethical principle of impartiality as an external dimension of ethics.

6 Discussion

In the AUSIT Code of Ethics, concerning the external dimension of ethics, translators must be impartial in all contexts by avoiding any bias towards either the ST author or TT readers, and they are not responsible for what they communicate. The Code of Ethics also stipulates that translators should not play an advocative role. The open-ended answer data give some examples of the translators' perceptions of their roles that directly reflect the external dimension of professional ethics. However, the results of the quantitative and qualitative analyses revealed that NAATI-certified translators have more diverse attitudes towards the professional ethical notion of impartiality than may be anticipated by external ethics institutions.

The construct of impartiality that emerged from the PCA suggests that impartiality may actually include the assumption of certain responsibilities and agency in producing a TT and in making stylistic decisions. Therefore, impartiality in this sense is not necessarily in binary opposition to advocacy, but instead these values can coexist within an individual's image or collective images of ethical translators. Such coexistence of impartiality, agency, and advocacy, as a mix of external and personal ethics, was also observed in the open-ended responses centring on translators' aims and responsibilities, as presented in Section 5. One certified translator even stated that she believed in translators' responsibility for the TT beyond accuracy and style and, therefore, her own personal ethics and moral values may stop her from accepting certain translations if they violate these values. This comment is consistent with the tendency identified by Kruger and Crots (2014) that the refusal to translate is mostly motivated by translators' personal ethics.

The certified translators' open comments on responsibilities also yield insights into how they may negotiate between the external and personal dimensions of professional ethics. One such way is by identifying exceptional situations for reasoning. The translators generally seemed to acknowledge and respect externally shared ethical values and principles, such as impartiality and accuracy, which is broadly consistent with the finding of Takimoto (2006) about business interpreters in Australia. However, when they hypothesised that they had encountered an exceptional situation (e.g., where the topics and themes of the translation breached their own sense of morality), they discussed the possibility of risking those principles (i.e., the personal dimension of ethics may need to be prioritised). Another exceptional situation discussed was, as reflected in T4's comment, actively making stylistic decisions as justified – or even necessitated – by a reason based on essential linguistic characteristics of the TT. The other way of negotiating between the external and personal dimensions is by relativising the importance of externally shared values. In other words, these values do not seem to be considered in the "narrower professional, codified view of ethics being used as a frame of reference for translation decisions" (Kruger & Crots, 2014, p. 178). Rather, their importance is judged relative to other professional values also shared in the external dimension and to their own personal moral values in individual situations.

These ways of ethical negotiation are founded on the translators' understandings of context. In the open response data clustered around the theme of translators' aims, there was also evidence that certified translators are highly conscious of translation contexts, especially the purposes of translation. They interpret these contexts and purposes and work as translators to achieve these purposes in an optimal way rather than being constrained by external values of accuracy and impartiality. These purpose-driven translation practices may reflect that *Skopos* theory and pragmatism in translation have been considered important enough to be widely taught in Australian translator training (Hao, 2019).

This study revealed diversity in the nationally certified translators' perceptions of, and attitudes towards, their ethical roles as translators. On the one hand, some translators seemed to closely adhere to externally shared ethical values; on the other, some translators actively negotiated between external and personal dimensions of ethics by interpreting contexts and the relative importance of potentially conflicting values. These aspects of interpretive work concerning professional ethics are considered to comprise part of the hermeneutic model of translation (Venuti, 2019). In this model, translation is viewed as an interpretive act by which translators produce a translation necessarily divergent from the ST according to the needs and interests of the TL and associated cultural system (Venuti, 2019). This alteration is inevitable because translators transform an ST into a TT by applying their interpretants, either formal (e.g., concerning style and equivalence) or thematic (e.g., concerning values, beliefs, and representations of social groups; Venuti, 2019). Situated in this hermeneutic model, the present findings suggest that translators also deploy ethical interpretants, which interact and overlap with formal and thematic interpretants, but are distinctive in their interpretations, evaluations, and negotiations of ethical principles and personal moral values according to individual translation contexts.

7 Implications for Community Translation Within and Outside of Australia

This study adopted a case study approach, focusing on the case of NAATI-certified English–Japanese translators. NAATI certifications are not only recognised in the field of community translation and interpreting but are also accepted in many other areas, including legal, health, academic, business, and tourism fields. The most common translation field for the NAATI-certified translators in this study was business and marketing, followed by community translation. However, in its annual report (2021), NAATI noted that their primary focus was on providing quality assurance and confidence to the translation and interpreting professions such that everyone can participate effectively in Australia's culturally and linguistically diverse society. Therefore, the ethical principles maintained by AUSIT and endorsed and tested by NAATI are intended to both create and externally enforce ethical role images of community translators and interpreters. Yet, the scope of NAATI certification is limited to Australia, and the study was also largely limited to situations and communities in Australia. Additionally, the research was not conducted on random samples; therefore, the findings should be interpreted with caution when applied to other cases involving, for example, other language combinations and other certification systems.

Building trust in the translation profession, whereby "information is scarce, asymmetrically distributed and typically hard to understand when foreign languages are involved" (Pym, 2021, p. 154), necessarily entails making promises about which the internal workings are not completely visible to everyone involved. However, dismissing observable phenomena poses an ethical question of misrepresentation. This question is of particular interest for community translation and interpreting, the fundamental purpose of which is to help multicultural societies achieve justice by intervening in power imbalances between dominant language users and those with less command of the language. Therefore, it is hoped that this study can contribute to better understanding how professional translators internalise and interact with such ethical principles and role images by highlighting diversity in their interpretations, perceptions, and negotiations of key ethical values. To construct meaningful dialogues about what community translators and other stakeholders can do to realise a more just society, it is essential to acknowledge the existence of various versions of ethical roles as imagined and negotiated by translators.

Since NAATI certification was determined to be an influential factor in translators' diverse attitudes towards translator impartiality in this study, a certification body like NAATI could play an important role in initiating and engaging in a more dynamic, heteroglot, and self-critical discourse on translator ethics beyond the binary ideologies around impartiality, bias, and accuracy. In turn, these discourses should be constantly updated through ethical dialogues among community translators, interpreters and other stakeholders through translator training and ongoing professional development events. Developing discourses on ethics that acknowledge the diversity, interpretive possibilities and, therefore, the creativity of translation work will benefit the community translators whose work is teleologically empowering and highlight the humanity of their translation practice such that it can be more valued in the pursuit of social justice in multicultural communities.

APPENDICES

Appendix A

Participants' Professional Data (*N* = 71)

Independent Variables		*Frequency (%)*
NAATI certification status (translation, interpreting, or both)	No (= 0)	16 (22.5)
	Yes (= 1)	55 (77.5)
	Mean (*SD*)	0.77 (0.42)
Translation training	None (= 0)	22 (31.0)
	NAATI-endorsed training (= 1)	38 (53.5)
	Training in Japan (= 2)	7 (9.9)
	Other (= 3)	4 (5.6)
	Mean (*SD*)	0.90 (0.80)
Duration of translation experience	Less than 3 months (= 1)	1 (1.4)
	3–6 months (= 2)	1 (1.4)
	6 months to 1 year (= 3)	–
	1–3 years (= 4)	8 (11.3)
	3–5 years (= 5)	7 (9.9)
	5–10 years (= 6)	21 (29.6)
	More than 10 years (= 7)	33 (46.5)
	Mean (*SD*)	6.01 (1.27)
How often translators refer to a code of ethics	Not at all (= 1)	28 (39.4)
	2	18 (25.4)
	3	18 (25.4)
	4	3 (4.2)
	Always (= 5)	4 (5.6)
	Mean (*SD*)	2.11 (1.15)

Independent Variables		Frequency (%)
Reference to AUSIT Code of Ethics	No (= 0)	31 (43.7)
	Yes (= 1)	40 (56.3)
	Mean (*SD*)	7.56 (0.50)

Appendix B

Participants' Fields of Translation (*N* = 71; Participants Chose All Fields That Applied)

		NAATI-Certified (n = 55)	Not NAATI-Certified (n = 16)
Independent variables		*Frequency (%)*	*Frequency (%)*
Field of translation	**Business and marketing**	45 (81.8)	8 (50.0)
	Community and public services	27 (49.1)	5 (31.3)
	Finance	9 (16.4)	2 (12.5)
	Health and medicine	13 (23.6)	4 (25.0)
	Legal	11 (20.0)	1 (6.3)
	Entertainment	14 (25.5)	0 (0.0)
	Literature	3 (5.5)	1 (6.3)
	Academic	10 (18.2)	4 (25.0)
	Technology	12 (21.8)	1 (6.3)
	Patent	2 (3.6)	1 (6.3)
	Tourism	1 (1.8)	3 (18.8)

Appendix C

Participants' Demographic Data (*N* = 71)

		NAATI-Certified (n = 55)	*Not NAATI-Certified (n = 16)*
Independent Variables		*Frequency (%)*	*Frequency (%)*
Gender	Female (= 0)	45 (81.8)	10 (62.5)
	Male (= 1)	9 (16.4)	5 (31.3)
	Unspecified (= 2)	1 (1.8)	1 (6.3)
	Mean (*SD*)	0.20 (0.45)	0.44 (0.63)
Age	Range	43	28
	Minimum	25	34
	Maximum	68	62
	Mean (*SD*)	46.67 (10.7)	46.63 (8.6)
Country of residence	Japan (= 0)	9 (16.4)	6 (37.5)
	Australia (= 1)	42 (76.4)	10 (62.5)
	Both Japan and Australia (= 2)	2 (3.6)	–
	New Zealand (= 3)	1 (1.8)	–
	Other (= 4)	1 (1.8)	–
	Mean (*SD*)	0.96 (0.67)	0.63 (0.50)
Cultural identity	Japanese (= 0)	36 (65.5)	14 (87.5)
	Australian (= 1)	10 (18.2)	1 (6.3)
	Australian Japanese (= 2)	3 (5.5)	–
	Japanese Australian (= 3)	3 (5.5)	–
	Other (= 4)	3 (5.5)	1 (6.3)
	Mean (*SD*)	0.67 (1.16)	0.31 (1.01)

Appendix D

Participants' Level of Agreement With Statement About Translators' Roles (*N* = 71)

	Strongly disagree (= 1)	*Disagree (= 2)*	*Neither agree nor disagree (= 3)*	*Agree (= 4)*	*Strongly agree (= 5)*	*Mean (SD)*
S1	2 (2.8)	5 (7.0)	9 (12.7)	39 (54.9)	16 (22.5)	3.87 (0.94)
S2	–	4 (5.6)	13 (18.3)	41 (57.7)	13 (18.3%)	3.89 (0.77)
S3	7 (9.9)	19 (26.8)	35 (49.3)	9 (12.7)	1 (1.4)	2.69 (0.87)
S4	5 (7.0)	21 (29.6)	28 (39.4)	13 (18.3)	4 (5.6)	2.86 (0.99)
S5	5 (7.0)	12 (16.9)	24 (33.8)	26 (36.6)	4 (5.6)	3.17 (1.01)
S6	2 (2.8)	7 (9.9)	38 (53.5)	18 (25.4)	6 (8.5)	3.27 (0.86)

(Frequency; %) — Level of Agreement

Appendix E

Importance of Key Ethical Principles of AUSIT as Perceived by Participants (N = 71)

	\multicolumn{6}{c}{Level of Importance}
	Not important at all (= 1)	2	2	4	Extremely important (= 5)	Mean (SD)
Impartiality	–	3 (4.2)	4 (5.6)	17 (23.9)	47 (66.2)	4.52 (0.49)
Accuracy	–	–	1 (1.4)	15 (21.1)	55 (77.5)	4.76 (0.46)
Role boundaries	–	2 (2.8)	11 (15.5)	22 (31.0)	36 (50.7)	4.3 (0.84)
Professional conduct	–	–	1 (1.4)	6 (8.5)	64 (90.1)	4.9 (0.36)
Competence	1 (1.4)	1 (1.4)	2 (2.8)	10 (14.1)	57 (80.3)	4.7 (0.73)
Maintaining professional relationships	–	2 (2.8)	14 (19.7)	24 (33.8)	31 (43.7)	4.18 (0.85)
Confidentiality	–	–	1 (1.4)	5 (7.0)	65 (91.5)	4.9 (0.35)
Professional development	–	2 (2.8)	4 (5.6)	17 (23.9)	48 (67.6)	4.6 (0.73)
Professional solidarity	1 (1.4)	4 (5.6)	21 (29.6)	27 (38.0)	18 (25.4)	3.8 (0.94)

(Frequency; %)

Notes

1 Hereafter, the examined statements are labelled with the abbreviations (S#) as listed in Table 3.1.
2 The acceptable value of α is argued to vary from 0.70–0.95 (Tavakol & Dennick, 2011).
3 A Spearman's correlation was used because the values assigned by the translators to ethical notions formed ordinal data according to the order of importance.

References

Asociación Argentina de Traductores e Intérpretes. (2018). *Código de ética* [Code of ethics]. https://aati.org.ar/aati

Abdallah, K. (2011). Towards empowerment: Students' ethical reflections on translating in production networks. *The Interpreter and Translator Trainer*, 5(1), 129–154. https://doi.org/10.1080/13556509.2011.10798815

Angelelli, C. V. (2004). *Revisiting the interpreter's role: A study of conference, court, and medical interpreters in Canada, Mexico, and the United States*. John Benjamins Publishing Company. https://doi.org/10.1075/btl.55

American Translators Association. (2010). *Code of ethics and professional practice*. www.atanet.org/about-us/code-of-ethics/

Australian Institute of Interpreters and Translators. (2012). *AUSIT code of ethics and code of conduct*. https://ausit.org/wp-content/uploads/2020/02/Code_Of_Ethics_Full.pdf

Baixauli-Olmos, L. (2021). Ethics codes for interpreters and translators. In K. Koskinen & N. K. Pokorn (Eds.), *The Routledge handbook of translation and ethics* (pp. 297–319). Routledge.

Baker, M. (2006). *Translation and conflict: A narrative account*. Routledge.

Creswell, J. W., Plano Clark, V. L., Gutmann, M. L., & Hanson, W. E. (2003). Advanced mixed methods research designs. In A. Tashakkori & C. Teddlie (Eds.), *Handbook of mixed methods in social & behavioral research* (pp. 209–240). Sage Publications.

Fraser, J. (1993). Public accounts: Using verbal protocols to investigate community translation. *Applied Linguistics*, 14(4), 325–343. https://doi.org/10.1093/applin/14.4.325

Hao, Y. (2019). Bridging the gap between translator training and practice: Can theory help translators? *Flinders University Languages Group Online Review*, 6(1), 33–49. https://docs.wixstatic.com/ugd/7fbb78_9d0babc8032d4311b4e1572cd1d5631a.pdf

Hox, J. J. (1997). From theoretical concept to survey question. In L. Lyberg, P. Biemer, M. Collins, E. de Leeuw, C. Dippo, N. Schwarz, & D. Trewin (Eds.), *Survey measurement and process quality* (pp. 47–70). John Wiley & Sons, Inc.

Kruger, H., & Crots, E. (2014). Professional and personal ethics in translation: A survey of South African translators' strategies and motivations. *Stellenbosch Papers in Linguistics Plus*, 43, 147–181. https://doi.org/10.5842/43-0-613

Lambert, J. (2018). How ethical are codes of ethics? Using illusions of neutrality to sell translations. *The Journal of Specialised Translation*, 30, 269–290.

Lambert, J. (2021). Professional translator ethics. In K. Koskinen & N. K. Pokorn (Eds.), *The Routledge handbook of translation and ethics* (pp. 165–179). Routledge.

Lesch, H. (1999). Community translation: Right or privilege. In M. Erasmus (Ed.), *Liaison interpreting in the community* (pp. 90–98). Van Schaik.

Lesch, H. (2004). Societal factors and translation practice. *Perspectives*, 12(4), 256–269. https://doi.org/10.1080/0907676X.2004.9961506

Lesch, H. (2017). From practice to theory: Societal factors as a norm governing principle for community translation. In M. Taibi (Ed.), *Translating for the community*. Multilingual Matters.

Ministry of Business, Innovation and Employment. (2021, July 8). *New standards and certification requirements.* www.mbie.govt.nz/cross-government-functions/language-assistance-services/new-standards-and-certification-requirements/

National Accreditation Authority for Translators and Interpreters. (2021). *2020–2021 Annual report: Breaking down language barriers.* www.naati.com.au/wp-content/uploads/2021/11/Annual-Report-2020-2021-1.pdf

Nord, C. (1991). *Text analysis in translation: Theory, methodology, and didactic application of a model for translation-oriented text analysis.* Rodopi.

Prunč, E. (2007). Priests, princes and pariahs: Constructing the professional field of translation. In M. Wolf & A. Fukari (Eds.), *Constructing a sociology of translation* (pp. 39–56). John Benjamins Publishing Company. https://doi.org/10.1075/btl.74.03pru

Pym, A. (2021). Translator ethics. In K. Koskinen & N. K. Pokorn (Eds.), *The Routledge handbook of translation and ethics* (pp. 147–161). Routledge.

QSR International. (2018). *NVivo* (Version 12) [Computer software]. www.qsrinternational.com/nvivo-qualitative-data-analysis-software/home

Simeoni, D. (1998). The pivotal status of the translator's habitus. *Target: International Journal of Translation Studies, 10*(1), 1–39. https://doi.org/10.1075/target.10.1.02sim

Tack, L. (2001). Review of beyond ambivalence. *The Translator, 7*(2), 297–321.

Taibi, M. (2011). Public service translation. In K. Malmkjær & K. Windle (Eds.), *The Oxford handbook of translation studies* (pp. 214–227). Oxford University Press. https://doi.org/10.1093/oxfordhb/9780199239306.013.0016

Taibi, M. (Ed.). (2017). *Translating for the community.* Multilingual Matters.

Taibi, M., & Ozolins, U. (2016). *Community translation.* Bloomsbury Academic.

Takimoto, M. (2006). AUSIT Rinrikitei to Tsuuyakusya No Koudou – Bijinesubunya Ni Okeru Daiarogu Tsuuyaku No Baai [The professional code of ethics of AUSIT and interpreters' behaviour – the case of dialogue interpreting in the business domain]. *Interpreting and Translation Studies: The Journal of the Japan Association for Interpreting and Translation Studies, 6,* 143–154.

Tavakol, M., & Dennick, R. (2011). Making sense of Cronbach's alpha. *International Journal of Medical Education, 2,* 53–55. https://doi.org/10.5116/ijme.4dfb.8dfd

Tymoczko, M. (2007). *Enlarging translation, empowering translators.* St Jerome Publishing.

Valero-Garcés, C. (2014). *Communicating across cultures: A coursebook on interpreting and translating in public services and institutions.* University Press of America.

Venuti, L. (1995). *The translator's invisibility: A history of translation.* Routledge.

Venuti, L. (2019). *Contra instrumentalism: A translation polemic.* University of Nebraska Press.

4

YOU DON'T SEE WHAT I SEE

Assessing Contextual Meanings in Translated Health Care Texts in New Zealand

Wei Teng

1 Introduction

The multiple outbreaks of the COVID-19 pandemic in Victoria, Australia, said to be related to vital information not being available in migrant languages (Grey, 2020; Yu, 2020), demonstrated the importance of translation and interpreting services in disseminating information related to the virus to linguistically disadvantaged people (e.g., refugees and migrants) in multicultural and multilinguistic societies. Recent studies (Crezee et al., 2017; Crezee et al., 2020; Teng, 2019; Teng et al., 2018) have shown that achieving pragmatic equivalence can help ensure the quality of translation and interpreting services which deliver information related to people's basic rights such as health care services and legal aid. In these studies and in the present chapter, pragmatic equivalence is defined as translation/interpreting that achieves the pragmatic function expected in the source text such as to inform or to persuade (Hale, 2004, 2014; House, 2006).

In a recent study (Teng, 2020), I used a set of translation assessment criteria developed in my previous studies (Crezee et al., 2017; Teng, 2019; Teng et al., 2018) and revealed conflicting opinions on translation quality perception between professional translators and lay readers in New Zealand. Specifically, the lay readers often did not respond to a translation in the way the translators had expected. This chapter adopted that set of assessment criteria to investigate the conflicting opinions and revealed that the established set of assessment criteria is aligned with the ideational, interpersonal, and textual meanings of systemic functional linguistics (Halliday & Matthiessen, 2004). This chapter also shows that consideration of these three contextual meanings is in line with lay readers' perspectives.

DOI: 10.4324/9781003247333-5

2 Background and Theoretical Framework

2.1 Health Care Translation for Communities

Community translation facilitates the social inclusion of members of minority communities in multicultural and multilingual societies by delivering crucial information related to a person's basic rights, such as their legal rights and their right to receive health services (Taibi & Ozolins, 2016). The pragmatic nature of community translation provides a perspective from which to investigate the quality of translated health care texts written to inform the general public, as well as patients and/or their families, about certain health conditions and treatment options.

In this study, health care translation refers to the translation of health care texts from the dominant language (i.e., English) into a community language (i.e., Mandarin Chinese). If the quality of translation is poor, members of minority communities may not have equal access to information. Having language access to information can improve social inclusion and improve an individual's ability, opportunity, and dignity in mainstream society (The World Bank, n.d.). Therefore, providing good quality health care translations may not only lead to positive health outcomes for minority communities, but also benefit society overall.

2.2 Pragmatic Equivalence in Health Care Translation

Health care translation is of particular interest in this study as health care texts (e.g., health care pamphlets) often perform the pragmatic functions of informing and persuading the target audience to take actions in relation to managing their own health (Fischbach, 1962). Therefore, a good quality health care translation informs and persuades the reader of the translated text in the same way that the source text does for the reader of the source text, which means the translation has achieved pragmatic equivalence.

The importance of achieving pragmatic equivalence has already been reflected in a number of studies (e.g., Burns & Kim, 2011; Crezee & Grant, 2016; Crezee et al., 2017; Hale, 2014; Schuster et al., 2010; Taibi & Ozolins, 2016; Teng, 2019; Teng et al., 2018) showing that while cross-cultural features are a crucial aspect of determining the achievement of expected pragmatic functions, ignoring cross-linguistic features may lead to "pragmalinguistic failures" (Hale, 2014, p. 323; Thomas, 1983), meaning that linguistic features fail to achieve the expected pragmatic functions. The study described here aims to offer a set of assessment criteria that can assess the quality of health care translations bearing in mind the three contextual meanings of a text: ideational, interpersonal, and textual.

2.3 Three Contextual Meanings

To achieve pragmatic equivalence, translators need to consider possible aspects of the contextual features of a text. In this respect, I chose to conduct analyses in the framework of systemic functional linguistics (SFL), which has been widely used to investigate issues in the study of translation (House, 1977, 2008). This framework considers that language functions to "express our experiences of the world that is around us or inside us" and to "act out our social relationships" (Halliday & Matthiessen, 2004, p. 29). While the function of "express[ing] our experiences of the world" requires linguistic representations (e.g., syntactical rules) to construe meanings, the function of "act[ing] out our social relationships" requires considerations of sociocultural contexts that encompass the linguistic representations (Halliday & Matthiessen, 2004, p. 29). When applying SFL to explain the functions of translation, translators express the source text writers' experiences of the world and act out the writers' social relationships with the audience through translation.

Therefore, consideration of the three contextual meanings of a text-ideational, interpersonal, and textual-can help achieve pragmatic equivalence. Such equivalence is what Matthiessen (2001) terms "the maximum equivalence" (p. 78) at a sociocultural contextual level (see Table 4.1).

3 Methodological Approach

3.1 The Assessed Health Care Translations

A total of 15 English–Chinese health care translations distributed in New Zealand were collected for the purpose of assessment in this study. Table 4.2 shows that a number of selection criteria were applied to ensure that all the translations were of a similar sociopragmatic nature.

TABLE 4.1 Three Contextual Meanings in Systemic Functional Linguistics

Contextual Meanings	*Explanation*
Ideational meaning	represents **logical reality** encountered by human beings (e.g. "John threw the ball" versus "The ball threw John"); represents the **experiential reality** encountered by human beings (e.g. "the doctor has treated the patient" versus "the doctor has dealt with the patient").
Interpersonal meaning	represents **the social relationship** between participants (e.g. teacher–student, government–general public).
Textual meaning	represents **the starting point of messages** – what is to be presented first, and what is later (e.g. "Today, I bought a car" versus "I bought a car today"); represents **information status** – what is shared between participants, and what is not (e.g. "I bought a car today" versus "I bought the car today").

TABLE 4.2 Criteria for Selection of Translations

Content	• The health care texts must have a primary pragmatic nature of being informative, not the ones with a commercial purpose
	• The health care texts must deliver health information mainly through words, so as to identify failed pragmatic functions caused by cross-linguistic features
	• The health care texts must cover a range of health topics from general health care services to socially sensitive health issues, so as to present a comprehensive selection of health translation
Distributors	• The health care texts must be distributed by different medical service providers and institutes, so as to minimise the possibility of repeatedly including the translations of a few translators
	• The health care texts must be distributed, physically or online, by a government body or authoritative health care service providers/institutes
Target readers	• The health care texts must be publicly accessible
	• The health care texts must be aimed at the general public, not medical specialists or experts

The translations were provided in a layout that followed the English source text's paragraph and sentence structure, for example, when there was a paragraph/sentence in the source text, the translation was presented as one paragraph/sentence (referred to as a *passage* for the purpose of the present study). The 15 translated texts comprised a total of 256 passages, and some texts had more passages than others: the shortest text had seven passages, while the longest had 28 passages.

In this chapter, I will present a number of passages from Texts 2 and 8 as examples to explain why consideration of the three contextual meanings is in line with lay readers' perspectives in assessing translation quality.

Text 2 (Appendix A) is a pamphlet informing diabetic patients of dietary suggestions and blood glucose monitoring. Text 8 (Appendix B) is a leaflet explaining the effects and side effects of spironolactone, a diuretic medication used to treat patients who are at risk of heart failure.

3.2 The Participants: Professional Translators and Lay Readers

I recruited a total of 30 participants for this study: 15 professional Chinese language translators and 15 Chinese lay readers based in New Zealand. The participants were all native Mandarin Chinese speakers. All the professional translators were holders of (or qualified to apply for) membership in the New Zealand Society of Translators and Interpreters (NZSTI). All the Chinese lay readers were 57 years old or older when participating in the study, and they were all immigrants born in China who had followed their adult children to immigrate to New Zealand. That means the lay readers in this study may often have difficulties in accessing health care information intended for the general public (Tang, 2017).

Before attending assessment sessions, the translators were reminded of the pragmatic intention of the English original to be informative and persuasive (Fischbach, 1962; Sin, 2004). They were instructed to bear that intention in mind when assessing the texts. The Chinese lay readers were encouraged to make their own judgements without worrying about not being professional translators. When making the assessments, neither group of participants had access to the English original. Thus, they made their judgements on an equally informed basis since both groups only saw the translations as native Chinese speakers.

3.3 Suitability of the Proposed Criteria Set

Adopting Nida's dynamic equivalence, I have argued that when a translation Sounds Natural, it can Make Sense to the target reader (Crezee et al., 2017; Teng, 2019; Teng et al., 2018). When a translation Makes Sense, it maintains the Original Manner (the original pragmatic functions, such as to inform, to persuade, or to make assumptions). When the Original Manner is maintained, it is then possible for the translation to elicit a Similar Response. In other words, a translated text would elicit a similar response from the reader of the translated text as the source text would elicit from the reader of the source text. I later observed that the achievement of a Similar Response closely depends on the linguistic features of the translation, and whether these features can fulfil the pragmatic functions (expected in the source text) in the target sociocultural context (Teng, 2019, 2020). That then leads to the achievement of pragmatic equivalence. This argument is presented in Figure 4.1.

For instance, if the English tag question, "you like pizza, correct?" (with a falling tone), is literally translated into Chinese as "nǐ xǐhuān pīsà, duì ma/你喜歡披薩, 對嗎?/you like pizza, correct?", the original illocutionary intent of making an assumption that the listener will agree with the speaker's statement is lost in the Chinese translation because the translation delivers the illocutionary intent to seek information without clear assumptions (Teng et al., 2018). The Chinese translation Sounds Natural, yet the linguistic features of the tag question "duì ma/對嗎/correct" does not maintain the Original Manner and elicit a Similar Response as the English original.

Based on the argument proposed in Figure 4.1, I developed and tested the suitability of a set of assessment criteria (Table 4.3; hereafter, the Criteria Set[1]).

You Don't See What I See 73

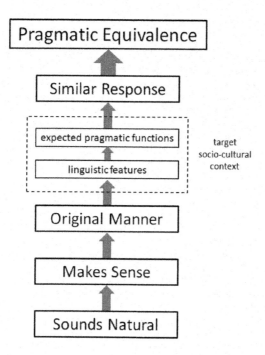

FIGURE 4.1 Relationship in producing a pragmatically equivalent translation

TABLE 4.3 Pragmatic Equivalence Assessment Criteria

Evaluation Criteria

Linguistic/Sociocultural System		*Sociocultural System*		*Possible Outcomes*
Sounds Natural (SN)	Makes Sense (MS)	Maintains Original Manner (OM)	Elicits Similar Response (SR)	
✓	✓	✓	✓	Total Equivalence
✓	✓	✓	✗	SR-F
✓	✓	✗	✓	OM-F
✓	✓	✗	✗	OM-SR-F
✗	✓	✗	✗	SN-OM-SR-F
✓	✗	✗	✗	MS-OM-SR-F
✗	✗	✗	✗	Totally Lost

Note: The letter F stands for Failed, denoting criteria not achieved in the translation; the symbol ✓ refers to the achievement of a criterion; and the symbol ✗ refers to instances where a criterion has not been achieved.

Following is a description of the seven assessment outcomes:

- Total Equivalence (achieved all four criteria; achieved pragmatic equivalence)
- SR-F (failed to achieve Similar Response, but achieved the other three criteria)
- OM-F (failed to achieve Original Manner, but achieved the other three criteria)
- OM-SR-F (failed to achieve Original Manner and Similar Response, but achieved Sounds Natural and Makes Sense)
- SN-OM-SR-F (failed to achieve Sounds Natural, Original Manner, and Similar Response, but achieved Makes Sense)
- MS-OM-SR-F (failed to achieve Makes Sense, Original Manner, and Similar Response, but achieved Sounds Natural)
- Totally Lost (failed to achieve all four criteria)

For instance, if participants assessed the Chinese translation of the English tag question, "you like pizza, correct?" (with a falling tone), and assigned it OM-SR-F, they would believe that the translation Sounded Natural and Made Sense, but that it does not convey the assumption that the addresser knows or believes the addressee likes pizza (i.e., the passage failed to maintain the Original Manner), or whether the addressee is expected to provide further explanation or defend his (un)fondness of pizza (i.e., the passage failed to elicit a Similar Response).

Because there are four criteria, the combination of these four criteria could lead to 16 possible assessment outcomes. That means it was possible that the participants' assessment results should have shown all 16 possible assessment outcomes. However, Table 4.4 shows that while all 16 possible outcomes appeared in the professional translators' assessment results, the outcomes that lay readers assigned were mostly the ones included in the Criteria Set. Outcomes included in the Criteria Set were also seen with a relatively higher average percentage compared

TABLE 4.4 Comparing Assessment Results of the 15 Texts

Possible Outcomes	Professional Translators	Chinese Lay Readers
	Average Percentage of Assigned Outcome	
Total Equivalence (Achieved all four criteria)	58.15%	5.23%
SR-F (Failed to achieve Similar Response)	0.38%	44.63%
OM-F (Failed to achieve Original Manner)	2.98%	0.02%
OM-SR-F (Failed to achieve Original Manner and Similar Response)	2.04%	7.62%

Possible Outcomes	Professional Translators	Chinese Lay Readers
	Average Percentage of Assigned Outcome	
SN-OM-SR-F	3.06%	1.91%
(Failed to achieve Sounds Natural, Original Manner, and Similar Response)		
MS-OM-SR-F	1.11%	16.27%
(Failed to achieve Make Sense, Original Manner, and Similar Response)		
<u>Totally Lost</u>	4.81%	21.55%
(Failed to achieve all four criteria)		
SN-SR-F	0.76%	2.66%
(Failed to achieve Sounds Natural and Similar Response)		
SN-F	21.33%	0.00%
(Failed to achieve Sounds Natural)		
MS-F	0.57%	0.00%
(Failed to achieve Makes Sense)		
SN-OM-F	1.10%	0.03%
(Failed to achieve Sounds Natural and Original Manner)		
SN-MS-F	2.69%	0.00%
(Failed to achieve Sounds Natural and Similar Response)		
MS-OM-F	0.05%	0.00%
(Failed to achieve Makes Sense and Original Manner)		
MS-SR-F	0.02%	0.02%
(Failed to achieve Makes Sense and Similar Response)		
SN-MS-SR-F	0.45%	0.02%
(Failed to achieve Sounds Natural, Makes Sense, and Similar Response)		
SN-MS-OM-F	0.49%	0.04%
(Failed to achieve Sound Natural, Makes Sense, and Original Manner)		

Note: Underlined outcomes are the ones included in the Criteria Set (see Table 4.3).

to the outcomes not included in the Criteria Set. In other words, the seven outcomes listed in the Criteria Set were consistent with the outcomes appearing in the assessment results of the lay readers.

4 Translators' Emphasis on Semantic Meanings

Eight of the 15 professional translators participated in a survey, which examined their views on what characterises a good quality translation (detailed discussion presented in Teng, 2020). The survey revealed that the professional translators' emphasis on the importance of (maintaining) semantic meanings seemed to be a cause of the significant divergence between their assessment results and those of the lay readers (Teng, 2020). Passages assessed by the professional translators as "good" translations (i.e., assigned Total Equivalence) were often assessed by the lay readers as "poor" translations (i.e., assigned Totally Lost or SR-F), as shown in Table 4.4.

To explain the divergence, I relied on two contextual meanings: ideational and interpersonal (Halliday & Matthiessen, 2004; Kim & Matthiessen, 2015). While interpersonal meaning projects the relationship between the author and the reader (of the translation assessed in this study), ideational meaning represents both the logical and experiential reality (see Table 4.1). Since both interpersonal and ideational meaning are realised through semantic meanings of words, translators' assessment results seem to show that the translators could see only the realisation of semantic meaning in the experiential reality. Hence, I could see that the professional translators had ignored the logical reality in the ideational meaning, as well as overlooking the interpersonal meaning when making their assessments. This postulation explains the difference between translators' perspectives and those of the lay readers, as shown in Figure 4.2. Figure 4.2 shows the following:

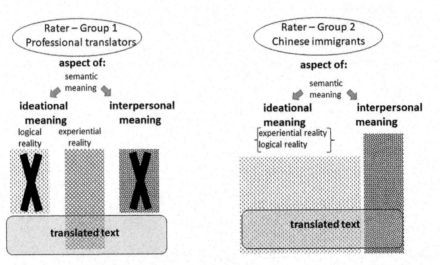

FIGURE 4.2 The difference between professional translators' and lay readers' perspectives on semantic meaning

- The professional translators seemed to ignore the logical reality in the ideational meaning and interpersonal meanings when assessing translation quality. They focused only on the experiential reality projected by the semantics. Their emphasis on semantic meaning was consistent with Crezee and Burn's (2019) observation of professionals' tendency to make comments on the messages in the translation.
- The lay readers, while assessing the appropriateness of the semantic meanings of the assessed translation (i.e., assessing whether the translation Sounded Natural and Made Sense) were, however, also sensitive to ideational (both logical and experiential reality) and interpersonal meanings. Both aspects of ideational and interpersonal meanings therefore seemed to be present in their perception of what characterises a good quality translation.

The delivery of semantic meaning is closely related to the criteria Sounds Natural and Makes Sense and Sounds Natural is a fundamental factor in eliciting a Similar Response and achieving pragmatic equivalence (Figure 4.1). Therefore, I examined assessment outcomes which indicated that the participants believed that a passage had achieved all three criteria except Similar Response (SR-F).

5 Divergence in the Assessment of Similar Response

Of the 16 possible assessment outcomes, SR-F was the outcome most frequently assigned by the lay readers with an average of 44.63% (see Table 4.4). Table 4.5 shows that of the 15 translated texts, lay readers assigned Text 8 the highest percentage of SR-F (55.11%); the professional translators, however, assigned this text the third highest percentage of Total Equivalence (69.33%). In other words, while the translators believed that almost 70% of the passages were "good" translations, the lay readers believed that they did not know what they were instructed to do after reading more than half of the passages in Text 8 (see Appendix C for the assessment results of all the passages in Text 8).

Despite assigning SR-F to a high percentage of passages in Text 8, the lay readers did not believe that these passages constituted "poor" translations. While the passages were unsuccessful in eliciting a Similar Response, the lay readers nevertheless believed that the passages Sounded Natural and Made Sense. They also believed that they knew the intention of the passages (i.e., to inform), hence achieving Original Manner. Therefore, it is necessary to investigate what had caused a passage to fail to elicit a Similar Response from the lay readers that the professional translators appeared to have expected.

Table 4.6 shows that 73.33% of lay readers assigned SR-F to Passage 3, while 80% of professional translators assigned the passage Total Equivalence.

The assessment results for Passage 3 illustrate that both groups of participants believed that the passage Sounded Natural, Made Sense, and achieved Original Manner). However, the high percentage of lay readers that assigned SR-F to Passage 3 indicates that the professional translators detached the aspect of semantic meanings

TABLE 4.5 Comparing Percentages of the Two Most Frequently Assigned Outcomes: Total Equivalence and SR-F

Text Number	Total Equivalence		SR-F	
	Professional Translators	*Chinese Lay Readers*	*Professional Translators*	*Chinese Lay Readers*
Text 1	49.12%	18.95%	0.35%	45.26%
Text 2	46.06%	17.58%	0.61%	43.03%
Text 3	52.63%	10.53%	0.35%	32.98%
Text 4	70.83% (second highest)	4.58%	0.42%	46.67%
Text 5	49.26%	3.33%	0.37%	34.44%
Text 6	74.67% (highest)	4.00%	0.27%	35.73%
Text 7	68.10%	6.43%	0.24%	50.95%
Text 8	69.33% (third highest)	4.44%	0.89%	55.11% (highest)
Text 9	44.76%	0.00%	0.00%	54.29%
Text 10	62.22%	0.44%	0.44%	46.67%
Text 11	45.26%	3.16%	1.05%	50.18%
Text 12	68.89%	2.67%	0.44%	48.44%
Text 13	42.90%	0.29%	0.29%	40.58%
Text 14	61.03%	1.54%	0.00%	46.15%
Text 15	67.18%	0.51%	0.00%	38.97%

TABLE 4.6 Comparing Percentages of Outcomes Assigned to Passage 3 in Text 8

Possible Outcomes Assigned to Passage 3, Text 8	Professional Translators	Chinese Lay Readers
	Average Percentage of Assigned Outcome	
Total Equivalence (Achieved all four criteria)	80.00%	6.67%
SR-F (Failed to achieve Similar Response)	0.00%	73.33%
OM-F (Failed to achieve Original Manner)	6.67%	0.00%
OM-SR-F (Failed to achieve Original Manner and Similar Response)	0.00%	6.67%

SN-OM-SR-F	0.00%	0.00%
(Failed to achieve Sounds Natural, Original Manner and Similar Response)		
MS-OM-SR-F	0.00%	13.33%
(Failed to achieve Makes Sense, Original Manner, and Similar Response)		
Totally Lost	0.00%	0.00%
(Failed to achieve all four criteria)		
SN-SR-F	0.00%	0.00%
(Failed to achieve Sounds Natural and Similar Response)		
SN-F	13.33%	0.00%
(Failed to achieve Sounds Natural)		
MS-F	0.00%	0.00%
(Failed to achieve Makes Sense)		
SN-OM-F	0.00%	0.00%
(Failed to achieve Sounds Natural and Original Manner)		
SN-MS-F	0.00%	0.00%
(Failed to achieve Sounds Natural and Similar Response)		
MS-OM-F	0.00%	0.00%
(Failed to achieve Makes Sense and Original Manner)		
MS-SR-F	0.00%	0.00%
(Failed to achieve Makes Sense and Similar Response)		
SN-MS-SR-F	0.00%	0.00%
(Failed to achieve Sounds Natural, Makes Sense and Similar Response)		
SN-MS-OM-F	0.00%	0.00%
(Failed to achieve Sounds Natural, Makes Sense and Original Manner)		

Note: Underlined outcomes are the ones included in the Criteria Set (see Table 4.3).

from ideational meanings and considered only the experiential reality, while ignoring logical reality (see Table 4.1 for ideational meanings). In contrast, the lay readers considered both the interpersonal meanings and the ideational meanings, seeing both experiential and logical reality projected through semantic meaning (see Figure 4.2).

Passage 3 was a subheading in Text 8 which provided information about spironolactone, a diuretic medication used to treat patients who are at risk of heart failure. The subheading was preceded by a description of the effects of spironolactone (Passage 2) and followed by a list of side effects that could be caused by this drug (Passage 4 and 5). Passage 3 (underlined) is presented in Example 4.1 along with Passage 2 and the first two of the five side effects described in Passages 4–5.

The following two Chinese linguistic features in Passage 3 provide a possible explanation as to why most participants in the two groups believed that the passage Sounded Natural, Made Sense, and achieved Original Manner.

- The subject "spironolactone" was absent in Passage 3 (see the back translation in Example 4.1). It is common in both written and spoken Chinese for the subject to be omitted from a sentence (i.e. a null subject) when it is understandable within the context of the sentence (Chu, 2018; Li & Thompson, 1981; Liu et al., 1996). Hence, the omission of "spironolactone" in Passage 3 did not affect the grammaticality of the sentence and the accessibility of the message.

EXAMPLE 4.1 Text 8

Original text	Spironolactone (Spiractin Spirotone) helps to reduce symptoms and improve survival in patients who have heart failure....
Passage 2	有證據顯示螺內酯能使患心臟衰竭的人情況好轉和延長壽命....
BT	There is evidence showing that spironolactone can improve the condition of patients who have heart failure and extend their life....
Original text	*What are some of the side effects?*
Passage 3	有什麼副作用？
BT	What side effects does [spironolactone] have?
Original text	Upset stomach or diarrhoea
Passage 4	腸胃不適
BT	Upset intestines and stomach
Original text	Rash
Passage 5	紅疹
BT	Rash

- Passage 3 involved the interrogative word "shénme/什麼/what", which may have made the participants believe that the passage was produced to inform the reader and provide answers to the question in the passage.

Therefore, in terms of the accessibility of the message and questioning tone, a majority of participants in both groups assessed Passage 3 as having achieved Sounds Natural, Makes Sense, and Original Manner (see percentage of Total Equivalence and SR-F in Table 4.6). The lay readers, however, did not believe that they knew how to respond to the passage or what they were expected to do, and they thus assessed it as SR-F.

The examination of the semantic meaning and syntactical structure of Passage 3 did not explain the contrasting assessment results between the two groups. Therefore, I looked at the lexico-grammatical features of the passage. Although Passage 3 included the interrogative word "shénme/什麼/what" to form a question, it lacked the sentence-final particle "ne/呢" to express the interpersonal meaning that could have elicited a Similar Response from the lay readers.

Since the pragmatic function of health care texts is to inform the reader (Fischbach, 1962), a question such as Passage 3 may not be a genuine question that seeks an answer from the reader. Therefore, the English original of Passage 3 put a question to its reader in order to deliver a particular interpersonal meaning. That is, the question could make the reader believe (i.e., respond) that *the author knows what I want to ask and here is the question that I wanted to ask*. The interpersonal meaning in the English original created a context whereby the author was in the same position as the reader. However, Passage 3 – the translated text – would not have successfully elicited that particular response from the lay readers.

A question in Chinese can be formed using a number of sentence particles – such as ma/嗎, ba/吧, or ne/呢 – the pragmatic intention of which may vary from making strong assumptions to simply seeking opinions (Crezee et al., 2017; Teng, 2019). For example, the sentence-final particle ne/呢, when it is attached to a question which is closely related to previous messages, does not express the expectation of an answer but instead introduces additional information related to those messages (Li & Thompson, 1981; Lin, 2003). In other words, while an interrogative question involving "shénme/什麼/what" expects the reader to give an answer to the question, the addition of the particle ne/呢 mitigates the questioning tone and draws the reader's attention to the information that follows. Therefore, without ne/呢 mitigating the questioning tone, the lay readers seemed to be confused by the question in Passage 3, because they were being asked to answer a question in a health care pamphlet that was supposed to provide information about spironolactone. That means, if the sentence-final particle ne/呢 had been attached to the question, Passage 3, making it "yǒu shén me fù zuò yòng ne/有什麼副作用呢?/What are the side effects?", the lay readers would have believed that they could expect to read the side effects in Passage 4 and 5.

When making their assessment, neither group of participants had access to the English original and thus were not able to judge the pragmatic function that I postulate here. However, it is this equally informed basis (whereby both groups saw only the translation as a Chinese native speaker) that again revealed the divergent perspectives of the two participant groups when they assessed a translated text. Even though a majority of participants in both groups believed that Passage 3 had expressed the intention of asking a question and seeking an answer (achieving Original Manner), the interpersonal meaning the participants (in both groups) believed about the passage was not a sense of empathy. In other words, Passage 3 did not make the lay readers believe that *the author knows what I want to ask, and he/she is going to give me the answers*. Hence, confusion occurred, leading to more than 73.33% of the lay readers assigning SR-F to Passage 3.

The brief linguistic analysis of Passage 3, based on the three aspects of meaning (see Figure 4.2), shows again that the Criteria Set seems to be in line with the lay readers' perspectives. In other words, the professional translators seemed to see only the semantic meaning (i.e., the experiential reality) of Passage 3. This is consistent with the findings in my previous study (Teng, 2020) in which professional translators responded to a survey and placed an emphasis on the semantic meanings of and faithfulness to the message. However, the assessment results presented in this study show that the lay readers considered both the experiential and the logical reality delivered by way of the ideational meanings when making their assessments.

In addition, the professional translators' apparent lack of awareness of the inappropriate interpersonal meaning of Passage 3 was also consistent with observations of translators not being aware of the potential pragmatic function of Chinese particles in previous studies (Crezee et al., 2017; Teng, 2019; Teng et al., 2018). In this respect, the findings from the lay readers' results and the linguistic analysis of Passage 3 showed that the achievement of the criterion Similar Response was not a definite result of the achievement of the other three criteria (Sounds Natural, Makes Sense, and Original Manner). The achievement of Similar Response also relies on whether the linguistic features of the translation can fulfil pragmatic functions (expected in the source text) in the target sociocultural context (see Figure 4.1).

This section has revealed that the lay readers in my study seemed to be quite sensitive to the contextual meanings (i.e., ideational and interpersonal) delivered by the linguistic features in the example, while believing that the translation Sounded Natural. The professional translators, who also believed that the translation Sounded Natural, did not, however, seem to have such awareness and sensitivity. Bearing in mind the criterion Sounds Natural, I then turned to look at passages that the lay readers believed Sounded Natural, while the professional translators did not believe that, yet still assessed those passages as achieving a Similar Response.

6 Divergence in the Assessment of Sounds Natural

Assigning SN-F (Sounds Natural Failed) to a passage indicated that the participants believed that the passage did not Sound Natural to a native speaker of the language, but had achieved the other three criteria, including Similar Response. Among the 16 possible outcomes, SN-F was the outcome second most frequently assigned by the professional translators with an average percentage of 21.33% (second only to Total Equivalence; see Table 4.4). However, none of the lay readers assigned this outcome to any of the 15 translated texts. In other words, when a passage did not Sound Natural, the lay readers did not seem to perceive the message of the passage (Makes Sense), or the intention of the passage

(Original Manner), or how they were supposed to respond to the passage (Similar Response). However, the high percentage of SN-F in the professional translators' assessment results appeared to contradict my argument that achieving the criterion Sounds Natural is of fundamental importance to a translated text achieving Similar Response (Figure 4.1). Therefore, it is necessary to discuss this and re-examine my argument (Figure 4.1) and the suitability of the Criteria Set.

Among the 15 translated texts, Text 2 was assigned the highest percentage of SN-F by the professional translators (33.33%; see Table 4.7). However, none of the passages in this text were assigned SN-F by any of the lay readers.

I then looked at the results of passages in Text 2 that had failed to achieve Sound Natural, as well as Make Sense and/or Original Manner, yet still achieved a Similar Response (i.e., outcomes SN-F, SN-OM-F, SN-MS-F, and SN-MS-OM-F). Table 4.8 shows that the lay readers did not assign any of those outcomes to any passages; the professional translators, by contrast, assigned one of these outcomes to 41.21% of the passages.

Among the 11 passages in Text 2, Passage 3 and Passage 10 were assigned the highest percentage of SN-F (46.67%) by the professional translators. Analysis of the assessment results for the two passages showed a difference in opinion on the achievement of Sounds Natural, as shown in Table 4.9 and Table 4.10. An overall view of contrasting assessment results for the passages in Text 2 from the perspectives of the two groups for each passage can be found in Appendix D.

Table 4.9 and Table 4.10 show that while Passage 3 and Passage 10 did not Sound Natural to almost half of the 15 professional translators (see 46.67%;

TABLE 4.7 Comparing Percentages of Texts Assessed as SN-F

Text Number	SN-F	
	Professional Translators	Chinese Lay Readers
Text 1	24.56%	0.00%
Text 2	*33.33%*	0.00%
Text 3	22.46%	0.00%
Text 4	11.25%	0.00%
Text 5	23.33%	0.00%
Text 6	8.00%	0.00%
Text 7	18.10%	0.00%
Text 8	13.33%	0.00%
Text 9	26.67%	0.00%
Text 10	22.22%	0.00%
Text 11	27.37%	0.00%
Text 12	15.56%	0.00%
Text 13	28.70%	0.00%
Text 14	23.08%	0.00%
Text 15	22.05%	0.00%

TABLE 4.8 Comparing Percentages of Outcomes Indicating That Sound Natural Had Not Been Achieved (SN-F), While Similar Response (SR) Had Been Achieved

Possible Outcomes	Text 2	
	Professional Translators	Chinese Lay Readers
SN-F	33.33%	0.00%
SN-OM-F	1.21%	0.00%
SN-MS-F	4.85%	0.00%
SN-MS-OM-F	1.82%	0.00%
Sub-total percentage	41.21%	0.00%

Note: The percentages do not add up to 100 percent because this table includes only outcomes indicating passages when Sound Natural had not been achieved, and when Similar Response had been achieved; thus, SN is seen in outcomes listed in this table, while SR is not.

TABLE 4.9 Comparing Percentages of Outcomes Assigned to Passage 3 in Text 2

Possible Outcomes Assigned to Passage 3, Text 2	Professional Translators	Chinese Lay Readers
	Average Percentage of Assigned Outcome	
Total Equivalence (Achieved all four criteria)	26.67%	26.67%
SR-F (Failed to achieve Similar Response)	6.67%	46.67%
OM-F (Failed to achieve Original Manner)	6.67%	0.00%
OM-SR-F (Failed to achieve Original Manner and Similar Response)	0.00%	6.67%
SN-OM-SR-F (Failed to achieve Sounds Natural, Original Manner, and Similar Response)	0.00%	0.00%
MS-OM-SR-F (Failed to achieve Makes Sense, Original Manner, and Similar Response)	0.00%	13.33%
Totally Lost (Failed to achieve all four criteria)	13.33%	6.67%
SN-SR-F (Failed to achieve Sounds Natural, and Similar Response)	0.00%	0.00%

(*Continued*)

You Don't See What I See 85

Possible Outcomes Assigned to Passage 3, Text 2	Professional Translators	Chinese Lay Readers
	Average Percentage of Assigned Outcome	
SN-F (Failed to achieve Sounds Natural)	46.67%	0.00%
MS-F (Failed to achieve Makes Sense)	0.00%	0.00%
SN-OM-F (Failed to achieve Sounds Natural and Original Manner)	0.00%	0.00%
SN-MS-F (Failed to achieve Sounds Natural and Similar Response)	0.00%	0.00%
MS-OM-F (Failed to achieve Makes Sense and Original Manner)	0.00%	0.00%
MS-SR-F (Failed to achieve Makes Sense and Similar Response)	0.00%	0.00%
SN-MS-SR-F (Failed to achieve Sounds Natural, Makes Sense, and Similar Response)	0.00%	0.00%
SN-MS-OM-F (Failed to achieve Sounds Natural, Makes Sense, and Original Manner)	0.00%	0.00%

Note: Underlined outcomes are the ones included in the Criteria Set (see Table 4.3).

TABLE 4.10 Comparing Percentages of Outcomes Assigned to Passage 10 in Text 2

Possible Outcomes Assigned to Passage 10, Text 2	Professional Translators	Chinese Lay Readers
	Average Percentage of Assigned Outcome	
Total Equivalence (Achieved all four criteria)	13.33%	13.33%
SR-F (Failed to achieve Similar Response)	0.00%	33.33%
OM-F (Failed to achieve Original Manner)	0.00%	0.00%
OM-SR-F (Failed to achieve Original Manner and Similar Response)	6.67%	20.00%

(*Continued*)

TABLE 4.10 (Continued)

Possible Outcomes Assigned to Passage 10, Text 2	Professional Translators	Chinese Lay Readers
	Average Percentage of Assigned Outcome	
<u>SN-OM-SR-F</u>	0.00%	0.00%
(Failed to achieve Sounds Natural, Original Manner and Similar Response)		
MS-OM-SR-F	6.67%	26.67%
(Failed to achieve Makes Sense, Original Manner, and Similar Response)		
<u>Totally Lost</u>	20.00%	6.67%
(Failed to achieve all four criteria)		
SN-SR-F	0.00%	0.00%
(Failed to achieve Sounds Natural and Similar Response)		
SN-F	46.67%	0.00%
(Failed to achieve Sounds Natural)		
MS-F	0.00%	0.00%
(Failed to achieve Makes Sense)		
SN-OM-F	6.67%	0.00%
(Failed to achieve Sounds Natural and Original Manner)		
SN-MS-F	0.00%	0.00%
(Failed to achieve Sounds Natural and Similar Response)		
MS-OM-F	0.00%	0.00%
(Failed to achieve Makes Sense and Original Manner)		
MS-SR-F	0.00%	0.00%
(Failed to achieve Makes Sense and Similar Response)		
SN-MS-SR-F	0.00%	0.00%
(Failed to achieve Sounds Natural, Makes Sense and Similar Response)		
SN-MS-OM-F	0.00%	0.00%
(Failed to achieve Sounds Natural, Makes Sense and Original Manner)		

Note: Underlined outcomes are the ones included in the Criteria Set (see Table 4.3).

SN-F), the two passages Sounded Natural to most of the lay readers, with the exception of one lay reader who did not believe that (see 6.67%; Totally Lost).

The low percentage of lay readers who assigned Totally Lost (6.67%) seemed to indicate that the lay readers were not as sensitive as the professional translators to the naturalness of expressions. However, this is my interpretation of the findings, viewing them from the perspective of a professional translator. In other words, I could not help but wonder why the lay readers had a different view from us translators (including myself among the latter here) because, after all, it is the lay readers who are the end users of a translated text (cf. also García-Izquierdo & Montalt i Resurrecció, 2017). It is only when the end users are able to fully grasp the purpose of the information contained in the original text that a translated text can be considered to be successful.

I therefore analysed the Chinese linguistic features of both Passage 3 and Passage 10. The result of the analyses seemed to be consistent with the observation (Teng, 2020) of the professional translators' belief in the importance of semantic meanings in the achievement of Makes Sense, Original Manner, and Similar Response, and their lack of awareness of certain Chinese pragmalinguistic features.

7 Assessing Similar Response Without Considering Sounds Natural

In terms of naturalness of expression, I agreed with the professional translators' assessment that Passage 3 did not Sound Natural when first seeing the passage. This passage, however, Sounded Natural to more than 90% of the lay readers (Total Equivalence 26.67%, SR-F 46.67%, OM-SR-F 6.67%, and MS-OM-SR-F 13.33%; see Table 4.9). Aligning myself with the perspectives of the lay readers (the end users), I analysed the linguistic features of Passage 3 and realised that the passage was indeed in accordance with Chinese syntax. The linguistic analysis also revealed the professional translators' belief that:

- Whether a translation Makes Sense or not relies only on the semantic meanings of individual words in the translation, and once the translation Makes Sense, the translation could elicit a Similar Response even if the translation does not Sound Natural.

This belief is apparently contrary to my argument that there is a correlative relationship between the achievement of the four criteria, whereby Sounds Natural is a fundamental factor in a translated text achieving Similar Response.

Passage 3 is presented in Example 4.2 with the pronouns nǐ/你/you and nǐde/你的/your in bold.

EXAMPLE 4.2 Passage 3 – Text 2

Original text:	**You** are also likely to put on extra weight if **you** eat more food than **your** body needs for energy.
Passage 3:	如果你的進食量超過你身體需要的能量，你將會增加體重。
BT:	If the amount of **your** intake of food exceeds the energy that **your** body needs, **you** will gain weight.

The back translation of Passage 3 shows that the English pronouns "you" and "your" were kept in the Chinese translation. The passage was produced in accordance with Chinese syntactical rules and the semantic meanings of content words also fitted the context surrounding the passage itself (i.e., the use of insulin and diet control). In other words, there was nothing amiss in Passage 3 either syntactically or semantically. Hence, the passage Sounded Natural to the lay readers, even though the professional translators did not believe the same. One linguistic feature of the Chinese language can help explain why the passage did not Sound Natural to the translators and may have again revealed their lack of awareness of potential pragmatic functions delivered through certain pragmalinguistic features of the language.

Chinese is a language which allows pronouns to be omitted from a sentence when the context surrounding that sentence allows the reader to have a clear idea of to what or whom the omitted pronouns refer (Li & Thompson, 1981; Xiao & Hu, 2015). When a pronoun (particularly a personal pronoun) frequently appears in a translated sentence, it is often the result of anglicisation (Dai, 2016; Xiao & Hu, 2015). The frequent use of the pronoun nǐ/你/you in Passage 3 could explain why the passage did not Sound Natural to almost half of the professional translators (see SN-F 46.7% in Table 4.9). However, what should also be noted is that frequent use of a personal pronoun in a sentence does not affect the grammaticality of the sentence, meaning that the sentence may still sound like Chinese. That could explain why more than 90% of the lay readers believed that Passage 3 Sounded Natural (Total Equivalence 26.67%, SR-F 46.67%, OM-SR-F 6.67, and MS-OM-SR-F 13.33%; see Table 4.9).

Even though there are no clear rules as to when a pronoun should be omitted, a pronoun present in a sentence (when it can be omitted) functions to deliver the textual meaning that the speaker/writer intended to emphasise that pronoun (Li & Thompson, 1976, 1981). Particularly when this pronoun is nǐ/你/you, the speaker/writer is making it clear that it is *you* I am talking to (Hsiao, 2011; Li & Thompson, 1981). In addition, because the imperative structure in Chinese allows keeping the pronoun nǐ/你/you in the sentence, the emphatic function of the pronoun nǐ/你/you is amplified. That then achieves the interpersonal function of delivering the message with an authoritative and imperative tone, and this tone is consistent with Sin's (2004) observation that the tone used in the delivery of health care related messages is more of an imperative one in the mainland Chinese context.

The imperative tone of Passage 3 was consistent with the interpersonal function expected from health care related messages in the mainland Chinese context. However, this passage did not elicit a Similar Response from almost 70% of the Chinese immigrant participants (SR-F 46.67%, OM-SR-F 6.67, and MS-OM-SR-F 13.33%; see Table 4.9) regarding the point that *they get to know they should not eat more than their bodies need*.

Further, even though there was no obvious indication that the imperative tone of Passage 3 had caused the lay readers to not know how to respond to the passage, such an imperative tone did not seem to facilitate the delivery of the message to the lay readers. More than 70% of them did not get the message that *they should not eat more than their bodies need.* The exact causes of the lay readers not having a Similar Response to Passage 3 may not be clear. However, the previously discussed pragmalinguistic feature of the pronoun nǐ/你/you revealed that the proposed Criteria Set again seemed to be in line with the perspectives of lay readers (the end users), because Table 4.9 shows that the Criteria Set included only the outcomes that would appear in the end user's assessment results.

The proposed Criteria Set did not include the assessment outcome SN-F (Sounds Natural is Failed, while the other three criteria have been achieved) because of my argument that Sounds Natural is a fundamental factor in achieving a Similar Response. This argument is consistent with the lay readers' assessment results because once the lay readers did not believe that the translated passage Sounded Natural, they did not understand what the passage meant (failed Makes Sense), what the passage intended to do with the message (failed Original Manner), and what they should or should not do (failed Similar Response).

In addition, the Criteria Set helped identify Passage 3 for linguistic analysis, which then revealed the professional translators' lack of awareness of potential ideational and interpersonal meanings (see Table 4.1) delivered through the content words. Regarding the third contextual meaning, textual meaning, I also found that the Criteria Set could help in a discussion of translators' (un)awareness of this contextual meaning.

8 Participants Not Considering the Three Contextual Meanings

While looking at SN-F, I also noticed interesting findings in the assessment results of Passage 10 in the same text, Text 2. Contrary to the assessment results of Passage 3, the assessment results of Passage 10 did not Sound Natural to almost half of the professional translators (SN-F 46.67%; see Table 4.10); the passage Sounded Natural to more than 90% of the lay readers (Total Equivalence 13.33%, SR-F 33.33%, OM-SR-F 20%, and MS-OM-SR-F 26.67%; see Table 4.10).

To explain why Passage 10 Sounded Natural to the majority of the lay readers, I analysed the linguistic features of the passage and realised that the passage was, again, indeed in accordance with Chinese syntax. The linguistic analysis seemed to reveal again the professional translators' belief that:

- A translation may still achieve Similar Response even if the translation does not Sound Natural

The analysis also revealed their lack of awareness of:

- The influences of a potentially anglicised Chinese sentence structure in translation
- The textual function of the copular verb shì/是/be in terms of giving affirmation to or assertion of the following or preceding messages (Chao, 1965; Li & Thompson, 1981; McDonald, 1992)

I have presented Passage 10 in Example 4.3 with the copular verb shì/是/be in bold.

EXAMPLE 4.3 Passage 10 – Text 2

Original text:	If you are unwell, it is important you do more testing because it can change your blood glucose level.
Passage 10:	如果你感覺不舒服，增加驗血次數是很重要。
BT:	If you feel unwell, increase the number of blood testing **is** very important.

The copular verb shì/是/be in Passage 10 could help explain why the professional translators did not believe that the passage Sounded Natural. The copular verb *shì*/是/*be* was not used in conjunction with the particle de/的 to form a "shì . . . de structure", which is a commonly seen anglicised Chinese structure in English to Chinese translation (Xiao & Hu, 2015). In other words, if Passage 10 had involved the particle de/的 at the end of the sentence, making it read "增加驗血次數是很重要的", the professional translators assigning the passage SN-F would most probably have believed that it Sounded Natural.

However, Passage 10 was indeed a grammatical sentence and did Sound Natural (without the particle de/的). The illocutionary force of Passage 10 seemed to trigger an argument by weakening the importance of 增加驗血次數/increase the number of blood testing. This illocutionary force was exerted by the copular verb shì/是/be for its textual functions; even though functioning to affirm or assert the following or preceding message (Chao, 1965; Li & Thompson, 1981; McDonald, 1992), the copular verb shì/是/be could also deliver an expression that may be similar to a softened expression of English *even though* (Liu et al., 1996). That softened expression of "even though" may then lead to a concession of the importance of messages both preceding and following the copular verb shì/是/be, and hence detach those messages from being the focal point of the information.

For instance, the copular verb shì/是/be, while weakening the importance of "study hard" in the sentence "yònggōng dúshū shì hěn zhòngyào/用功讀書是很重要/study[ing] hard is very important", implies that there are other matters more important than "study hard". Therefore, the attention of the target audience may be drawn away from "study hard" to, for instance, "health" in the sentence: "yònggōng dúshū shì hěn zhòngyào, dàn jiànkāng gèng zhòngyào/用功讀書是很重要，但健康更重要/study[ing] hard is very important, but health is more important". In other words, a sentence with the copular verb shì/是/be may cause the target audience to expect that what follows deserves more attention. The "something" that deserved more attention was, however, absent from Passage 10, and hence the textual meanings delivered in the passage seemed to have hindered the lay readers' understanding of the passage in terms of what or how to respond to the passage.

The textual meaning (the emphasised information) of "increase the number of blood testing" was attenuated by the copular verb shì/是/be. The copular verb weakened the illocutionary force of advising patients to do more testing, while implying that there was something else more important than that advice. That is, the textual meaning of "增加驗血次數/increase the number of blood testing" in

Passage 10 was distorted because it delivered the implied message that increasing the number of blood tests was less important than messages that followed; yet such messages were not provided to the target reader. The lay readers would very possibly believe that it is important to increase the number of blood testing, but then what? That may explain why 80% of the lay readers did not know how to respond to Passage 10 (SR-F 33.33%, OM-SR-F 20%, and MS-OM-SR-F 26.67%; see Table 4.10) even though they all believed that the passage Sounded Natural.

This brief linguistic analysis of Passage 10 again seemed to indicate that the professional translators were only paying attention to the message delivered through the content words in the passage. In other words, their assessment seemed to be based on their judgement of whether the semantic meaning of words themselves Made Sense in the passage. In this example, they did not seem to consider the textual meaning associated with certain words (e.g., the copular verb shì/是/be). My analysis also seemed to reveal that the professional translators' concept of natural expression may have been influenced by the commonly used anglicised translational "shì . . . de structure" (Xiao & Hu, 2015). This may possibly have led them to assess the passage as not Sounding Natural. This may also have resulted in their lack of awareness of the textual meanings of the copular verb shì/是/be.

The lay readers, by contrast, seemed to be more sensitive to the textual meanings of certain pragmalinguistic features, such as the copular verb shì/是/be in this example. In other words, the difference in assessment between the two groups of participants was not only reflected in their consideration of semantic, ideational, and interpersonal meanings (see Figure 4.1), but the consideration of textual meanings also seemed evident in the lay readers' concept of what characterises a good quality translation. Hence, the discussion in this section has further revealed how the professional translators' emphasis on the experiential reality of semantic meanings reflected a different view to that of the lay readers' assessments, as represented in Figure 4.3.

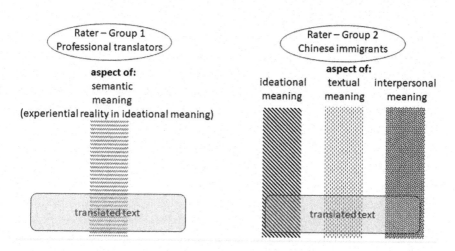

FIGURE 4.3 Difference in two participant groups' perspectives on three contextual meanings

Figure 4.3 shows the lay readers' sensitivity to the three contextual meanings, namely ideational, interpersonal, and textual meanings, as reflected in their assessment results and revealed in the previously discussed linguistic analysis. Figure 4.3 also shows again that the proposed Criteria Set seemed to be in line and compatible with the perspectives of the end users (the lay readers) when they looked at a translated text. The Criteria Set may therefore be a set of criteria applicable to the real-life practice of community translation in terms of determining translation quality at the level of context.

9 Conclusion

The discussion in this chapter relied on theoretical frameworks that are end user–oriented. To be specific, if the end user does not clearly understand the message or know what they are meant to do, then the translation has not been successful. Through brief linguistic analyses of sample passages in this chapter, it appeared that the proposed Criteria Set had been developed using such theoretical frameworks. The discussion therefore indicated that the Criteria Set seemed to be able to help assess translation quality with a consideration of all three contextual values of ideational, interpersonal, and textual meanings. This consideration of all three contextual meanings was in line with the end users' perspectives, as represented in Figure 4.3. Assessing translation quality in this way is important because only when the lay readers' conceptions are considered and appreciated can we produce a translation that duly provides them with language access to crucial information related to their basic rights such as access to health care services, legal aid, and other forms of social welfare.

This chapter also indicates that the Criteria Set could include SN-F for its applicability in translator education. While the four criteria – Sounds Natural, Makes Sense, Original Manner, and Similar Response – are equally important in achieving pragmatic equivalence, the criterion Sounds Natural is the fundamental factor in achieving the other three criteria. Therefore, the assessment outcome SN-F can serve to reveal student translators' awareness or unawareness of how and why achieving/failing Sounds Natural could be of fundamental importance in achieving Similar Response.

Further, while the assessment of Original Manner and Similar Response are closely related to the pragmatic functions of words, the two criteria may be especially significant in reminding student translators of the importance of achieving pragmatic equivalence. These criteria do this by showing student translators the significance of assessing whether the three contextual meanings of a translation – ideational, interpersonal, and textual meanings – fit the sociocultural context that encompasses the translation. The Criteria Set therefore can serve as a pedagogical model in translator education.

APPENDICES

Appendix A

Text 2 English Original and Chinese Translation

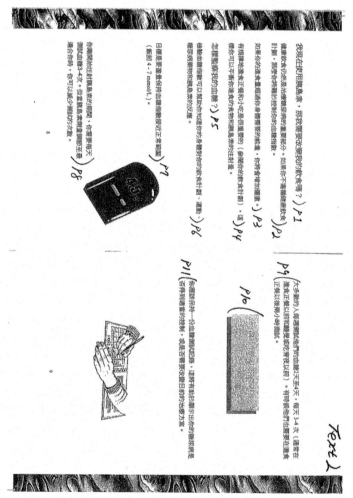

Note: Due to the low legibility of Passage 10, transcription of the passage is provided as follows

如果你感覺不舒服，增加驗血次數是很重要

On page 11 we will tell you what to do if you have a 'hypo'.

If you have any side effects that you think may be caused by your insulin, talk to your doctor.

Do I need to change what I eat?

Healthy eating will still be an important part of your diabetes treatment. If you do not follow a healthy food plan, it will be harder to control your blood glucose levels.

You are also likely to put on extra weight if you eat more food than your body needs for energy. The more weight you have, the more insulin you many need.

It is important that you have regular meals containing carbohydrate so that you balance what you eat with how much insulin you inject. Some people need snacks between meals, but if you want to control your weight, snacks may not be necessary. Check with your doctor or nurse for advice.

Monitoring my blood glucose

Your nurse or pharmacist will show you how to check your own blood glucose levels using your blood glucose meter. Checking your levels at home will help you to see how well your body responds to your food plan, exercise, diabetes tablets and insulin. The goal for most people is to keep blood glucose levels as close to the normal range as possible (5-7mmol/L before meals).

When you first start insulin you will need to test your blood glucose at least 3 to 4 times a day. But once you have found the insulin dose that best suits you, you can do less testing. Sometimes people also need to test their levels 2 hours after meals. Occasionally you may be asked to test overnight.

If you are unwell it is important you do more testing because it can change your blood glucose level.

Appendix B

Text 8 English Original and Chinese Translation

Text 8

螺內酯 Spironolactone（Spirotone - 螺內酯製劑的商品名）

它有什麼作用？) P1

有證明顯示螺內酯能使患心臟衰竭的人情況有好轉和延長壽命。
它防止體內的水份累積起來，而你也只需要服食低的劑量。) P2

有什麼副作用？) P3

- 腸胃不適) P4
- 紅疹) P5
- 男性 — 乳房壓痛和/或略微變大) P6
- 頭痛) P7
- 精神混亂) P8

其他需知的重要訊息) P9

- 你將需要定期做血液檢驗以檢查你的腎功能和含鉀指數。你將需要在服藥後的一週、四週，然後三個月進行血液檢驗。有些人需要更多的血液檢驗。) P10
- 如果你有嘔吐和/或腹瀉 …) P11
  - 增加你的飲水量) P12
  - 停止服此藥（參閱下面有關重新服藥的訊息）) P13
  - 如果你腹瀉超過三天，請約見醫生。) P14
  - 不要再次開始服藥，直至腹瀉停止以後的兩天) P15

有什麼我需要避免的？

- 螺內酯可能增加你體內的鉀含量，因此要避免使用鹽的替代品，因為這些替代品含有鉀的成分。
- 一些止痛藥會影響螺內酯的作用或使你的心臟衰竭情況惡化。更多的信息請參閱第十五頁。

Text 8

Spironolactone

Spironolactone (Spiractin® Spirotone®) helps to reduce symptoms and improve survival in patients who have heart failure because of weak heart muscle. Spironolactone has a weak diuretic effect, so will also help to rid your body of extra fluid.

What are some of the side effects?

- Upset stomach or diarrhoea
- Rash
- Leg cramps at night
- Headache
- Confusion
- In men – breast tenderness and/or enlargement

You will need to have regular blood tests to check your kidneys and the potassium level in your blood. You will need a blood test after the first week, then again in another 4 weeks, and then every 3 months.

If you are vomiting or have diarrhoea

- Stop taking this tablet
- Drink more fluids, especially water
- Do not start your tablet again until 2 days after the diarrhoea has stopped

If you have diarrhoea for more than 3 days, see your doctor.

Appendix C

Assessment Results of Text 8

Assessment results - Text 8

Raters - Group 1: professional translators

	Passage 1	Passage 2	Passage 3	Passage 4	Passage 5	Passage 6	Passage 7	Passage 8	Passage 9	Passage 10	Passage 11	Passage 12	Passage 13	Passage 14	Passage 15
Total Equivalence	80.00%	13.33%	80.00%	100.00%	100.00%	60.00%	100.00%	66.67%	66.67%	40.00%	73.33%	86.67%	80.00%	80.00%	13.33%
SR-F	0.00%	0.00%	0.00%	0.00%	0.00%	0.00%	0.00%	6.67%	6.67%	6.67%	0.00%	0.00%	0.00%	0.00%	0.00%
OM-F	6.67%	0.00%	6.67%	0.00%	0.00%	0.00%	0.00%	0.00%	0.00%	0.00%	6.67%	6.67%	0.00%	6.67%	0.00%
OM-SR-F	0.00%	0.00%	0.00%	0.00%	0.00%	0.00%	0.00%	0.00%	0.00%	0.00%	6.67%	0.00%	0.00%	0.00%	0.00%
SN-OM-SR-F	0.00%	13.33%	0.00%	0.00%	0.00%	13.33%	0.00%	0.00%	6.67%	13.33%	0.00%	0.00%	0.00%	0.00%	20.00%
MS-OM-SR-F	0.00%	0.00%	0.00%	0.00%	0.00%	0.00%	0.00%	0.00%	0.00%	6.67%	0.00%	0.00%	0.00%	0.00%	0.00%
Totally Lost	0.00%	13.33%	0.00%	0.00%	0.00%	6.67%	0.00%	26.67%	0.00%	0.00%	0.00%	0.00%	6.67%	0.00%	26.67%
SN-SR-F	0.00%	0.00%	0.00%	0.00%	0.00%	0.00%	0.00%	0.00%	0.00%	0.00%	0.00%	0.00%	6.67%	0.00%	0.00%
SN-F	13.33%	46.67%	13.33%	0.00%	0.00%	20.00%	0.00%	6.67%	13.33%	26.67%	13.33%	0.00%	6.67%	13.33%	20.00%
MS-F	0.00%	0.00%	0.00%	0.00%	0.00%	0.00%	0.00%	0.00%	0.00%	0.00%	0.00%	0.00%	0.00%	0.00%	0.00%
SN-OM-F	0.00%	6.67%	0.00%	0.00%	0.00%	0.00%	0.00%	0.00%	0.00%	0.00%	0.00%	0.00%	0.00%	0.00%	6.67%
SN-MS-F	0.00%	6.67%	0.00%	0.00%	0.00%	0.00%	0.00%	0.00%	0.00%	0.00%	0.00%	0.00%	0.00%	0.00%	0.00%
MS-OM-F	0.00%	0.00%	0.00%	0.00%	0.00%	0.00%	0.00%	0.00%	0.00%	0.00%	0.00%	0.00%	0.00%	0.00%	0.00%
MS-SR-F	0.00%	0.00%	0.00%	0.00%	0.00%	0.00%	0.00%	0.00%	0.00%	0.00%	0.00%	0.00%	0.00%	0.00%	0.00%
SN-MS-SR-F	0.00%	0.00%	0.00%	0.00%	0.00%	0.00%	0.00%	0.00%	0.00%	6.67%	0.00%	0.00%	0.00%	0.00%	6.67%
SN-MS-OM-F	0.00%	0.00%	0.00%	0.00%	0.00%	0.00%	0.00%	0.00%	6.67%	0.00%	0.00%	0.00%	0.00%	0.00%	6.67%

Raters - Group 2: Chinese immigrants

	Passage 1	Passage 2	Passage 3	Passage 4	Passage 5	Passage 6	Passage 7	Passage 8	Passage 9	Passage 10	Passage 11	Passage 12	Passage 13	Passage 14	Passage 15
Total Equivalence	0.00%	6.67%	6.67%	6.67%	6.67%	6.67%	6.67%	0.00%	0.00%	6.67%	6.67%	6.67%	0.00%	0.00%	6.67%
SR-F	53.33%	40.00%	73.33%	66.67%	66.67%	53.33%	46.67%	40.00%	46.67%	46.67%	60.00%	66.67%	60.00%	60.00%	46.67%
OM-F	0.00%	0.00%	0.00%	0.00%	0.00%	0.00%	0.00%	0.00%	0.00%	0.00%	0.00%	0.00%	0.00%	0.00%	0.00%
OM-SR-F	6.67%	6.67%	6.67%	13.33%	13.33%	13.33%	13.33%	6.67%	6.67%	6.67%	13.33%	6.67%	13.33%	6.67%	0.00%
SN-OM-SR-F	0.00%	0.00%	0.00%	0.00%	0.00%	0.00%	0.00%	0.00%	0.00%	0.00%	0.00%	0.00%	0.00%	0.00%	0.00%
MS-OM-SR-F	26.67%	20.00%	13.33%	6.67%	6.67%	20.00%	6.67%	26.67%	26.67%	20.00%	6.67%	6.67%	6.67%	13.33%	20.00%
Totally Lost	13.33%	20.00%	0.00%	6.67%	6.67%	6.67%	26.67%	26.67%	20.00%	13.33%	13.33%	13.33%	20.00%	20.00%	26.67%
SN-SR-F	0.00%	6.67%	0.00%	0.00%	0.00%	0.00%	0.00%	0.00%	0.00%	6.67%	0.00%	0.00%	0.00%	0.00%	0.00%
SN-F	0.00%	0.00%	0.00%	0.00%	0.00%	0.00%	0.00%	0.00%	0.00%	0.00%	0.00%	0.00%	0.00%	0.00%	0.00%
MS-F	0.00%	0.00%	0.00%	0.00%	0.00%	0.00%	0.00%	0.00%	0.00%	0.00%	0.00%	0.00%	0.00%	0.00%	0.00%
SN-OM-F	0.00%	0.00%	0.00%	0.00%	0.00%	0.00%	0.00%	0.00%	0.00%	0.00%	0.00%	0.00%	0.00%	0.00%	0.00%
SN-MS-F	0.00%	0.00%	0.00%	0.00%	0.00%	0.00%	0.00%	0.00%	0.00%	0.00%	0.00%	0.00%	0.00%	0.00%	0.00%
MS-OM-F	0.00%	0.00%	0.00%	0.00%	0.00%	0.00%	0.00%	0.00%	0.00%	0.00%	0.00%	0.00%	0.00%	0.00%	0.00%
MS-SR-F	0.00%	0.00%	0.00%	0.00%	0.00%	0.00%	0.00%	0.00%	0.00%	0.00%	0.00%	0.00%	0.00%	0.00%	0.00%
SN-MS-SR-F	0.00%	0.00%	0.00%	0.00%	0.00%	0.00%	0.00%	0.00%	0.00%	0.00%	0.00%	0.00%	0.00%	0.00%	0.00%
SN-MS-OM-F	0.00%	0.00%	0.00%	0.00%	0.00%	0.00%	0.00%	0.00%	0.00%	0.00%	0.00%	0.00%	0.00%	0.00%	0.00%

Appendix D

Assessment Results of Text 2

Assessment results - Text 2

Raters - Group 1 professional translators

	Passage 1	Passage 2	Passage 3	Passage 4	Passage 5	Passage 6	Passage 7	Passage 8	Passage 9	Passage 10	Passage 11
Total Equivalence	53.33%	66.67%	26.67%	40.00%	73.33%	46.67%	60.00%	46.67%	26.67%	13.33%	53.33%
SR-F	0.00%	0.00%	6.67%	0.00%	0.00%	0.00%	0.00%	0.00%	0.00%	0.00%	0.00%
OM-F	0.00%	6.67%	6.67%	0.00%	0.00%	6.67%	6.67%	6.67%	0.00%	6.67%	0.00%
OM-SR-F	0.00%	0.00%	0.00%	0.00%	0.00%	0.00%	0.00%	0.00%	0.00%	6.67%	0.00%
SN-OM-SR-F	6.67%	0.00%	0.00%	0.00%	0.00%	0.00%	0.00%	6.67%	6.67%	0.00%	0.00%
MS-OM-SR-F	0.00%	0.00%	0.00%	0.00%	0.00%	0.00%	0.00%	0.00%	0.00%	6.67%	0.00%
Totally Lost	0.00%	0.00%	13.33%	13.33%	0.00%	6.67%	0.00%	0.00%	0.00%	20.00%	0.00%
SN-SR-F	0.00%	0.00%	0.00%	6.67%	0.00%	0.00%	0.00%	6.67%	0.00%	0.00%	0.00%
SN-F	40.00%	26.67%	46.67%	26.67%	26.67%	33.33%	13.33%	33.33%	33.33%	46.67%	40.00%
MS-F	0.00%	0.00%	0.00%	0.00%	0.00%	0.00%	0.00%	0.00%	0.00%	0.00%	0.00%
SN-OM-F	0.00%	0.00%	0.00%	0.00%	0.00%	0.00%	0.00%	0.00%	6.67%	6.67%	0.00%
SN-MS-F	0.00%	0.00%	0.00%	6.67%	0.00%	6.67%	20.00%	0.00%	13.33%	0.00%	6.67%
MS-OM-F	0.00%	0.00%	0.00%	0.00%	0.00%	0.00%	0.00%	0.00%	0.00%	0.00%	0.00%
MS-SR-F	0.00%	0.00%	0.00%	0.00%	0.00%	0.00%	0.00%	0.00%	0.00%	0.00%	0.00%
SN-MS-SR-F	0.00%	0.00%	0.00%	0.00%	0.00%	0.00%	0.00%	0.00%	13.33%	0.00%	0.00%
SN-MS-OM-F	0.00%	0.00%	0.00%	6.67%	0.00%	0.00%	0.00%	0.00%	0.00%	0.00%	0.00%

Raters - Group 2 Chinese immigrants

	Passage 1	Passage 2	Passage 3	Passage 4	Passage 5	Passage 6	Passage 7	Passage 8	Passage 9	Passage 10	Passage 11
Total Equivalence	26.67%	33.33%	26.67%	13.33%	13.33%	13.33%	13.33%	13.33%	13.33%	13.33%	13.33%
SR-F	60.00%	40.00%	46.67%	40.00%	60.00%	33.33%	40.00%	40.00%	26.67%	33.33%	53.33%
OM-F	0.00%	0.00%	0.00%	0.00%	0.00%	0.00%	0.00%	0.00%	0.00%	0.00%	0.00%
OM-SR-F	13.33%	20.00%	6.67%	20.00%	6.67%	20.00%	13.33%	20.00%	20.00%	20.00%	13.33%
SN-OM-SR-F	0.00%	0.00%	0.00%	0.00%	0.00%	6.67%	0.00%	0.00%	0.00%	0.00%	0.00%
MS-OM-SR-F	0.00%	0.00%	13.33%	20.00%	6.67%	6.67%	20.00%	13.33%	26.67%	26.67%	6.67%
Totally Lost	0.00%	6.67%	6.67%	6.67%	13.33%	20.00%	13.33%	13.33%	13.33%	6.67%	13.33%
SN-SR-F	0.00%	0.00%	0.00%	0.00%	0.00%	0.00%	0.00%	0.00%	0.00%	0.00%	0.00%
SN-F	0.00%	0.00%	0.00%	0.00%	0.00%	0.00%	0.00%	0.00%	0.00%	0.00%	0.00%
MS-F	0.00%	0.00%	0.00%	0.00%	0.00%	0.00%	0.00%	0.00%	0.00%	0.00%	0.00%
SN-OM-F	0.00%	0.00%	0.00%	0.00%	0.00%	0.00%	0.00%	0.00%	0.00%	0.00%	0.00%
SN-MS-F	0.00%	0.00%	0.00%	0.00%	0.00%	0.00%	0.00%	0.00%	0.00%	0.00%	0.00%
MS-OM-F	0.00%	0.00%	0.00%	0.00%	0.00%	0.00%	0.00%	0.00%	0.00%	0.00%	0.00%
MS-SR-F	0.00%	0.00%	0.00%	0.00%	0.00%	0.00%	0.00%	0.00%	0.00%	0.00%	0.00%
SN-MS-SR-F	0.00%	0.00%	0.00%	0.00%	0.00%	0.00%	0.00%	0.00%	0.00%	0.00%	0.00%
SN-MS-OM-F	0.00%	0.00%	0.00%	0.00%	0.00%	0.00%	0.00%	0.00%	0.00%	0.00%	0.00%

Note

1 For a detailed explanation of the Criteria Set (see Crezee et al., 2017; Teng et al., 2018; Teng, 2019, 2020).

References

Burns, A., & Kim, M. (2011). Community accessibility of health information and the consequent impact for translation into community languages. *Translation & Interpreting*, *3*(1), 58–75. https://doi.org/10.12807/T&I.V3I1.107

Chao, Y. R. (1965). *A grammar of spoken Chinese*. University of California Press.

Chu, C. (2018). *Hanyuyufazhilu* [A journey of Chinese syntax]. Hungyeh Publishing.

Crezee, I. H. M., & Burn, J. A. (2019). Action research and its impact on the development of pragmatic competence in the translation and interpreting classroom. In R. Tipton & L. Desilla (Eds.), *The Routledge handbook of translation and pragmatics* (pp. 355–372). Routledge.

Crezee, I. H. M., Burn, J. A., & Teng, W. (2020). Community translation in New Zealand. In S. Laviosa & M. González-Davies (Eds.), *The Routledge handbook of translation and education* (pp. 245–263). Routledge.

Crezee, I. H. M., & Grant, L. (2016). Thrown in the deep end: Challenges of interpreting informal paramedic language. *Translation & Interpreting*, *8*(2), 1–12.

Crezee, I. H. M., Teng, W., & Burn, J. A. (2017). Teething problems? Chinese student interpreters' performance when interpreting authentic (cross-) examination questions in the legal interpreting classroom. *The Interpreter and Translator Trainer*, *11*(4), 337–356. https://doi.org/10.1080/1750399X.2017.1359756

Dai, G. (2016). *Hybridity in translated Chinese*. Springer.

Fischbach, H. (1962). Problems of medical translation. *Bulletin of the Medical Library Association*, *50*(3), 462–472.

García-Izquierdo, I., & Montalt i Resurrecció, V. (2017). Understanding and enhancing comprehensibility in texts for patients in an institutional health care context in Spain: A mixed methods analysis. *Revista Española de Lingüística Aplicada*, *30*(2), 592–610.

Grey, A. (2020, June 29). Australia's multilingual communities are missing out on vital coronavirus information. *ABC News*. www.abc.net.au/news/2020-06-29/coronavirus-multilingual-australia-missing-out-covid-19-info/12403510

Hale, S. (2004). *The discourse of court interpreting: Discourse practices of the law, the witness, and the interpreter*. John Benjamins Publishing Company.

Hale, S. (2014). Interpreting culture. Dealing with cross-cultural issues in court interpreting. *Perspectives*, *22*(3), 321–331. https://doi.org/10.1080/0907676X.2013.827226

Halliday, M. A. K., & Matthiessen, C. (2004). *An introduction to functional grammar*. Oxford University Press.

House, J. (1977). A model for assessing translation quality. *Meta*, *22*(2), 103–109. https://doi.org/10.7202/003140ar

House, J. (2006). Text and context in translation. *Journal of Pragmatics*, *38*, 338–358. https://doi.org/10.1016/j.pragma.2005.06.021

House, J. (2008). Beyond intervention: Universals in translation. *Trans-Kom*, *1*(1), 6–19.

Hsiao, C. (2011). Personal pronoun interchanges in Mandarin Chinese conversation. *Language Sciences*, *33*(5), 799–821. https://doi.org/10.1016/j.langsci.2011.02.001

Kim, M., & Matthiessen, C. (2015). Ways to move forward in translation studies: A textual perspective. *Target*, *27*(3), 335–350.

Li, C. N., & Thompson, S. A. (1976). Subject and topic: A new typology of language. In C. N. Li (Ed.), *Subject and topic* (pp. 457–489). Academic Press.

Li, C. N., & Thompson, S. A. (1981). *Mandarin Chinese: A functional reference grammar*. University of California Press.

Lin, C. (2003). *Hanyu yuweizhuci"ne"zhi jiaoxuefa chutan* [A preliminary investigation of pedagogy of Mandarin utterance-final particle "ne"]. National Taiwan Normal University.

Liu, Y., Pan, W., & Gu, W. (1996). *Modern Chinese grammar for teachers of Chinese as a second language and advanced learners of modern Chinese*. Shidashuyuan.

Matthiessen, C. (2001). The environments of translation. In E. Steiner & C. Yallop (Eds.), *Exploring translation and multilingual text production: Beyond Content* (pp. 47–124). Mouton de Gruyter.

McDonald, E. (1992). Outline of a functional grammar of Chinese for teaching purposes. *Language Science, 14*(4), 435–458.

Schuster, C. R., Schuster, P., & Nykolyn, L. (2010). *Communication for nurses: How to prevent harmful events and promote patient safety*. F.A. Davis Company.

Sin, K. F. (2004). *Language and culture in community translation* [Unpublished master's thesis]. Auckland University of Technology.

Taibi, M., & Ozolins, U. (2016). *Community translation*. Bloomsbury Academic.

Tang, A. (2017). *What are the experiences of older Mandarin-speaking migrants in Auckland when accessing health and support services in New Zealand?* [Unpublished master's thesis]. Auckland University of Technology.

Teng, W. (2019). When pragmatic equivalence fails: Assessing a New Zealand English to Chinese health translation from a functional perspective. In C. Ji, M. Taibi, & I. H. M. Crezee (Eds.), *Multicultural health translation, interpreting and communication* (pp. 85–122). Routledge.

Teng, W. (2020). *It makes sense, but I just don't get it. Translators' and end-users' perspectives on the English to Chinese community translation of health texts* [Unpublished doctoral dissertation]. Auckland University of Technology.

Teng, W., Burn, J. A., & Crezee, I. H. M. (2018). I'm asking you again! Chinese student interpreters' performance when interpreting declaratives with tag questions in the legal interpreting classroom. *Perspectives, 26*(5), 745–766.

The World Bank. (n.d.). *Social inclusion*. Retrieved December 5, 2018, from www.worldbank.org/en/topic/social-inclusion

Thomas, J. (1983). Cross-cultural pragmatic failure. *Applied Linguistics, 4*(2), 91–112. https://doi.org/10.1093/applin/4.2.91

Xiao, R., & Hu, X. (2015). *Corpus-based studies of translational Chinese in English-Chinese translation*. Shanghai Jiao Tong University Press; Springer. https://doi.org/10.1007/978-3-642-41363-6

Yu, A. (2020, June 24). "There was nothing": Translation delay raises questions about virus information to migrant communities. *The Age*. www.theage.com.au/national/victoria/there-was-nothing-translation-delay-raises-questions-about-virus-information-to-migrant-communities-20200624-p555us.html

5

SPEAK MY LANGUAGE!

The Important Role of Community Translation in the Promotion of Health Literacy

Ineke Crezee and Hoy Neng Wong Soon

1 Introduction

In this chapter, we explore the role of community translation in the promotion of health literacy. The chapter begins by presenting some background information on Aotearoa New Zealand (Aotearoa NZ) as a culturally and linguistically diverse society, while also briefly touching on the earliest community translator and interpreter training and service provision in the 1990s.

The literature review section focuses on community translation, health literacy, and the community translation of health texts. We explore definitions of community translation before moving to the concept of health literacy, focusing also on the refugee and migrant populations for whom we translate and touching on some of the many barriers to accessing health information. The final part of the literature review briefly outlines different approaches to translation studies in general, involving a product or process approach, before moving to reception studies involving a participatory action research approach in health translation.

In the following sections, we examine our own approach to community translation as part of health promotion efforts, providing glimpses into the different experiences that prompted this approach. We explore what we might need to do to achieve a 'just right' outcome when engaged in community translation for the purposes of health literacy and how this should involve the end users of the translations.

Section 4 discusses some of our own research relating to community translation in Aotearoa NZ. Hoy Neng Wong Soon outlines some of the difficulties involved in providing coherent and accurate translations of health information from English into Samoan in the Aotearoa NZ context. Community translation into Samoan involves a number of issues not previously explored or discussed in the literature. Hoy Neng Wong Soon's comments in this chapter are based on her experience as a translator and reviewer of multiple Samoan/English translations for many years since 2007, and from doing pro bono translation and interpreting work before 2007 for District Health Boards (DHBs) and translation and interpreting agencies,[1] both in Aotearoa NZ and abroad. She will discuss some examples of the translation issues that she is continuing to see when reviewing other translators' work.

Following this, Ineke Crezee reports on some of her own approaches to ensuring health translations are accessible to members of the target audience. This section touches on some of Crezee's experiences as a Fulbright New Zealand Scholar (Public Health) at the Center for Diversity and Health Equity at Seattle Children's Hospital in Seattle, Washington (USA).

The discussion and conclusion sections will discuss some questions regarding the translation of important health information for culturally and linguistically diverse communities.

2 Background

2.1 Linguistic Diversity and Language Access

The linguistic makeup of the Aotearoa NZ community is continually evolving, and this has an impact on both demand for and supply of community translation and interpreting services (cf. Eser, 2020). Information for the Office of Ethnic Communities (OEC, 2018) showed that "twelve per cent of the Asian population, 7 per cent of the MELAA population and 5 per cent of Pacific Peoples could only communicate in a language 'other than English', Te Reo Māori and New Zealand Sign Language" (para. 4, "Ethnic Group by Languages Spoken" section). It is clear that many of these people would not be able to access health or other public services without quality interpreting and translation services.

Auckland is the largest and most diverse urban centre in Aotearoa NZ (Statistics New Zealand, 2021). Migrants tend to settle in Auckland, not only because the city offers the most work and business opportunities, but also because of the presence of people from the same cultural and linguistic background. Aotearoa NZ has an ongoing need for public service interpreters and translators, particularly in the health setting. Auckland was the first large urban centre to offer health and public service interpreter and translator education in the late 1980s and early 1990s, while the country's first interpreting and translation services were established by South Auckland Health[2] in 1991. In May 2021, the top six languages for language access at Counties Manukau District Health Board in its very culturally diverse catchment area in South Auckland were Mandarin, Cantonese, Samoan, Tongan, Hindi, and Punjabi.

The need for trained and credentialled translators in a significant number of different languages explains the need for non–language-specific translator and interpreter education. Translator education needs to include the knowledge, skills, and attributes set out by the National Accreditation Authority for Translators and Interpreters (NAATI, 2015), as well as the core cultural competencies for community translators (Katan & Taibi, 2021). There have been no previous studies on the number of Samoan translators working in Aotearoa NZ, and this includes any international statistics.

2.2 Community Translation

The most common form of translation in the country is community translation (Taibi & Ozolins, 2016). This principally involves the translation of important national or local government information for members of minority language communities and – to a lesser degree – the translation of official documents such as birth and marriage certificates, qualifications, work references, and academic transcripts from minority languages into English (Taibi & Ozolins, 2016). This chapter will also use the term *heritage languages*, defined as language spoken by a "heterogeneous group ranging from fluent native speakers to non-speakers who may be generations removed but who may feel culturally connected to a language" (Van Deusen-Scholl, 2003, p. 221).

3 Literature Review

3.1 Community Translation

Community translation is defined here as translation in and for communities (Taibi & Ozolins, 2016). Community translation fulfils a social function in that it aims to ensure equal access to official information. Community translation of health information may be said to empower members of minority communities to take the actions necessary to maintain good health. This became particularly evident during the COVID-19 pandemic, when it became crucial that information was disseminated among different minority language communities in an accurate and efficient manner.

The question needs to be asked as to whether written texts are always the most effective. It could be argued that each target community is different and that the (health) authorities' preconceptions of what works best for them may be incorrect. As Taibi (2017) asks: "How can the needs of the end users be determined and accommodated?" (p. 9). The needs of the target readership must be explored first.

In this chapter, we argue that a range of questions need to be considered, including – but not limited to – whether translations are culturally appropriate, since culture affects unspoken beliefs, expectations, acceptable topics, register, manner of interaction, and length of sentences.

Many of the (often elderly) first-generation migrants and refugees are neither literate nor health literate. To be effective, translators and interpreters need to have a very good understanding of anatomy, physiology, and pathology – in other words, they need to be health literate (cf. Crezee, 2013) and able to unpack complex medical concepts. The next section will look at the concept of health literacy and why it is important for translators and interpreters.

3.2 Health Literacy

Fleary et al. (2018) defined health literacy as "the extent to which individuals attain, manage, and understand health information and apply that information in health decision-making" (p. 117). Nutbeam (2009) distinguishes three different types of health literacy: functional, interactive, and critical health literacy, whereby the latter "empowers individuals to act on the social, economic, and environmental determinants of health through individual and collective efforts" (Fleary et al., 2018, p. 117).

Several authors have described the prevalence of limited health literacy across populations and its association with poorer health outcomes (Paasche-Orlow et al., 2005; Berkman et al., 2011; Rudd et al., 2007; Weiss, 2015). Health literacy may also affect the health outcomes of migrants and refugees. Several scholars have studied the link between health literacy and timely use of prevention and treatment services (Abdel-Latif, 2020; Wångdahl et al., 2021; Yu et al., 2021), especially during the COVID-19 pandemic (Abdel-Latif, 2020). Abdel-Latif (2020) emphasises that migrants, members of ethnic minorities, people with lower education levels, and older adults are more likely to experience low health literacy, and this is also confirmed by studies relating to Aotearoa NZ (Crezee & Roat, 2019; Crezee & Tupou Gordon, 2019; Magill, 2017; Shrestha-Ranjit et al., 2020). Samoan translator and interpreter Wong Soon (Burn & Wong Soon, 2020) demonstrates the importance of health literacy for interpreters to be able to unpack complex medical concepts into accessible Samoan. Taibi et al. (2019) describe the importance of exploring the most effective methods of disseminating translated health information material in either written or spoken form. Their pilot study described the role of community engagement combined with translation expert input, as well as testing any translated material with members of the intended target audience (Taibi et al., 2019).

3.2 Community Translation of Health Texts

Community translation of health texts can combine a number of different approaches, including a *product-oriented* approach (Alves & Vale, 2017) or a *process-oriented* approach (Angelone, 2016). In a product-oriented approach, researchers focus on the translation product rather than on the process of translation. An example of this approach is presented in Section 4, in which Samoan translations are examined as end-products. In a process-oriented approach, researchers focus on the translation process – from conceiving the idea for a text to commissioning the text, providing translation and editing guidelines, through to the translation and editing process. An example of this approach is also presented in this chapter.

One could argue that *reception studies* are a target readership type of product-oriented approach. Some scholars (Di Giovanni & Gambier, 2018) focus on audiovisual translation, while others (e.g., Taibi et al., 2019; Teng, 2019) explore how community health translations are received by members of the target audience. Teng (2019) involved both professional translators and members of the target audience in the assessment of translated health information. He argues that the community translation of health texts provides equal access to important information, but that translators and end users had different perspectives on what constituted a good translation. Work by Taibi et al. (2019) and Teng (2019) seems to suggest that translators, professionals, and end users must be involved in shaping the target text and end users must be consulted on the cultural and linguistic appropriacy of the target text. Research by other scholars has also reported on involving representatives of target readers when preparing or translating fact sheets for patients (García-Izquierdo & Montalt, 2017), arguing that it is important to involve representatives of the intended target audience in this process.

The authors believe that representatives of the target readership should be asked if there is anything unclear or ambiguous, any information overload, or anything culturally inappropriate within the target text. Such research may involve a participatory action research (PAR) approach (Kemmis et al., 2014), whereby participants are considered co-researchers. PAR would seem the more appropriate since it aims to achieve social change and – in this case – improve health literacy among minority groups.

4 Community Translation Research in Aotearoa, NZ

This section reports on some of our research into the community translation of health information in Aotearoa NZ. The first example follows a product-oriented approach: presenting issues uncovered by Wong Soon when editing and reviewing Samoan translations of English health texts. Providing written translations for different communities without checking whether this is their preferred way of disseminating health information is still the conventional approach. Crezee then presents the process-oriented approach followed in two small studies, both of which sought health consumer feedback on information presented by way of voice-overs in the target language.

4.1 Samoan Translations of Health Texts: A Product-Oriented Approach

4.1.1 Background

Samoans originate from the independent island state of Samoa, formerly known as Western Samoa, comprising the four main inhabited islands of Savai'i, 'Upolu, Apolima, and Manono (Biewer, 2021). Within Aotearoa NZ, Samoan speakers include those who were born and raised in Samoa and moved to Aotearoa NZ, often in search of education or a better life. They also include descendants of Samoan migrants who were born and/or raised in Aotearoa NZ. The Samoan language is one of the most widely spoken Pasefika languages in Aotearoa NZ, and much official information is translated into Samoan.

4.1.2 Method

In this section, we present excerpts of translations which were published and made publicly accessible either in paper pamphlet form, or on the websites of different health organisations. Both the English source texts and the Samoan target texts are included, as well as Hoy Neng Wong Soon's suggested revisions and her rationale for these. We first present examples of omissions of articles, prepositions, and particles which are needed for readers to make sense of the Samoan text.

4.1.3 Omission of Articles

The following points analyse and discuss the implications of omitting articles, prepositions, and particles with in the Samoan target text (as shown in Example 5.1 and Example 5.2).

Example 5.1 Omission of Necessary Articles, Prepositions, and Particles in the Target Text

English source text	Babies start moving early in pregnancy, but at first you will not feel them. Slowly you will start to feel little flutters, between 16 – 22 weeks, and these will build up to being strong movements as baby grows in size and strength.
Samoan translation (original translation)	E ʻāmata ona gāoioi i le ʻāmataga o le maʻitō, ʻae e tau lē lagonaina. ʻAe faʻasolosolo lava ona ʻe faʻalogoina, i le va o le 16 – 22 vaiaso, ma ʻo le ʻā faʻasolosolo lava ina mālolosi gāoioiga ʻaʻo tuputupu aʻe pepe i lona lāpoʻa ma lona mālosi.
Back translation of original translation	It begins to move at the start of/in early pregnancy, but at first you will not feel it. But slowly you will feel, between 16 – 22 weeks, and these will become stronger movements as baby grows in size and strength.
Author's suggested Samoan translation	ʻO pepe ʻe ʻāmata ona gāoioi i le ʻāmataga o le maʻitō, ʻae ʻe te tau lē lagonaina. ʻE amata faʻasolosolo lava ʻona ʻe lagonaina ni minōiga laiti rna ʻe mālū, i le va o le 16 – 22 vaiaso, ma ʻo le ʻā faʻasolosolo lava ʻina mālolosi gāoioiga ʻaʻo tuputupu aʻe pepe i lona lāpoʻa ma lona mālosi.
Author's back translation of suggested translation	The babies start to move at the start of/in early pregnancy, but you will not feel them. You will slowly start to feel little and gentle movements/flutters, between 16-22 weeks, and these movements will start to build up/become stronger as baby grows in size and strength.

1. Omission of "Babies" (red font). The translation starts with "It begins . . .". The "It" here does not refer to "babies" but is the general start of a sentence. Wong Soon has used the article "*The*" to start the sentence in Samoan as it is appropriate for sentence structure to have an article, unless it is in speech marks, in which case Samoan does not need an article to begin the sentence.
2. Omission of the particle needed to formulate the pronoun "you". In the original translation, the translator should have used the particle "*te*" to form the pronoun "you" in the sentence structure (i.e., " ʻ*e te*").
3. Omission of "*E amata* [Start to]".

4. Use of incorrect term *"fa'alogoina* [hearing]" instead of *"lagonaina* [feeling]"*. Using *"fa'alogoina"* in this sentence may sound 'correct' in spoken language, but in written format, we must use the correct word or equivalent (i.e., *"lagonaina"*).
5. Omission of "little flutters" as suggested in Wong Soon's translation as *"ni minōiga laiti ma 'e mālū"*, which back translates to "little and gentle movements/flutters". She added *"gentle"* to explain the type of movement (i.e., flutters), as Samoan does not have an equivalent for "flutter", so the translator needs to add this semantic aspect to achieve pragmatic equivalence.

Example 5.2 Omission of Articles in Samoan

English source text	Eligibility and pricing structure for maternity care
Samoan translation (original)	Fa'atagaga ma le fa'atulagaga o totogi mo le tausiga o ma'itō
Back translation	Eligibility and pricing structure for maternity care
Suggested Samoan translation	O le Āgava'a ma le fa'atulagana o totogi mo le tausiga o ma'itō
Author's back translation of suggested translation	The Eligibility and pricing structure for maternity care

1. *"O le"* (*The*) before *"Āgava'a* [Eligibility]" is used as an article referred to as *"fa'asino 'autū"*, which in Samoan linguistics is the article that is referring to the noun. In this case, Samoan sentence structure would start off with an article. There are other sentence structures such as quotes in speech marks and so forth, when Samoan may not need to include the article to begin a sentence. Also, the use of *Fa'atagaga* to refer to "Eligibility" is incorrect. *Fa'atagaga* is "allow" but the translator should have used the equivalent of "eligibility" which is *Āgava'a* as included in the suggested translation. Also, the incorrect use of the apostrophe which should be the glottal stop as shown in the suggested equivalent of 'Eligibility'. i.e. *Āgava'a*.
2. Spoken versus written form of the Samoan language. The translator used the 'informal' or colloquial pronunciation of the noun in his/her translation (i.e.) *Fa'atagaga* (Allowing); this is the same term that the translator used to refer to "Eligibility" (see preceding example point 1). The use of informal words in written texts is inappropriate when translating a formal text. Samoans know to always use 'formal pronunciation' of any words in a written text – referred to as *Gagana t/n* in Samoan. There is an exception in this case, and in other texts representing dialogues – since in that case the translator can use the pronunciation style that the characters are using, because these will be considered as quotations, presented between double speech marks.

4.1.4 Unpacking Specialist Health Vocabulary in Samoan

Samoan lacks specialist health vocabulary, which means all words must be unpacked and that can only happen if translators have a health background or a very good level of health literacy. Example 5.3 illustrates the process of unpacking the medical terminologies: *motor neurone disease* and *dementia*.

Example 5.3 Incorrect Translation of Health-Related Concepts in Samoan

English source text	1. Palliative care supports people of any age who have been told that they have a life-limiting illness that cannot be cured.
	2. It can assist people with illnesses such as cancer, motor neurone disease, advanced dementia and end-stage kidney, heart or lung disease.
Samoan translation (original)	1. E lagolagoina fo'i e le palliative care tagata o so'o se matua 'ua iloa 'o ia 'ua maua i se ma'i e fa'aumatia ai le soifua.
	2. E mafai ona fesoasoani i tagata e maua i le kanesa, ma'i o le motor neurone (lē lelei sela neura o le fai'ai), **māfaufau lē 'ātoa** ma le ma'i o le lata ina leaga 'atoa fatuga'o, fatu po'o māmā fo'i.
Back translation	1. Palliative care supports people of any age who know that they have a condition that ends life.
	2. It can also help people who have cancer, illness of the motor neurone (neurone cells of the brains are not good), **mind not fully good** and condition that kidneys are nearly /fully not working/functioning well, heart or lungs too.
Suggested Samoan translation	1. E lagolagoina 'e le Tausiga o gasegase 'ua ui (palliative care) o tagata o so'o se matua 'ua fa'ailoaina ia i latou 'ua maua i se gasegase e fa'atapula'ainaai le soifua ma ua ui le ma'i.
	Or
	1. E lagolagoina 'e le Tausiga o gasegase 'ua ui togafitiga/fofō (palliative care) o tagata o so'o se matua lava 'ua fa'ailoaina ia i latou 'ua maua i se gasegase e fa'atapula'ainaai le soifua ma 'ua lē 'o toe aogā i ai se fofō/togafitiga.
	2. E mafai ona fesoasoani i tagata 'ua maua i gasegase e pei o le kanesa, ma'i o sela neura maile fai 'aii lona 'au poole maeā ario (motor neurone disease), matuia/ōgaōga tele le gasegase o le galogalo o mea i le mafaufau/ valevale matua ma 'ua matuā fa'aletonu/leaga 'atoafatuga'o, ma'i fatu po'o le māmā fo'i.

Author's back translation of suggested translation	1. Palliative care supports/assists people of any age who have been told that they have a condition that is life limiting and it cannot be cured/there is no cure.
	2. It can assist/help people with conditions/illnesses such as cancer, motor neurone disease(s), condition of advanced/severe forgetfulness of the mind/brain (dementia), and terminal/end stage kidney, heart or lung disease.

1. The Original translator (OTr) used plural for *lungs*, but the source text uses a singular structure (i.e.) lung. Obviously, we have '*lobes of lungs*', but the text specifically refers to 'lung' in the singular form.
2. Use of English language in the target text (i.e., *palliative care*) in the target translation instead of unpacking and paraphrasing the medical term (i.e., *palliative care*) in Samoan – i.e., *Tausiga o gasegase 'ua ui togafitiga/fofō (palliative care)*, which translates to *care for conditions that have no treatment or cure*. This explanation of *palliative care* includes the fact that this concerns specialised medical care for people with serious or terminal illnesses. The described unpacking in Samoan emphasises the fact that although the patient is receiving care from health professionals and being treated with multiple medications, these treatments are to help enhance the patient's quality of life. The suggested Samoan translation of *palliative care* also uses the language and tone that is culturally appropriate for the patient's family and support persons to understand the extent of their loved one's medical condition and progress. *Palliative care* can also be translated into Samoan as *tausiga mo gasegase ua lē toe aogā i ai se fofō po'o se togafitiga*[3] or *tausiga o gasegase ua leai se togafitiga/fofō*,[4] but this may be too long in written translation. However, these phrases are culturally acceptable and appropriate in both written and spoken language.
3. Use of *motor neurone disease* in the English language in the target text (Samoan) – the translation uses the English terminology instead of unpacking and paraphrasing for the target readers (see Example 5.3) for the suggested translation.

4.1.5 The Misunderstanding of Medical Concepts by Translators

Based on Hoy Neng Wong Soon's reviews of health translations, it seems that most Samoan translators do not have a health background and make errors conveying the meaning of health-specific terminology, some of which can be quite serious. Example 5.4 illustrates examples of such errors.

110 Ineke Crezee and Hoy Neng Wong Soon

Example 5.4 Incorrect Understanding and Translation of Medical Concepts

English source text	**Tetanus** Tetanus is a disease that can enter the body through a cut or a graze. It causes muscles to stiffen and spasm. It may affect the breathing muscles.
Samoan translation (original)	**'Ona (tetanus)** O le 'ona o se ma'i e mafai ona sao i totonu o le tino e mafua mai se vaega o le tino ua lavea pe ma'osia. E mafua ai ona maló faafuasei uaua o le tino ma migi. E ono aafia ai foi maso o le vaega o loo mānava ai.
Back translationv	Tetanus is a disease that can enter the body through a cut or a graze. It causes veins of the body to stiffen and spasm. It may also affect the muscles of the part where you breathe (from).
Suggested Samoan translation	**'Ona (tetanus)** O le 'ona o se ma'i e mafai ona sao i totonu o le tino ma 'e mafua mai i se vaega o le tino ua lavea pe ma'osia. E mafua ona malō ma migi ai maso. E ono aafia ai maso mānava.
Author's back translation of suggested translation	Tetanus is a disease that can enter the body through a cut or a graze. It causes muscles to stiffen and spasm. It may affect the breathing muscles.

In Example 5.4, the back-translated text is shown in red as that is the focus of the example. A review of the translation shows that "and" *(ma)* is omitted in the Samoan translation. Also, the preposition 'i' must be inserted to show that it is referring to the body (part) which was cut or grazed. Wong Soon has underlined these omissions in her suggested translation.

Health-literate translators will know that there are in fact many "*breathing muscles*" involved in respiration. Respiratory muscles are complex; however, the source text (English) provides the most basic overarching terminology when it talks about "*breathing muscles*".

1   Samoan has an equivalent for *breathing muscles* (i.e., *maso mānava*) as provided in the suggested translation (see Example 5.4).
2   The Original Translator (OTr) needs to review their translations – especially the sentence structure. If the translator is unable to understand what "*breathing muscles*" are (maybe due to not having health background), then they should at least check and write it in plural form, just as the

English source text does. Ideally, they should disclose their lack of health knowledge to the client and decline this type of specialised translation assignment.

3   If the translator opts to paraphrase and use "*o le vaega e mānava aī*" (the part where you breathe [from]), it is his/her responsibility to check this against the source text which had "*breathing muscles*" and research the respiratory muscles of the body. There are many parts of the body that help with breathing, including respiratory muscles in the abdominal region, in the thoracic area, and the diaphragm.

4   Another issue is that the translator used the plural in the beginning of the clause to refer to "*muscles*" (i.e., It may affect the breathing muscles). However, in the second clause, the OTr used a singular sentence structure to refer to "*part of the body*". In the table "part" has been underlined since it is a singular noun instead of plural (see the following example). If the OTr had used plural in this clause (e.g., "*o vaega*"; the parts) without the singular preposition "*le*", the translation would have been more accurate.

It may also affect the muscle of the part where you breathe (from).
E ono aafia ai foi maso o le vaega o loo 'e mānava mai ai.

5   An incorrect equivalent is used in the target translation to refer to *muscles*, where the OTr used *uaua* which is the equivalent of *vein*, instead of *maso*. This can cause confusion and result in the target reader being misinformed.

Example 5.5 provides another example of the importance of translators understanding medical concepts to ensure accurate message transfer.

Example 5.5 Incorrect Understanding and Translation of Medical Concepts

English source text	What is warfarin?
	Warfarin is a medicine that helps to prevent blood clots.
Samoan translation (original)	'O le ā le warfarin?
	'O le warfarin 'o se fuālā'au e fa'ataga mai e le fōma'i e fesoasoani e taofia le māfiafia o le toto (coagulating).
Back translation	What is warfarin?
	Warfarin is a medicine that has been allowed/prescribed by the doctor to help stop/prevent blood from thickening (coagulating).
Suggested Samoan translation	'O le ā le warfarin?
	'O le warfarin 'o se fuālā'au e fesoasoani e taofia le toto mai le potopotoi
Author's back translation of suggested translation	What is warfarin?
	Warfarin is a medicine that helps to prevent the blood from clotting

1 The translation shows a lack of understanding of the difference between blood coagulation, blood clots/clotting and blood thickening. The OTr translated coagulation/blood clotting as *mafiafia o le toto*, meaning blood is thickening. There is a difference between blood clotting and thickening of the blood, with the latter being referred to as hypercoagulation. Again, anyone undertaking medical translations should have completed appropriate training in translation and should have acquired a sound knowledge of anatomy, physiology, and pathology (Crezee, 2013). Translators are responsible for the work that they do, and this can affect the patients and target readers' ability to make informed decisions if they are provided with translated information that does not match the source text.
2 Incorrect use of glottal stops in the target text.

4.1.6 Lack of Reflection on Issues in Translation and Rationale for Choices

When translators have not had any translator education, they may not be used to reflecting on translation issues, approaches to resolving these, or a rationale for any strategies implemented.

The original translation in Example 5.6 has two meanings, which will be discussed. It shows an incorrect translation of information from the source text (English) to the target text (Samoan), which can create detrimental issues to the target readers, and most importantly parents who need to give their informed consent for their children to receive the Boostrix™ vaccine. Incorrect translations can influence the parents' and caregivers' consent to immunisations for their children. This can also result in vaccine hesitancy and anti-vaccination beliefs (Gavaruzzi et al., 2021) because of incorrect information being published for healthcare end users. As a translator and healthcare consumer, Wong Soon believes that most of these health pamphlets are reviewed well by other translators, but unfortunately those reviews cannot come into being if the original translator rejects any of the reviewer's recommendations/suggestions – as has happened in my own experience.

Example 5.6 Ambiguous and Potentially Misleading Translation Choices

English source text	Parent consent form
Samoan translation (original translation)	Pepa faatumu a le aoga mo le maliega
Back translation	Paper to complete/form of the school for consent Or School's Paper to complete/ form for consent ** It may be that the translator assumes that the reader will understand that the form is from the school and to be completed by another but the 'person to complete/give consent' is omitted in the translation.

Suggested Samoan translation	Pepa o le maliega a matua
Author's back translation of suggested translation	Paper/form of consent by parent(s), which is 'Parent consent form', as stated in the English source text

In this translation, the translator should avoid ambiguities in his/her translation.

The parental consent form has been translated well, but it can have a double meaning in Samoan. As translators, we try to avoid ambiguities in our translations. In this example, the translation is ambiguous if read.

1. The translator should have rephrased the translation so that it does not confuse the reader, because as it stands, the chosen translation can mean two things:

    i The form is from the school and needs to be completed to show consent – the issue is here is the omission of "Parent", which is very important as the aim of the text is for parents to be give their consent for their children to receive the vaccine.

    ii The form is to be completed by the school for consent – this is an incorrect meaning, and some readers may indeed interpret the translated section incorrectly, thinking that they do not give consent but the school will. This can be very dangerous, not only for the parents/caregivers of the children on their decisions to vaccinate, but also the lives of the children who need to be immunised.

2. The OTr has omitted the most important information in the source text, i.e. parents, who are the target readers to be informed so they can give their consent for their children to receive the vaccine. Misinformation such as this can create concern amongst the communities, starting with the target readers of the translated texts, because they are provided with detailed information that is in fact not correct.

4.1.7 Omitting or Adding Information

Examples 5.7 and 5.8 reveal the omission and addition of information by the Samoan translator.

Example 5.7 Omission and Addition of Information

English source text	an immune deficiency condition (e.g., your child is HIV positive)
Samoan translation (original)	ua faaletonu le vaega o le tino e teena faama'i (e pei o le aafia o lou alo i le siama o le HIV)

Back translation	Part of the body that defends itself/fights off diseases is affected/compromised (such as your child is affected by the bacteria/virus of HIV)
Suggested Samoan translation	ua fa'alētonu le vaega o le tino e te'ena ai fa'ama'i (fa'ata'ita'iga., ua maua lau tama i le siama o le HIV)
Author's back translation of suggested translation	a condition that malfunction of the immune system of the body that fends off infections/diseases (for example, your child has the HIV virus)

1. Unnecessary addition and omission of information in the target translation, e.g. *fa'ata'ita'iga*.
2. The translator used "*e pei*", which is the equivalent of "such as". Samoan has the equivalent of "e.g."/"for example" in and that is *fa'ata'ita'iga*. This is included in the suggested translation in the table in Example E2 at the end of this chapter.

Example 5.8 Omission of Information

English source text	See the Consumer Medical information published at www.medsafe.govt.nz/consumers/ cmi/b/boostrix.pdf
Samoan translation (original)	Omission in target text
Back translation	n/a
Suggested Samoan translation	Silasila ane i fa'amatalaga Fa'alesoifua Maloloina mo Tagata o lo'o fa'ailoaina atu i le www.medsafe.govt.nz/consumers/ cmi/b/boostrix. pdf Or Taga'i ane i fa'amatalaga Fa'alesoifua Maloloina mo le Tagata o lo'o fa'ailoaina atu i le www.medsafe.govt.nz/consumers/ cmi/b/boostrix.pdf
Author's back translation of suggested translation	See Consumer Medical information made known/ published/ presented at www.medsafe.govt.nz/consumers/ cmi/b/boostrix.pdf

1. The original translator omitted this information in one of the most important sections of the English source text. The omitted information empowers healthcare end users to know where they can access information regarding the Boostrix vaccine. In Wong Soon's suggested translations, she bolded "*fa'ailoaina*" (published/presented), which has many equivalents in Samoan.
2. Wong Soon often notices Samoan translators' apparent inability to use different equivalents available in Samoan, which is useful where there is a repetition of a specific term (e.g.) *"fa'ailoaina"* – Samoan can use any of these equiva-

lents to mean *"fa'ailoaina" (published/presented)lomia, fa'asalalauina, lomia fa'asalalau, fa'alauiloaina.*

3   Choosing the correct Samoan equivalents may depend on the context, but if translators understand the 'essence' of the source text, they will be able to translate accordingly.
4   If we use *"fa'asalalau"* in this context, it will mean "(to) publish/published"; however, this term can also mean "to spread" or "to broadcast" in media settings. This latter equivalent is used with reference to a radio host or TV presenter.

4.1.8 Changing Information in the Target Text

Example 5.9 Change of information in the target text

English source text	Why not try:…
	Swimming or aqua fitness – there's lots you can do in the water
Samoan translation (original)	Aisea e lē faataitai ai?:
	Aau poo le malosi i le vai – e tele mea e mafai ona faia i le vai
Back translation	Why not try?:
	Swimming or strength in the water – there's lots you can do in the water
Suggested Samoan translation	Aiseā e lē fa'ata'ita'i ai:
	Le 'a'au poo le fa'amalositino i le vai
	Or
	Le 'a'au poo le fa'amalositino e faia i totonu o le vaita'ele/ sami
Author's back translation of suggested translation	Why not try:
	Swimming or exercise(s) in the water
	Or
	Swimming or exercise(s) in the pool/sea

This text was taken from a so-called Green Prescription pamphlet, which entails written advice from the general practitioner (GP) that is supported/ subsidised by the Ministry of Health for patients to be active and stay healthy. Patients are then referred to community exercise programmes.

Most of the patients who are given this referral have medical problems such as being overweight, having type 2 diabetes or high blood pressure, and many other diagnoses.

1. In this translation, it would be better to use "pool", as most Green Prescription programmes are delivered at community swimming pools.
2. It is very important to have knowledge of the healthcare system, e.g. in Aotearoa NZ. In translator training, learning about the healthcare system of the country will enable the translator to know how to translate the source text in such a way that it is appropriate for the target readers. In this example, *aqua fitness* is a common exercise programme that the Green Prescription professionals deliver at community swimming pools, which is convenient for attendees who reside in the area. Translators should be responsible for their own ongoing professional development in familiarising themselves with the healthcare system of the country where the target readers reside. This should include keeping abreast of changes relating to government and non-government policies and so on. Such ongoing professional development is also emphasised in the NAATI guidelines for translators (2015).
3. The original translator did not include the preposition "**le**", and without this, the Samoan target text does not read well and is not grammatically correct.

Example 5.10 Change of Information in the Target Text

English source text	1. You could wrap your baby gently in a towel/wrap to stop baby's arms getting in the way of your medicine giving.
	2. Use an oral medicine syringe and squirt *a little medicine* into the mouth onto the inside cheek *where there are no bitter taste buds*. Usually baby will swallow if the syringe is far enough back in the mouth.
Samoan translation (original)	1. Afifi lelei pepe ise solo poʻo se palanikete tautuana ona lima ia afifi lelei ia aua neʻi faʻalavelave ile taimi e faʻainu ai lana vai.
	2. Faʻaaoga se tui faʻapitoa mole faʻainuina o vai ona faga lea I totonu o lona gutu mai le itu. E vave ai lava ona mimiti ele pepe le vai pea tuʻu saʻo i totonu o lona gutu.
Back translation	1. Properly wrap baby in a towel or blanket make sure to wrap his/her arms/hands so that they are not in the way at the time you give his/her medicine.
	2. Use a syringe specialised for administering oral medicine then shoot inside his/her mouth from the side.

Suggested Samoan translation	1. E mafai lava ona 'e afifi lēmū lelei pepe i se solo po'o se palanikeke e taofi ai ōna lima, ina ia 'aua ne'i fa'alavelave i lou fa'ainuina ai o lana vai. 2.1 Fa'aaogā se tui fa'apitoa mo le fa'ainuina o vai ona fa'apasī la'itiiti lea o lana vai i totonu o lona gutu i le itu i totonu o lona alafau, *ma o 'iina e lē lagona tele ai se 'oona o le vai.* E masani lava 'ona foloina e pepe le vai pe 'a tu'utu'u tele i totonu o lona gutu. **2.1 OR** Fa'aaogā se tui fa'ainuvai ona fa'apasī la'itiiti lea o lana vai i totonu o lona gutu i le itu i totonu o lona alafau i totonu o lona gutu, *ma o 'iina e lē lagona tele ai se 'oona o le vai.* E masani lava 'ona foloina e pepe le vai pe 'a tu'utu'u tele i totonu o lona gutu.
Author's back translation of suggested translation	1. You could wrap baby gently in a towel or a blanket to stop his/her arms/hands from being in the way of you giving him/her medicine. 2. Use a special syringe for taking medicine, then squirt a little of his/her medicine inside his/her mouth onto the inside of her/his cheek, and this way baby will not taste the sourness of the medicine. Usually baby will swallow his/her medicine if you put it further inside/towards the back of the mouth

In this example, the OTr has not used the correct equivalents, and there were many omissions and additions in their work.

4.1.9 Lack of a Standard Guide for the Writing and Spelling of Samoan

The lack of a uniform guide for the writing and spelling of Samoan is also evident from a number of Samoan translations.

Example 5.11 Not Following the Conventions of Written Samoan

English	Samoan Translation 1 (SamT1)	Samoan Translation 2 (SamT2)
Your doctor will tell you: • The INR level that is best for you • The warfarin dose you need to take • How often you need an INR blood test When should you take it?	'Ole'ā ta'u atu e lau fōma'i po'o le ā le sini o le INR, po'o le ā fo'i le fua o le warfarin 'e te mana'omia, ma pē fa'afia fo'i ona 'e mana'omia le su'ega o lou toto 'O ā taimi e inu ai a'u fuālā'au?	O le 'a ta'u atu e lau foma'i poo le ā le sini o le INR, poo le ā fo'i le fua o le warfarine te mana'omia, ma pe fa'afia fo'i ona e mana'omia le su'ega o lou toto O ā taimi e inu ai a'u fualaau?
Move more for better health	Minoi atili mo le faaleleia o lou soifua maloloina	Minoi atili mo le fa'aleleia o lou soifua mālōlōina

The writing and spelling of the Samoan language used in pamphlets in health and other settings differ based on the translator(s) undertaking the translations. The examples of differences are shown in red and the table shows the same words/terms written/spelled differently. These examples are very common in the published Samoan translations that are used by health consumers.

1. The preceding examples show a difference in how the two translators start their sentences. The beginning of the sentence starts with the particle that denotes future tenses i.e., 'Ole'a or O le 'a in SamT1, it is 'Ole'ā and the SamT2 writes O le 'a. Wong Soon agrees with SamT1's translation even though, growing up, she was taught the way it is in SamT2's translation i.e., O le 'a. Wong Soon agrees with SamT1's translation 'Ole'ā in view of the written evidence provided by Milner (1966, p. 163); however, the apostrophe before the *a* is incorrect. The correct spelling should have the glottal stop before the *a* as the emphasis is on the *a* to indicate the time aspect – in this case, the future. With the correct use of the glottal stop in place, the particle should be written as *Ole'ā*.

2. *Foma'i* vs *foma'i* vs *fomai* (doctor) – the correct spelling is shown in SamT2's translation. It should always be written this way because the glottal stop should be used, as the emphasis is on the " *'i*" in *doctor* (i.e.) *foma'i* and not *foma'i*. For those born and educated in Samoa, the idea of using diacritical symbols was not a major concern in the past; however, it has since become evident that there is indeed a great need to use diacritical symbols. The written Samoan language should consider emphasising the importance of using these grammatical symbols to help the reader to correctly pronounce words when reading the text. The use of diacritical symbols would also help translators follow a 'uniform approach' to writing Samoan in their translations. In Wong Soon's view, it is fortunate that Samoa introduced the Samoan Language Commission Act 2014 No.5 (Ministry of Education, Sports and Culture, 2014), amended in 2019, which enshrined Samoan as the official language of Samoa. The development for standardised spelling and writing conventions is a logical next step. This is also a way of maintaining the language in its correct form for the future generations of Samoan speakers.

Again, this is an example of public services employing the conventional written translation approach as a 'one size fits all' for different ethnic communities – Wong Soon argues that interviewing Samoan speaking health professionals on Radio Samoa would be a more effective approach to reaching Samoan communities. Radio Samoa posts audiovisual recordings of such interviews, and statistics show that these are watched by a great many viewers.

4.2 Talking Cards

In 2014, Ineke Crezee conducted her Fulbright (Public Health) research at the Center for Diversity and Health Equity at Seattle Children's Hospital (SCH). The

Center was engaged with outreach involving various communities (e.g., African, First Nations) and employed bilingual patient navigators. The navigator role included empowering limited English proficient (LEP) parents to advocate for their children, by helping them develop an understanding of their child's condition and proposed treatment plan (see Crezee & Roat, 2019). Navigators not only helped identify barriers to understanding, but also barriers to accessing the healthcare system and following prescribed treatment. Navigators often used narratives to convey complex health messages (Crezee, 2015). This involved identifying the crux of the message. As an example, one navigator suggested the analogy of Mom and Dad making a stew during a genetics counselling session with a couple who both reportedly had mosaic genetic mutations (cf. Rohlin et al., 2009).

4.2.1 Talking Cards with Discharge Instructions

Staff at SCH also explored other ways of ensuring important information was conveyed or reinforced. In 2014, Ali Adem, one of the Somali-speaking patient navigators, took part in a Talking Cards project whereby discharge instructions were recorded in the patient's preferred language of medical care – in this case Somali. The small pilot study involved ten Somali-speaking families, who were phoned post-discharge to assess their understanding of the instructions. The study was repeated in 2016, with a larger number of families, and most families expressed their satisfaction with the Talking Cards, sharing these with others and listening to the instructions several times (Lion et al., 2019). The Talking Cards project inspired Crezee to run a similar project in Aotearoa NZ, which will be reported in what follows.

Following her sojourn as a Fulbright scholar in the United States, Crezee ran a Talking Cards project in Aotearoa NZ, inspired by the project at SCH – but with a difference.

In the Seattle pilot, physicians' discharge instructions for Somali-speaking patients had been recorded onto Talking Cards. This involved the researcher/interpreter being present at the discharge and recording the instructions before following up personally with the Somali-speaking patients. Crezee looked for a situation whereby patients are given the same instructions provided by health professionals and interpreted by healthcare interpreters. She decided to focus on gestational diabetes mellitus (GDM) – pregnancy diabetes – since this is a major issue in Aotearoa NZ, specifically among non-Caucasian communities. Poor management of GDM can have serious consequences for both mother and child. Crezee applied for funding to order Talking Cards from the United States and the cost of translating and recording the information into Mandarin, Cantonese, and Samoan. The cards were available at the special antenatal clinic for women with GDM at Auckland City Hospital. The cards contained the standard information on treatment of GDM (insulin, Metformin, or both) in spoken form. This information has been written by Dr Janet Rowan, one of the diabetes physicians at Auckland District Health Board. This was the same information as that normally conveyed to women by midwives in English, through interpreters and repeated by midwives several times, to ensure understanding. This information was translated into Mandarin and Cantonese and Samoan and voiced over onto the cards. Ethics approval was granted by the Auckland University of Technology Ethics Committee, but subject to very strict recruitment conditions, which unfortunately affected the number of participants recruited.

4.2.2 Findings

Only ten Chinese-speaking women took the cards home, with one card proving defective. Participants received a phone call from a Chinese-speaking research assistant who conducted a short telephone survey. Follow-up by the research assistant, who spoke both Mandarin and Cantonese, showed that all ten participating women were highly literate end users, who said they found the recorded information useful as a basis for doing their own research (on the Chinese social media platform Weibo). A small number of women ($n = 3$) commented that while the information was useful, it would be good to have information on how they might be able to manage their own pregnancy diabetes (GDM).

4.2.3 Limitations

Over 10% of the Talking Cards ordered from the United States proved to be defective (unable to record, or unable to play back recording). Although the company replaced these at no additional cost, this led to some delays in commencing the research study. An additional drawback was that cards only allowed for a 180-second message to be recorded. The Samoan translation had to be sped up by the (Samoan) sound technician to fit in the 180 seconds, resulting in the message sounding unnaturally rushed.

4.2.4 Take-Home Messages

What Crezee learned from this project was that even though medical information had been correctly translated and voiced over, there were no images – only words. In addition, we had not asked potential end users what sort of information they would have wanted. It turned out that the end users also wanted information on how to manage GDM themselves (agency), such as through diet. Even though the number of participants was small, the study shows a novel approach to community translation. The study was set up bearing in mind the fact that recipients might want to share information with older generations sharing their homes, by simply pressing 'Play' on the card. In other words, Crezee tried to approach the study from a collectivist perspective, rather than a more individualistic (Western) perspective (Hofstede Insights, 2021; Meyer, 2014). Older relatives may have a lot of influence on what food is provided in multigenerational households (Wong Soon, 2016), so their understanding of GDM was deemed important.

4.3 Community Translation With Visuals and Voice-Overs

4.3.1 Background

After the Talking Card project, Crezee decided to take a different approach to community translation, considering the focus of the New Zealand Ministry of Health (MoH). The focus of the MoH was on people living with long-term conditions (LTCs), which included non-communicable diseases, in particular conditions such as diabetes, cancer, cardiovascular diseases, respiratory diseases, mental illness, chronic pain, chronic kidney disease, and dementia.

Two groups particularly at risk are those among the elderly population with LTCs who may have trouble reading and processing information due to a lack of completed formal schooling (Baker et al., 2007; Bennett et al., 2009; Ward et al., 2019) and older health consumers who have limited English proficiency (Kreps & Sparks, 2008; Yeheskel & Rawal, 2019). Barriers to understanding may also include limited attention span and a lack of previous knowledge.

4.3.2 Method

Based on the findings of the Talking Card study, Crezee decided that it might be better to combine visuals (simple cartoons) with brief, rather than more in-depth information, intended to convey the most essential messages. Regarding the use of visual images, some research suggests that stick figures are best (Choi, 2013; Gaissmaier et al., 2012), while others suggest that health professionals such as nurses are best placed to decide on graphics. For the small study on the use of community translation on betablockers, Crezee used her experience as a registered nurse and cartoonist to develop the images, using a clean style (*ligne claire/klare lijn:* 'clear line') without too much distracting detail.

For this project, the lead author developed two different narratives:

1 Mr Lee is prescribed betablockers.
2 Tommy needs antibiotics.

The first topic was more in line with the MoH's focus, and after consulting a community pharmacist, Crezee designed a short story about an older man whose family doctor gives him a prescription for betablockers. See Diagram 5.1 for a brief overview of the process followed.

Diagram 5.1 Overview of Process

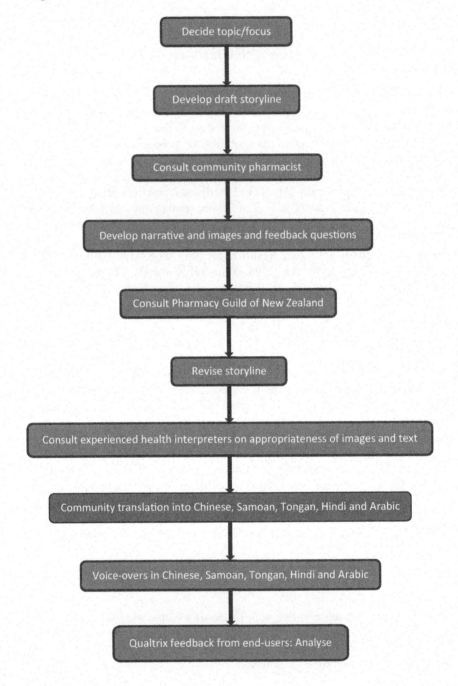

In the story, when the pharmacist asks the older man if he knows what beta blockers might be for, the man draws a blank. Consultation included the Pharmacy Guild of New Zealand and experienced healthcare interpreters working between English and Samoan, Tongan, Mandarin Chinese, Hindi, and Arabic. The story consists of seven visuals, accompanied by a narrative voiced over in these six most in-demand community or heritage languages, which are also among those most in demand for language access services. This research is currently in progress and involves the use of Qualtrics to gain user feedback on the way information is presented.

5 Further Discussion

There is no 'one-size-fits-all' solution, which means a uniform approach to community translation across different languages will not work, and is, moreover, disrespectful to members of minority communities. All heritage or community language translators will face a different set of issues, depending on the nature of their target readership and the nature of their language. In this chapter, we looked at a few small studies involving different approaches to health translation for different communities, including the use of Talking Cards and visual images supported by voice-overs. We also discussed a small sample of problems identified when translating health information into Samoan, based on Wong Soon's experience as a reviewer. She argued that community translation into Samoan involves the following issues not previously explored or discussed.

1. Translators are often Aotearoa NZ–born and only use the language in what Fishman (1964) called the home and friendship domains – this affects their ability to translate into culturally and linguistically appropriate Samoan.
2. The Samoan language lacks health specialist vocabulary, which means all words must be unpacked – and that can only happen if translators have a health background.
3. Most translators do not have a health background and make errors reflecting this; some of these errors can be quite serious.
4. Translators may not have had any translator education and are not used to reflecting on translation problems and strategies.
5. There is no uniform guide for the writing and spelling of the Samoan language.

Many questions remain when it comes to the community translation of health information, starting with the question as to who should write health information and in what form it should be presented (oral, written, or a combination of both) and disseminated. Commissioners of community translations should also ask themselves what input is needed before a source text is finalised.

The authors suggest involving the commissioner, actual text writers, translators, and target reader representatives from the outset (cf. García-Izquierdo & Montalt, 2017; Teng, 2019). They also suggest asking registered nurses to write material since they are used to communicating complex medical information to patients with varying levels of health literacy, and then inviting experienced health interpreters and translators and target readers to give their input on the appropriateness of the translated texts, ease of understanding, naturalness of language, too little/too much information, and any ambiguities or lack of clarity. It may be that translations need to involve more unpacking, as outlined in Section 4.1.4.

Another important point raised in Section 4.1 is that even when the translation is reviewed, the original translator (OTr) does not always accept the comments. This part of the translation process needs to be addressed further, particularly if there are examples when a necessary correction of the target text is ignored by the OTr.

The authors also suggest considering the use of audiovisuals with voiced-over texts then making translated material available on relevant websites and sending links to patients' smartphones. User feedback could then be collected using Qualtrics (or a similar platform) through multiple-choice or open-ended questions.

Health information presented by way of narratives may be remembered more readily than that presented in more traditional informative discursive style (Crezee, 2014, 2015). One argument in favour of using simple storylines when presenting health information is that narratives are about 'other people' and may therefore be perceived as less threatening. Research has shown that audiovisual medication information may improve health consumers' understanding of why they have been prescribed certain medication, as well as how and when they should take it (Dowse & Ehlers, 2003a, 2003b, 2011).

6 Conclusion

In terms of the best approach to community translation, the approach at the moment appears to be top-down in Aotearoa NZ, with the various ministries deciding what needs to be communicated and drafted, with the resulting texts then being sent off for translation. There appears to be no consultation with communities, which could be done by consulting with healthcare users (and their families), experienced health professionals working with those communities, or health interpreters and translators.

The authors recommend that the authorities consider the importance of key messages, asking themselves who should write it, who should be consulted and how, and who should review translated texts (involving back translation, see Ozolins et al., 2020). There also needs to be more emphasis on the importance of cultural appropriateness; the use of images, including types of images, and why those; and the importance of narratives and storylines. The use of narratives will mean readers can read about 'others' going through situations which they recognise, without feeling as though they are being directly addressed.

Translators working in healthcare should have appropriate health training to understand the source texts and undertake their translations accordingly.

Based on Wong Soon's review (Section 4.1.5, Example 5.4), she deduced that the translator either did not have a background or knowledge in health or did not undertake the required research on "breathing muscles". To be a competent translator in health – or in any area – translators must take all possible steps to provide the best quality in their work. Translators need to research the topic if they do not understand the text. Translators have a duty to uphold accuracy in their work and the responsibility to maintain the meaning of the message in the source text, and that also goes for translating into a heritage language such as Samoan.

In today's multicultural, superdiverse societies, health promotion seems to have traditionally involved the 'write first, translate second' approach. This needs to change. From the outset, health promotion involving culturally and linguistically diverse communities should involve representatives of end users, and translators/interpreters as intercultural experts. Input from the former is essential to check how translation is received by end users in terms of ease of reading (sounds natural, makes sense, cf. Teng, 2019) and cultural appropriateness (register, topic, choice of imagery). Without such an inclusive approach, health translations may not achieve the goals that the commissioners have in mind.

Acknowledgements/Fa'afetai tele lava i le 'oa o la outou fa'asoa

Hoy Neng Wong Soon would like to first acknowledge her beloved mother, Peleiupu Wong Soon-Bentley (may she rest in peace), for always encouraging her and supporting her to seek a fulfilling education. Fa'afetai tele i le asaina o le ala fitā auā se manuia o i matou lau fanau. E lē galo oe le tinā.

She would also like to acknowledge in gratitude the advice she received from the following people:

- Namulau'ulu Filipo Reupena, Cultural Advisor, Safotulafai, Samoa
- Namulau'ulu Au'apaau Tavita Leaumoana, Cultural Advisor, Lalomanu, Manono, Sapapalii, Samoa
- Tupa'i Gese Lealaitafea, Sala'ilua, Palauli, Cultural Advisor, Auckland, Aotearoa New Zealand
- Leulua'iali'i Perive Lelevaga, Principal/Coordinator, National Sexual Reproductive Health, Samoa
- Ta'ala Logomai Feterika Lualua Tele'a, Senior Nurse Specialist, (MT2 Clinical), Samoa
- Margaret Tuala-Lauese, Clinical Nurse Specialist Palliative Care, CMH, Auckland, Aoatearoa New Zealand
- Moelagi Leilani Jackson, Tausisoifua/Nurse, Auckland, Aotearoa New Zealand
- Papali'i Tulua Leaumoana, Faufautua/Advisor, Auckland, Aotearoa New Zealand

APPENDICES

Appendix A

EXAMPLE A1 Omissions of Necessary Articles, Prepositions, and Particles in the Target Text[5]

English source text	Babies start moving early in pregnancy, but at first you will not feel them.
	Slowly you will start to feel little flutters, between 16–22 weeks, and these will build up to being strong movements as baby grows in size and strength.
Samoan translation (original translation)	E 'āmata ona gāoioi i le 'āmataga o le ma'itō, 'ae e tau lē lagonaina. 'Ae fa'asolosolo lava ona 'e fa'alogoina, i le va o le 16–22 vaiaso, ma 'o le 'ā fa'asolosolo lava ina mālolosi gāoioiga 'a'o tuputupu a'e pepe i lona lāpo'a ma lona mālosi.
Back translation of original translation	It begins to move at the start of/in early pregnancy, but at first you will not feel it. But slowly you will feel, between 16–22 weeks, and these will become stronger movements as baby grows in size and strength.
Author's Suggested Samoan translation	'O pepe 'e 'āmata ona gāoioi i le 'āmataga o le ma'itō, 'ae 'e te tau lē lagonaina. 'E amata fa'asolosolo lava 'ona 'e lagonaina ni minōiga laiti ma 'e mālū, i le va o le 16–22 vaiaso, ma 'o le 'ā fa'asolosolo lava 'ina mālolosi gāoioiga 'a'o tuputupu a'e pepe i lona lāpo'a ma lona mālosi.
Author's back translation of suggested translation	*The* babies start to move at the start of/in early pregnancy, but you will not feel them. You will slowly start to feel little and gentle movements/flutters, between 16–22 weeks, and these movements will start to build up/become stronger as baby grows in size and strength.

EXAMPLE A2 Omission of Articles in Samoan[6]

English source text	*Eligibility and pricing structure for maternity care*
Samoan translation (original)	Fa'atagaga ma le fa'atulagaga o totogi mo le tausiga o ma'itō
Back translation	Eligibility and pricing structure for maternity care
Suggested Samoan translation	*O le* Āgava'a ma le **fa'**atulagana o totogi mo le tausiga o ma'itō
Author's back translation of suggested translation	*The* eligibility and pricing structure for maternity care

Speak My Language! **127**

Appendix B

Example B Incorrect Translations of Health-Related Concepts in Samoan7

English source text	1. Palliative care supports people of any age who have been told that they have a life-limiting illness that cannot be cured.
	2. It can assist people with illnesses such as cancer, motor neurone disease, advanced dementia and end-stage kidney, heart or lung disease.
Samoan translation (original)	1. E lagolagoina fo'i e le palliative care tagata o so'o se matua 'ua iloa 'o ia 'ua maua i se ma'i e fa'aumatia ai le soifua.
	2. E mafai ona fesoasoani i tagata e maua i le kanesa, ma'i o le motor neurone (lē lelei sela neura o le fai'ai), **māfaufau lē 'ātoa** ma le ma'i o le lata ina leaga 'atoa fatuga'o, fatu po'o māmā fo'i.
Back translation	1. Palliative care supports people of any age who know that they have a condition that ends life.
	2. It can also help people who have cancer, illness of the motor neurone (neurone cells of the brains are not good), **mind not fully good** and condition that kidneys are nearly/fully not working/functioning well, heart or lungs too.
Suggested Samoan translation	1. E lagolagoina 'e le Tausiga o gasegase 'ua ui (palliative care) o tagata o so'o se matua 'ua fa'ailoaina ia i latou 'ua maua i se gasegase e fa'atapula'aina ai le soifua ma ua ui le ma'i.
	Or
	1. E lagolagoina 'e le Tausiga o gasegase 'ua ui togafitiga/fofō (palliative care) o tagata o so'o se matua lava 'ua fa'ailoaina ia i latou 'ua maua i se gasegase e fa'atapula'aina ai le soifua ma 'ua lē 'o toe aogā i ai se fofō/togafitiga.
	2. E mafai ona fesoasoani i tagata 'ua maua i gasegase e pei o le kanesa, **ma'i o sela neura mai le fai'ai i lona 'au poo le maeā ario (motor neurone disease),** mātuiā/ōgaōga tele le gasegase o le galogalo o mea i le mafaufau/

Appendix C

EXAMPLE C1 Incorrect Understanding and Translation of Medical Concepts[8]

English source text	**Tetanus**
	Tetanus is a disease that can enter the body through a cut or a graze. It causes muscles to stiffen and spasm. It may affect the breathing muscles.
Samoan translation (original)	**'Ona (tetanus)**
	O le 'ona o se ma'i e mafai ona sao i totonu o le tino e mafua mai se vaega o le tino ua lavea pe ma'osia. E mafua ai ona malō faafuasei uaua o le tino ma migi. E ono aafia ai foi maso o le vaega o loo mānava ai.
Back translation	Tetanus is a disease that can enter the body through a cut or a graze. It causes veins of the body to stiffen and spasm. It may also affect the muscles of the part where you breathe (from).
Suggested Samoan translation	**'Ona (tetanus)**
	O le 'ona o se ma'i e mafai ona sao i totonu o le tino ma 'e mafua mai i se vaega o le tino ua lavea pe ma'osia. E mafua ona malō ma migi ai maso. E ono aafia ai maso mānava.
Author's back translation of suggested translation	Tetanus is a disease that can enter the body through a cut or a graze. It causes muscles to stiffen and spasm. It may affect the breathing muscles.

EXAMPLE C2 Incorrect Understanding and Translation of Medical Concepts[9]

English source text	What is warfarin?
	Warfarin is a medicine that helps to prevent blood clots.
Samoan translation (original)	'O le ā le warfarin?
	'O le warfarin 'o se fuālā'au e fa'ataga mai e le fōma'i e fesoasoani e taofia le māfiafia o le toto (coagulating).
Back translation	What is warfarin?
	Warfarin is a medicine that has been allowed/prescribed by the doctor to help stop/prevent blood from thickening (coagulating).
Suggested Samoan translation	'O le ā le warfarin?
	'O le warfarin 'o se fuāla'au e fesoasoani e taofia le toto mai le potopotoi.
Author's back translation of suggested translation	What is warfarin?
	Warfarin is a medicine that helps to prevent the blood from clotting.

Appendix D

EXAMPLE D: Ambiguous and Potentially Misleading Translation Choices[10]

English source text	Parent consent form
Samoan translation (original translation)	Pepa faatumu a le aoga mo le maliega
Back translation	Paper to complete/form of the school for consent
	Or
	School's Paper to complete/form for consent
	** It may be that the translator assumes that the reader will understand that the form is from the school and to be completed by another but the 'person to complete/give consent' is omitted in the translation
Suggested Samoan translation	Pepa o le maliega a matua
Author's back translation of suggested translation	Paper/form of consent by parent(s), which is 'Parent consent form', as stated in the English source text

Appendix E

EXAMPLE E1 **Omission and Addition of Information**[11]

English source text	an immune deficiency condition (e.g., your child is HIV positive)
Samoan translation (original)	ua faaletonu le vaega o le tino e teena faama'i (e pei o le aafia o lou alo i le siama o le HIV)
Back translation	Part of the body that defends itself/fights off diseases is affected/compromised (such as your child is affected by the bacteria/virus of HIV)
Suggested Samoan translation	ua fa'alētonu le vaega o le tino e te'ena ai fa'ama'i (fa'ata'ita'iga., ua maua lau tama i le siama o le HIV)
Author's back translation of suggested translation	(a condition that is the) malfunction of the immune system of the body that fends off infections/diseases (for example, your child has the HIV virus)

EXAMPLE E2 Omission of Information[12]

English source text	*See the Consumer Medical information published at www.medsafe.govt.nz/consumers/cmi/b/boostrix.pdf*
Samoan translation (original)	Omission in target text
Back translation	n/a

Suggested Samoan translation	Silasila ane i fa'amatalaga Fa'alesoifua Maloloina mo Tagata o lo'o **fa'ailoaina** atu i le www.medsafe.govt.nz/consumers/cmi/b/boostrix.pdf
	Or
	Taga'i ane i fa'amatalaga Fa'alesoifua Maloloina mo le Tagata o lo'o **fa'ailoaina** atu i le www.medsafe.govt.nz/consumers/cmi/b/boostrix.pdf
Author's back translation of suggested translation	See Consumer Medical information made known/published/presented at www.medsafe.govt.nz/consumers/cmi/b/boostrix.pdf

Appendix F

EXAMPLE F Change of Information in the Target Text[13]

English source text	Why not try: . . .
	Swimming or aqua fitness – there's lots you can do in the water
Samoan translation (original)	Aisea e lē faataitai ai?:
	Aau poo le malosi i le vai – e tele mea e mafai ona faia i le vai
Back translation	Why not try?:
	Swimming or strength in the water – there's lots you can do in the water
Suggested Samoan translation	Aiseā e lē fa'ata'ita'i ai:
	Le 'a'au poo le fa'amalositino i le vai
	Or
	Le 'a'au poo le fa'amalositino e faia i totonu o le vaita'ele/sami
Author's back translation of suggested translation	Why not try:
	Swimming or exercise(s) in the water
	Or
	Swimming or exercise(s) in the pool/sea

Appendix G

EXAMPLE G **Change of Information in the Target Text**[14]

English source text	1. You could wrap your baby gently in a towel/wrap **to stop** baby's arms getting in the way of your medicine giving.
	2. Use an oral medicine syringe and squirt *a little medicine* into the mouth onto the inside cheek *where there are no bitter taste buds*. Usually baby will swallow if the syringe is far enough back in the mouth.
Samoan translation (original)	1. Afifi lelei pepe **ise** solo poʻo se **palanikete** tautuana ona lima ia afifi lelei ia aua neʻi faʻalavelave ile taimi e faʻainu ai lana vai.
	2. Faʻaaoga se tui faʻapitoa mole faʻainuina o vai ona **faga** lea **I** totonu o lona gutu **mai** le itu. E vave ai lava ona mimiti ele pepe le vai pea tuʻu saʻo i totonu o lona gutu.
Back translation	1. Properly wrap baby in a towel or blanket make sure to wrap his/her arms/hands so that they are not in the way at the time you give his/her medicine.
	2. Use a syringe specialised for administering oral medicine then shoot inside his/her mouth from the side.
Suggested Samoan translation	1. E mafai lava ona ʻe afifi lēmū lelei pepe i se solo poʻo se palanikeke e taofi ai ōna lima, ina ia ʻaua neʻi faʻalavelave i lou faʻainuina ai o lana vai.
	a. Faʻaaogā se tui faʻapitoa mo le faʻainuina o vai ona faʻapasī laʻitiiti lea o lana vai i totonu o lona gutu i le itu i totonu o lona alafau, *ma o ʻiina e lē lagona tele ai se ʻoona o le vai*. E masani lava ʻona foloina e pepe le vai pe ʻa tuʻutuʻu tele i totonu o lona gutu.

OR

b. Fa'aoga se tui fa'ainuvai ona fa'apasī la'itiiti lea o lana vai i totonu o lona gutu i le itu i totonu o lona alafau **i** totonu o lona gutu, *ma o 'iina e lē lagona tele ai se 'oona o le vai.* E masani lava 'ona foloina e pepe le vai pe 'a tu'utu'u tele i totonu o lona gutu.

Author's back translation of suggested translation

1. You could wrap baby gently in a towel or a blanket to stop his/her arms/hands from being in the way of you giving him/her medicine.

2. Use a special syringe for taking medicine, then squirt a little of his/her medicine inside his/her mouth onto the inside of her/his cheek, and this way baby will not taste the sourness of the medicine. Usually baby will swallow his/her medicine if you put it further inside/towards the back of the mouth.

Appendix H

EXAMPLE H **Not Following Conventions of Written Samoan**[15]

English	Samoan Translation 1 (SamT1)	Samoan Translation 2 (SamT2)
Your doctor will tell you: • The INR level that is best for you • The warfarin dose you need to take • How often you need an INR blood test	'Ole'ā ta'u atu e lau fōma'i po'o le ā le sini o le INR, po'o le ā fo'i le fua o le warfarin te mana'omia, ma pē fa'afia fo'i ona 'e mana'omia le su'ega o lou toto	O le 'a ta'u atu e lau foma'i po'opoo le ā le sini o le INR, poo 'e le ā fo'i le fua o le warfarin e te mana'omia, ma pe fa'afia fo'i ona e mana'omia le su'ega o lou toto
When should you take it?	'O ā taimi e inu ai a'u fuālā'au?	O ā taimi e inu ai a'u fualaau?
Move more for better health	Minoi atili mo le faaleleia o lou soifua maloloina	Minoi atili mo le fa'aleleia o lou soifua mālōlōina

Notes

1. DHBs and translation and interpreting organisations will remain anonymous here when reviews of translation work are discussed, unless stated otherwise.
2. South Auckland Health provided publicly funded primary and secondary health care in the early 1990s (at the time of writing, it was referred to as Counties Manukau District Health Board).
3. English back translation: care for medical conditions for which there is no more use for any cure/treatment.
4. English back translation: care for medical conditions that have no cure/treatment.
5. Extract from the translation: *Women's Health Division – My Baby's Movements*.
6. Extract from a translation on Women's Health (11 April 2017)
7. Extract from a translation of a source text entitled: "What is Palliative Care?" Reviewed 24 January 2019. Available at: www.healthnavigator.org.nz/media/8227/mercy-hospice-poi-palliative-care-english.pdf
8. www.healthed.govt.nz/resource/year-7-immunisation-tetanus-diphtheria-and-whooping-cough-pertussis-boostrix%E2%84%A2-vaccine and www.healthed.govt.nz/resource/year-7-immunisation-tetanus-diphtheria-and-whooping-cough-pertussis-boostrix%E2%84%A2-vaccine-4
9. www.healthnavigator.org.nz/medicines/w/warfarin-and-diet/ and www.saferx.co.nz/assets/Documents/c1df5363db/warfarin-samoan.pdf
10. www.healthed.govt.nz/resource/year-7-immunisation-tetanus-diphtheria-and-whooping-cough-pertussis-boostrix%E2%84%A2-vaccine and www.healthed.govt.nz/resource/year-7-immunisation-tetanus-diphtheria-and-whooping-cough-pertussis-boostrix%E2%84%A2-vaccine-4
11. www.healthed.govt.nz/resource/year-7-immunisation-tetanus-diphtheria-and-whooping-cough-pertussis-boostrix%E2%84%A2-vaccine and www.healthed.govt.nz/resource/year-7-immunisation-tetanus-diphtheria-and-whooping-cough-pertussis-boostrix%E2%84%A2-vaccine-4
12. www.healthed.govt.nz/resource/year-7-immunisation-tetanus-diphtheria-and-whooping-cough-pertussis-boostrix%E2%84%A2-vaccine and www.healthed.govt.nz/resource/year-7-immunisation-tetanus-diphtheria-and-whooping-cough-pertussis-boostrix%E2%84%A2-vaccine-4
13. "Green Prescription: Need Help to Get ACTIVE?" www.health.govt.nz/system/files/documents/publications/need-help-to-get-active-english.pdf and: Green Prescription: Manaomia se fesoasoani ina ia GAIOI? www.health.govt.nz/system/files/documents/publications/need-help-to-get-active-samoan.pdf
14. Extracts from texts on the Health Navigator website with links to the Pharmaconline source text and translation into Samoan. Topic: "Giving medicines to children" www.healthnavigator.org.nz/videos/p/paracetamol-children/ https://pharmac.govt.nz/assets/tips-for-kids-english.pdf and www.pharmaconline.co.nz/webtop/bsg/product?client=Pharmac&prodid=PHMI037&version=&type=pdf
15. Samoan translation 1: www.healthnavigator.org.nz/medicines/w/warfarin-and-diet/ and www.saferx.co.nz/assets/Documents/c1df5363db/warfarin-samoan.pdf Samoan translation 2: www.health.govt.nz/system/files/documents/publications/need-help-to-get-active-english.pdf and www.health.govt.nz/system/files/documents/publications/need-help-to-get-active-samoan.pdf

References

Abdel-Latif, M. M. M. (2020). The enigma of health literacy and COVID-19 pandemic. *Public Health*, *185*, 95–96. https://doi.org/10.1016/j.puhe.2020.06.030

Alves, F., & Vale, D. C. (2017). On drafting and revision in translation: A corpus linguistics oriented analysis of translation process data. In S. Hansen-Schirra, O. Čulo,

& S. Neumann (Eds.), *Annotation, exploitation and evaluation of parallel corpora* (pp. 89–109). Language Science Press.

Angelone, E. (2016). A process-oriented approach for documenting and gauging intercultural competence in translation. *The Interpreter and Translator Trainer*, *10*(3), 304–317. https://doi.org/10.1080/1750399X.2016.1236560

Baker, D. W., Wolf, M. S., Feinglass, J., Thompson, J. A., Gazmararian, J. A., & Huang, J. (2007). Health literacy and mortality among elderly persons. *Archives of Internal Medicine*, *167*(14), 1503–1509. https://doi.org/10.1001/archinte.167.14.1503

Bennett, I. M., Chen, J., Soroui, J. S., & White, S. (2009). The contribution of health literacy to disparities in self-rated health status and preventive health behaviors in older adults. *The Annals of Family Medicine*, *7*(3), 204–211. https://doi.org/10.1370/afm.940

Berkman, N. D., Sheridan, S. L., Donahue, K. E., Halpern, D. J., & Crotty, K. (2011). Low health literacy and health outcomes: An updated systematic review. *Annals of Internal Medicine*, *155*(2), 97–107. https://doi.org/10.7326/0003-4819-155-2-201107190-00005

Biewer, C. (2021). Samoan English: An emerging variety in the South Pacific. *World Englishes*, *40*(3), 333–353. https://doi.org/10.1111/weng.12516

Burn, J. A., & Wong Soon, H. N. (2020). Interview with Samoan-English Specialist Mental Health Interpreter Hoy Neng Wong Soon. *International Journal of Interpreter Education*, *12*(2), Article 8.

Choi, J. (2013). Older adults' perceptions of pictograph-based discharge instructions after hip replacement surgery. *Journal of Gerontological Nursing*, *39*(7), 48–54.

Crezee, I. (2013). *Introduction to healthcare for interpreters and translators*. John Benjamins Publishing Company.

Crezee, I. (2014, December 10). *Laten we genetica uitleggen door te zeggen dat papa en mama samen een soep bereiden: Patient Navigators (Spaans en Somalisch) in het kinderziekenhuis in Seattle* [Let's explain genetics by saying that Mum and Dad are making a broth together: Patient navigators (Spanish and Somali) at Seattle Children's Hospital] [Keynote address] KU Leuven, Catholic University Leuven, Belgium.

Crezee, I. (2015, December 5). *Health literacy and narrative genres* [Presentation]. 5th New Zealand Discourse Conference, Auckland, New Zealand.

Crezee, I., & Roat, C. E. (2019). Bilingual patient navigator or healthcare interpreter: What's the difference and why does it matter? *Cogent Medicine*, *6*(1), Article 181087776. https://doi.org/10.1080/2331205X.2019.1582576

Crezee, I., & Tupou Gordon, M. (2019). Cross-cultural and cross-linguistic access to the healthcare system: Case studies from Seattle and Auckland. *Multicultural Health Translation, Interpreting and Communication*, 3–24.

Di Giovanni, E., & Gambier, Y. (2018). *Reception studies and audiovisual translation* (Vol. 141). John Benjamins Publishing Company.

Dowse, R., & Ehlers, M. S. (2003a). The influence of education on the interpretation of pharmaceutical pictograms for communicating medicine instructions. *International Journal of Pharmacy Practice*, *11*(1), 11–18. https://doi.org/10.1211/002235702810

Dowse, R., & Ehlers, M. S. (2003b). Pharmaceutical pictograms: Part 2: Weird and wonderful interpretations. *South African Pharmaceutical Journal*, *70*(3), 42–46.

Dowse, R., & Ehlers, M. S. (2011). Pictograms in pharmacy. *International Journal of Pharmacy Practice*, *6*(2), 109–118. https://doi.org/10.1111/j.2042-7174.1998.tb00924.x

Eser, O. (2020). *Understanding community interpreting services: Diversity and access in Australia and beyond*. Palgrave Macmillan. https://doi.org/10.1007/978-3-030-55861-1_3

Fishman, J. A. (1964). Language maintenance and language shift as a field of inquiry. A definition of the field and suggestions for its further development. *Linguistics*, *2*(9), 32–70. https://doi.org/doi:10.1515/ling.1964.2.9.32

Fleary, S. A., Joseph, P., & Pappagianopoulos, J. E. (2018). Adolescent health literacy and health behaviors: A systematic review. *Journal of Adolescence, 62*, 116–127. https://doi.org/10.1016/j.adolescence.2017.11.010

García-Izquierdo, I., & Montalt, V. (2017). Understanding and enhancing comprehensibility in texts for patients in an institutional health care context in Spain: A mixed methods analysis. *Revista Española de Lingüística Aplicada/Spanish Journal of Applied Linguistics, 30*(2), 592–610. https://doi.org/10.1075/resla.00008.gar

Gaissmaier, W., Wegwarth, O., Skopec, D., Müller, A. S., Broschinski, S., & Politi, M. C. (2012). Numbers can be worth a thousand pictures: Individual differences in understanding graphical and numerical representations of health-related information. *Health Psychology, 31*(3), 286.

Gavaruzzi, T., Caserotti, M., Leo, I., Tasso, A., Speri, L., Ferro, A., Fretti, E., Sannino, A., Rubaltelli, E., & Lotto, L. (2021). The role of emotional competences in parents' vaccine hesitancy. *Vaccines, 9*(3), 298. www.mdpi.com/2076-393X/9/3/298

Hofstede Insights. (2021). *Consulting, training, certification, tooling.* www.hofstede-insights.com/

Katan, D., & Taibi, M. (2021). *Translating cultures: An introduction for translators, interpreters and mediators* (3rd ed.). Routledge. https://doi.org/10.4324/9781003178170

Kemmis, S., McTaggart, R., & Nixon, R. (2014). Introducing critical participatory action research. In *The action research planner* (pp. 1–31). Springer. https://doi.org/10.1007/978-981-4560-67-2_1

Kreps, G. L., & Sparks, L. (2008). Meeting the health literacy needs of immigrant populations. *Patient Education and Counseling, 71*(3), 328–332. https://doi.org/10.1016/j.pec.2008.03.001

Lion, K. C., Kieran, K., Desai, A., Hencz, P., Ebel, B. E., Adem, A., Forbes, S., Kraus, J., Gutman, C., & Horn, I. (2019). Audio-recorded discharge instructions for limited english proficient parents: A pilot study. *The Joint Commission Journal on Quality and Patient Safety, 45*(2), 98–107. https://doi.org/10.1016/j.jcjq.2018.06.001

Magill, D. (2017). *Healthcare interpreting from a New Zealand sign language interpreters' perspective* [Master's thesis, Auckland University of Technology]. Tuwhera Open Access Theses & Dissertations. http://hdl.handle.net/10292/10317

Meyer, E. (2014). *The culture map: Breaking through the invisible boundaries of global business.* Public Affairs.

Milner, G. B. (1966). *Samoan dictionary: Samoan-English, English-Samoan.* Pasifka Press.

Ministry of Education, Sports and Culture. (2014). *The Samoan language commission act 2014.* www.palemene.ws/wp-content/uploads/01.Acts/Acts%202014/Samoan-Language-Commission-Act-2014-Eng.pdf

National Accreditation Authority for Translators and Interpreters. (2015). *NAATI translator certification: Knowledge, skills and attributes.* www.naati.com.au/wp-content/uploads/2020/02/Knowledge-Skills-and-Attributes_Translator.pdf

Nutbeam, D. (2009). Defining and measuring health literacy: What can we learn from literacy studies? *International Journal of Public Health, 54*(5), 303–305.

Office of Ethnic Communities. (2018). *Ethnic communities in New Zealand.* www.ethniccommunities.govt.nz/resources-2/ethnic-communities-in-new-zealand/

Ozolins, U., Hale, S., Cheng, X., Hyatt, A., & Schofield, P. (2020). Translation and back-translation methodology in health research – a critique. *Expert Review of Pharmacoeconomics & Outcomes Research, 20*(1), 69–77. https://doi.org/10.1080/14737167.2020.1734453

Paasche-Orlow, M. K., Parker, R. M., Gazmararian, J. A., Nielsen-Bohlman, L. T., & Rudd, R. R. (2005). The prevalence of limited health literacy. *Journal of General Internal Medicine, 20*(2), 175–184. https://doi.org/10.1111/j.1525-1497.2005.40245.x

Rohlin, A., Wernersson, J., Engwall, Y., Wiklund, L., Björk, J., & Nordling, M. (2009). Parallel sequencing used in detection of mosaic mutations: Comparison with four diagnostic DNA screening techniques. *Human Mutation*, *30*(6), 1012–1020. https://doi.org/10.1002/humu.20980

Rudd, R. E., Anderson, J. E., Oppenheimer, S., & Nath, C. (2007). Health literacy: An update of medical and public health literature. *Review of Adult Learning and Literacy*, *7*, 175–203.

Shrestha-Ranjit, J., Patterson, E., Manias, E., Payne, D., & Koziol-McLain, J. (2020). Accessibility and acceptability of health promotion services in New Zealand for minority refugee women. *Health Promotion International*, *35*(6), 1484–1494. https://doi.org/10.1093/heapro/daaa010

Statistics New Zealand. (2021). *2018 Census place summaries*. www.stats.govt.nz/tools/2018-census-place-summaries/

Taibi, M. (2017). Quality assurance in community translation. In M. Taibi (Ed.), *Translating for the community* (pp. 7–25). Multilingual Matters. https://doi.org/10.21832/9781783099146-005

Taibi, M., Liamputtong, P., & Polonsky, M. (2019). Impact of translated health information on CALD older people's health literacy: A pilot study. In M. Ji, M. Taibi, & I. H. Crezee (Eds.), *Multicultural health translation, interpreting and communication* (pp. 138–158). Routledge.

Taibi, M., & Ozolins, U. (2016). *Community translation*. Bloomsbury Academic.

Teng, W. (2019). When pragmatic equivalence fails: Assessing a New Zealand English to Chinese health translation from a functional perspective. In *Multicultural health translation, interpreting and communication* (pp. 85–122). Routledge.

Van Deusen-Scholl, N. (2003). Toward a definition of heritage language: Sociopolitcal and pedagogical considerations. *Journal of Language, Identity & Education*, *2*(3), 211–230. https://doi-org.ezproxy.aut.ac.nz/10.1207/S15327701JLIE0203_4

Wångdahl, J., Nilsson, U., Dahlberg, K., Jaensson, M., & Bergman, L. (2021). Health literacy and e-health literacy among Arabic speaking migrants in Sweden. *European Journal of Public Health*, *31*(Supplement 3), 1–12. https://doi.org/10.1093/eurpub/ckab164.700

Ward, M., Kristiansen, M., & Sørensen, K. (2019). Migrant health literacy in the European Union: A systematic literature review. *Health Education Journal*, *78*(1), 81–95. https://doi.org/10.1177/0017896918792700

Weiss, B. D. (2015). Health literacy research: Isn't there something better we could be doing? *Health Communication*, *30*(12), 1173–1175. https://doi.org/10.1080/10410236.2015.1037421

Wong Soon, H. N. (2016). *Food literacy: What does food literacy mean for Samoan families?* [Master's thesis, Auckland University of Technology]. Tuwhera Open Access Theses & Dissertations. http://hdl.handle.net/10292/10497

Yeheskel, A., & Rawal, S. (2019). Exploring the "patient experience" of individuals with limited English proficiency: A scoping Review. *Journal of Immigrant and Minority Health*, *21*(4), 853–878. https://doi.org/10.1007/s10903-018-0816-4

Yu, Y., He, A., Zheng, S., Jiang, J., Liang, J., Shrestha, B., & Wang, P. (2021). How does health literacy affect the utilization of basic public health services in Chinese migrants? *Health Promotion International*, *37*(1), 1–12. https://doi.org/10.1093/heapro/daab040

6
COMMUNITY TRANSLATION FOR ONCOLOGICAL AND PALLIATIVE CARE

Katarzyna Stachowiak-Szymczak and Karolina Stachowiak

1 Introduction: Community Translation

Community translation is a form of translation distinguishable by its human-oriented character. Community translators enable written communication of messages, documents, etc., between parties who do not (fluently) read and/or write the same language, or more specifically, for individuals and groups whose dominant language differs from that of the country or region in which they live/work (Taibi, 2011). Gouadec (2007) understands community translation as any translation that facilitates inter-community communication when there is a linguistically and/or culturally diverse society. Niska (2002) defines community translation in terms of the type of text and agents involved. As he proposes, community translation is the translation of texts of mainly informative character, such as alerts or communications of authorities or other institutions, addressed to "people" who do not understand the source language. Taibi (2011) takes a broader perspective on community translation, writing that it is not necessarily the type of text (e.g., informative vs. argumentative), nor the type of agent (e.g., authorities vs. people) that makes translation qualify as community translation. Instead, he proposes an initiative-oriented approach whereby community translation is understood as the translation of texts which are issued in the form of a message to the members of a community. The issuer, or the text provider, can be a formal group or institution (e.g., local authorities, hospital), or an informal one (e.g., local sales group, city revival project leaders), while individuals (potentially) interested or affected by the message constitute the addressee.

Therefore, community translation refers to public (or semi-public, if we refer to a closed group such as a neighbourhood community) communications, falling within the scope of public services, initiatives, actions, etc. In turn, the degree of text-provider formality and text character remain varied. This to some extent enables one to differentiate between community translation and either public

DOI: 10.4324/9781003247333-7

service or institutional translation. Institutional translation, according to Gouadec (2007), is any form of translating texts issued by, and for, formal institutions (e.g., the North Atlantic Treaty Organization [NATO]). On a similar note, community translation is not synonymous to sworn translation. In contrast to community translation, sworn translation is usually a legally regulated profession. However, this distinction is not universally applicable. Some countries, such as the United States and Australia, have introduced certification systems for translators which put community translation on a professionalisation level not dissimilar to that of sworn translation. In contrast, O'Hagan (2011) writes about translation done by internet (community) users, free of charge, usually for, or in cooperation with, an online community, referring to this type of volunteer translation also as community translation. This approach has recently lost popularity precisely due to the growing professionalisation of community translation.

Regardless of the communicative aspect of community translation, it does seem to share characteristics that may be succinctly put under the umbrella terms: *imbalance* and *diversity*. First, community translation involves a power imbalance between the receiver (e.g., a migrant) and the addresser (e.g., a public institution). Borrowing from community interpreting studies, Taibi and Ozolins (2016) comment on a triangular structure of the client–translator–text receiver relationship whereby the client's frequent "institutional" nature makes the receiver less powerful. This is visible both when, for example, a local authority communicates the rules of action, or when the power imbalance is in fact rooted in knowledge imbalance. Examples of knowledge imbalance can be found in medical translation (and interpreting), as communication may proceed from the medical staff representative to the patient, the latter being a layperson. By the same token, community translation can – but does not always – require vocabulary and register adjustment to the target text reader. Finally, minorities frequently constitute the target recipient of community translation, and therefore the previously mentioned triangular structure displays features of linguistic, ethnic, political, social, and/or cultural imbalance. To some extent, the mission of community translation is to level the playing field for those groups of people who are on the lower level of the power or social scale, by equipping under-represented and/or underprivileged groups with knowledge coming from access to information in their native language.

From a slightly different perspective, the community translation market displays linguistic, ethnic, political, and sociocultural diversity. First, community translation target readers include members of communities of different linguistic and sociocultural backgrounds. Second, the number of these members differs and changes over time. In highly multilingual countries, this translates into the demand for many language combinations. Imbalance and diversity also affect terminology. To borrow an example from Taibi and Ozolins (2016), terms "taken for granted" in some societies, such as "recycling" or "social security" may remain unknown in other societies (p. 14). This problem is not specific to community translation, as in general languages differ terminologically. However, it is frequent in community translation, precisely due to the fact that migrant minorities often come from countries differing in ethnic, cultural, technological, etc., backgrounds than the target country they migrate to. By the same token, translation strategies would remain different depending on how different the source and target language are in terms of, for instance, human rights or economy-rooted terminology. Finally, diversity may also affect a translator's choices in terms of the language variation or alphabet use. More importantly, from this chapter's point of view, the character of community translation requires the translator to be aware of different kinds of imbalance and diversity, and have related knowledge on the social, cultural, ethnic, and other differences between the source and target language communities, and the interplay between them.

2 Community Translation Policies and Quality Assurance

Quality criteria are not universal in translation studies and practice. At the same time, community translation takes from those approaches where target text function, context, and end-user needs are key factors in assessing the target text quality, as opposed to theories valuing equivalence above other criteria. The Skopos theory, developed by Reiss and Vermeer (1984/2014) and later expanded by Nord (1997), specifies that text function, purpose, and target reader needs should constitute the guiding dimensions of translation. Translators determine the approach towards translation they want to take, and the translation strategies to adopt, depending on the function and purpose of the text, and who the end users are. Koby et al. (2014) propose that "a quality translation demonstrates accuracy and fluency required for the audience and purpose and complies with all other specifications negotiated between the requester and provider, taking into account end-user needs" (p. 416). When understood intuitively, this definition seems accurate. At the same time, it raises further questions. Defining the end-user needs may be difficult, for instance, because not all groups of end users are involved in the decision-making process regarding what the target text should be like. Taibi (2018) observes that sometimes the end user needs may "clash" with the specifications of the requester and provider (p. 32).

House (1997, 2001, 2009, 2013) developed a system of parameters allowing to compare the original and translated texts. These include the text genre and register, the latter being further composed of field (i.e., the content), tenor (i.e., the social roles of the text provider and reader, and the asymmetry between them, which affects text formality) and mode (in very simplified terms: written vs. written-to-be-read text, and monologue vs. dialogue, etc.). Assessing the text based on these parameters allows for assessing the degree of "change of denotative meaning" (House, 1997). In practice, this means calculating the number of errors in translation, while the errors (or "mismatches", as House refers to them) are to some extent subjectively perceived by the assessor. In reference to this, Askari and Rahim (2015) rightly point out that none of House's models specify how many assessors are needed to form a sample big enough for reliable assessment. Practice shows that formal assessment (e.g., during certification exams or training) usually involves no more than several (frequently two or three) assessors. On a slightly different note, Taibi and Ozolins (2022) further observe that in many cases, the end user is the sole translation assessor, due to the confidentiality of information included in the source and target texts.

While local (e.g., university) translation assessment guidelines exist, there have been relatively few initiatives to propose international standards for assessing translation quality. Examples include the ISO 9000 standard and the Multidimensional Quality Metrics (MQM). The latter is a European Union (EU)-funded joint university initiative that offers a set of translation issues and different metrics that allow for translation quality assessment, depending on translation type. The same consortium also developed the Translation Automation User Society (TAUS) Dynamic Quality Framework (DQF) which is a set of tools enabling translation assessment. At the same time, standards and policies dedicated to community translation are still scarce.

2.1 Policies and Standards of Community Translation Quality Assurance

Methods of community translation quality assurance vary across countries and largely depend on the level of professionalisation. Australia has developed a world-leading translation certification system. The Australian National Accreditation Authority for Translators and Interpreters (NAATI) developed a set of translation assessment criteria, broadly used both during its own certification process and in courses offered by NAATI-endorsed institutions.

In short, NAATI offers testing to obtain credentials for the following.

- Certified Translator
- Certified Provisional Interpreter
- Certified Provisional (Auslan) Interpreter
- Certified Provisional Deaf Interpreter
- Certified (Auslan) Interpreter
- (Auslan) Certified Specialist Health Interpreter
- (Auslan) Certified Specialist Legal Interpreter
- (Auslan) Certified Conference Interpreter

Additionally, NAATI grants "Recognised Practising" credentials to practitioners working in rare or emerging languages, for whom testing is not (yet) available (NAATI, n.d.).

Other examples of unified criteria for community translation assessment can be found on the subnational level. For instance, the California Department of Education (2006) issued the "Quality Indicators for Translation and Interpretation in Kindergarten Through Grade Twelve Educational Settings Guidelines and Resources for Educators". The document proposes elements of assessment and includes a list of professional organisations that may help in the selection of translators for a given project. At the same time, it does not provide for a definite list of assessment criteria.

In general, there is still the need to develop community translation assessment criteria worldwide. Taibi (2018) rightly observes that:

> because end users are often disempowered people who speak minority languages, and also as a result of budgetary constraints in public services, it

is often the case that ad hoc measures are adopted, if at all, to cater for the communication needs of these community members.

(p. 33)

To verify whether general translation assessment criteria can be applied to evaluating community translation, Yamamoto (2011) used the framework proposed by Reiss and Vermeer (1984/2014) to assess community translations and concluded that it is "necessary to consider non-text factors, such as the consistency of information in the target language and timelines of the translation, in order to adapt the assessment framework for community translation" (Yamamoto, 2011, p. 101).

Taibi (2018) proposes a "multidimensional framework for quality in community translation" (p. 34) which includes the areas where quality can and should be ensured, for example, by means of proper translator briefing, adequate translator selection, and consultations with the community. Among other areas of quality provision, Taibi (2018) comments on proper source text preparation, stating that draftsmen should be aware of the differences between any text per se and a text that will serve for translation into different languages. To borrow the example from Taibi (2018), the Australian Multicultural Health Communication Service has created the "Guidelines for the Production of Multilingual Resources" (2014), advising on adequate source text style, register, and vocabulary level. This is particularly important in translated health communications as the reception of these elements is potentially affected by culture, demographics, and social issues, as well as health literacy.

2.2 Education

There are relatively few educational programmes offering specialised courses for community translators. Rather than specialising in community translation itself, translators tend to re-skill or upskill, changing or adding a community specialisation to their general translation portfolio (see e.g., Taibi & Ozolins [2016] for an overview of community translation courses worldwide). While some countries, such as Australia, offer community-oriented translation education, in other countries, the field still lacks dedicated training and upskilling programmes, which translates into "general" translators "self-specialising" in community translation.

As Taibi (2011) and Taibi and Ozolins (2016) comment, the basic skills a translator acquires, (e.g., at the university) are a good starting point for community translation. These go beyond pure language skills (Rothe-Neves, 2007) to include extralinguistic knowledge (i.e. subject-related knowledge and translation-specific knowledge such as translation strategies), instrumental skills (i.e., the knowledge and ability to work with translation-related infrastructure), strategic competence (i.e., the ability to plan and organise translation work), and psycho-physiological competence (i.e. the physiological and psychological resources needed in translation work) (PACTE, 2005, as cited in Taibi & Ozolins, 2016). At the same time,

> training programmes with a clear focus on community translation would expose trainees to the community texts they will ultimately be translating,

raise their awareness and understanding of the relevant local communities and public service settings, and develop the specific translation and intercultural communication skills they will need when translating for public services or for local communities.

(Taibi & Ozolins, 2016, p. 47)

In reference to this, it seems vital to distinguish between translation in general and community translation in translator education. On one hand, trainees may receive general translation training, also serving as a starting point for further specialisation. This is justifiable by a long process of gaining translation expertise, which is visible in studies on professional versus student translators. To give an example, Carl and Buch-Kromann (2010) investigated the translation process differences between professional translators and translation trainees, observing that students and professionals render equally accurate texts, while the texts of professional translators are more fluent. In addition, the authors propose a division of translation into three stages: skimming, drafting, and post-editing (Carl & Buch-Kromann, 2010). As they report, student translators devote more time to the initial phase, while professional translators pre-translate faster and spend more time on post-editing. On a different note, Redelinghuys (2016) hypothesised that less experienced translators would show less tendency to use different text registers than more experienced translators, while she in fact found no differences between experienced and inexperienced translators in this matter. She reports high register variation in three different corpora in both groups, regardless of experience. On the other hand, inexperienced translators were more inclined to emphasise logical and semantic relations in informal texts than experienced translators. Longer translation experience was also associated with higher vocabulary range in the translated texts (Redelinghuys, 2016). This shows the translator's long training and upskilling path, whereby general translation might serve as the baseline for future specialisations. At the same time, fully community translation-dedicated curricula can train translators with a clear focus on their future specialisation and maximise opportunities for developing the best quality community translation services. These two views are not mutually exclusive. They rather point attention towards the length and intensity of translator and community translator training. In fact, translation specialisations have increased in recent years, and are becoming, in turn, more and more narrow and demanding in terms of knowledge, skills, and resources. This is due to both increasing market variability with more diverse client needs and to the growing number of technological solutions and translation-assisting tools and processes.

3 Community Translation for Oncological and Palliative Care

Community translation for health care refers to intra- and interlingual translation rendered to ensure written communication within a broad array of services and places where health care occurs, among agents ranging from medical staff through local authorities and programmes to laypeople such as patients and their close ones. Community translation for health care may be understood as the translation of, for example, government health-related communications or hospital instructions for patients. In some settings, community translation for health care is not dissimilar to medical translation, although medical translation does not need to be conducted in community settings and may refer to, for example, translating a professional handbook of medicine. In contrast, community translation for health care gives the members of minorities access to health-related information in their dominant language which often differs from the language of the country in which they live (Taibi, 2011). This information may be personal or addressed at a wider audience, regardless of which community translation contributes to health literacy. By the same token, it plays a role in disease prevention, monitoring, and management, and the development of healthy habits among community members.

3.1 The Specificity of the Patient in Oncological and Palliative Care

Oncological and palliative cancer care differ primarily in their goals: while treatment in oncological care is curative, in palliative cancer care, it is symptomatic. In other words, oncological care aims at the patient's recovery from cancer, while the overarching aim of palliative care is to ensure the proper quality of life and dying, therefore managing physical (e.g., physical pain) and mental (e.g., anxiety) symptoms, and ensuring "good death" (see e.g., Saunders, 1959; Meier et al., 2016). In both oncological and palliative care, the patient's identity shifts. This shift might be subtle in oncological care, whereby patients face the need to adjust their lifestyle and priorities to what their treatment requires. It may be drastic, especially in palliative care, whereby the patient's identity may change from caregiver to care receiver. These shifts are related to family life and/or work, for instance when a breadwinner becomes a dependant, and some revolve around the social aspect of a person's life, for example, when an active member of a community (church, hobby, professional) becomes socially excluded due to the specificity of their disease and treatment. In palliative care, the patient's quality of life becomes shaped by short-term goals such as having a family visit, enjoying music, or – from a different perspective – living without pain.

Both oncological and palliative care cancer patients are considered particularly vulnerable. At the same time, lacking fluency in the main language of communication in a given health care setting adds to this vulnerability. Allophones in oncological and palliative cancer care may be considered "extra vulnerable" (Bischoff et al., 2003; de Moissac & Bowen, 2019) and require specific attention. They should be granted access to health-related information in their mother tongue or any other preferred language.

3.2 Translating Material to be Used in Oncological and Palliative Care

Translation for oncological and palliative cancer care should be governed by a very good knowledge of the specificity of these two types of care (and patients), as well as social, cultural, ethnic, and religious differences between the source and target reader. This refers to health communications, patient educational material (such as instructions after discharge or self-care manuals), promotional material to increase health literacy, guidelines, legal statements, and many others.

Community translation for health care helps to ensure the patient's basic rights. Current guidelines specify that every patient has the right to access health care and have good quality of life, laid down in national legislation, defined by the patient themselves and determined by their dignity, integrity, and autonomy (see e.g., Bahrami et al., 2008). This can be achieved, for example, by giving the patient enough information to give informed consent about treatment and care or by providing access to accurate and well-communicated information about one's health status, prognosis, options, and solutions, which are either ensured or facilitated by translation in the case of allophones or patients less fluent in the target language, respectively.

At this point, it seems vital to point out that in many countries, health communications are published in a selection of languages that are spoken by larger language minorities (e.g., Spanish in the United States). Minorities speaking so-called "rare" languages (e.g., Finnish or Korean in Poland) frequently have the option to use Medical English as Lingua Franca (MEFL). Using MEFL can be useful or even lifesaving in health care. In many cases, MEFL can function as an optimum alternative for the patient's mother tongue, while at the same time, access to communication in one's mother tongue should be promoted. Despite its applicability, Martin (2015) observes that the management of consultation routines can be affected by MEFL due to the language and cultural assumptions that are sometimes associated with it.

3.3 Translating Research Questionnaires in Health Care

As this chapter comments, among other things, on translating research questionnaires, it seems vital to discuss this now. Translating research questionnaires, or any research material in fact, does not guarantee their validity in the target language. Griffee (2001) observes that "validity is context specific and is not an abstract notion that transfers from one instrument to another" (p. 11). In other words, translated research material needs to be re-validated. At the same time, translation itself can pose problems, as it needs to take into account the cultural, social, demographic, etc., context. This is because human reactions to research material are affected by those different contexts. Studies on the interlingual adaptation of research questionnaires are quite numerous, albeit in non-translation studies (which have devoted less attention to this matter, see e.g., Ozolins, 2009; Przepiórkowska, 2016). For example, Kalfoss (2019) embarked on troubleshooting and describing the process of translating the Identity and Experiences Scale from English to Norwegian. She observed that words carrying an emotional load, action words, and lexical items "connected to complex operational concepts", such as "change, behaviour, attitudes, beliefs, goals, life, failures, doubts, and things" (Kalfoss, 2019, p. 9) posed problems in translation. Oliveira and Bandeira (2011) described the translation of a personality disorder assessment tool. More than a half of the items were modified in the translation from English to Brazilian Portuguese to maintain the tool's function. Finally, Bager et al. (2018)

had a quality-of-life questionnaire translated from English into Danish, followed by testing and back translation by different translators. They found that approximately two-thirds of the items in both forward and back translation included dissimilarities between the translated versions. In the pilot testing phase, the authors observed that lexical items related to sensory experiences (e.g., sense of smell), time (e.g., present vs. past), and the English pronoun "you" were challenging in translation and caused some confusion.

4 The Studies

This chapter will comment on two pilot studies we conducted within the Interpreting and Translating for Perinatal and End-of-Life Care project. The overarching aim of the project is to provide a framework for translator and interpreter education. At the same time, one of the specific aims of the project is to investigate the quality of community translation for health care.

4.1 Study 1: Translation Can be Perceived as Potentially Misleading

The aim of this study was to determine whether medical professionals in oncology and palliative care assess the components of the translated text's accuracy and quality, as well as identify and report issues in community translation.

Taking part in the study were 80 oncologists and 30 palliative care specialists (M = 68, F = 42). The average work experience of the participants was 15 years (SD = 4.26 years). They worked in municipality hospitals, regional oncology centres, city hospitals, and palliative care units.

The aim of the study was to investigate the accuracy and quality of texts translated from Polish into English. The texts came from a corpus created within the Interpreting and Translating for Perinatal and End-of-Life Care project. The goal of the corpus is to provide medical translation samples for research purposes. The corpus is currently composed of 96 bilingual sets of texts. There are 76 texts translated from English into Polish and 20 texts translated from Polish into English (both accompanied with originals). The database includes 23 research articles, 10 questionnaires, 26 health care communications, 15 anonymised case descriptions, and 16 expressions of the patient's will in health care. These texts were collected in three different ways: 37 texts are student translations, collected during the students' last semester of translator training; 43 texts are public record; 16 texts were collected from patients and anonymised. All contributors signed an informed consent for the texts to be included in the database.

Twelve samples of professional (i.e., non-student) translations from English into Polish were selected for this study. The samples were matched for the Gunning Fog Index Readability Formula and length. The study sample was composed of four health care guidelines (on how to self-treat a wound, how to keep a healthy diet being a cancer patient, how to manage diabetes mellitus being a cancer patient, and how to manage cancer pain), four questionnaires, four patient's wills and four hospital discharge documents, all related to oncological and palliative care.

These samples were subsequently presented to the participants of the study. Each participant read four samples, in the target text only. The order of reading was counterbalanced across the participants.

Each text was followed by a "debriefing"; that is, a description of the text's aim and the addresser's intentions. To give an example, one of the texts, originally written in English, described wound care and the way a patient should react to alarming symptoms: "Do not feel alarmed when the dressing is bloody but do not hesitate to contact your GP [general practitioner]. Proceed to immediate contact with the ER [emergency room] if the dressing becomes yellowish". This text was translated into Polish and presented to the participants in Polish. At the same time, a debriefing (also in Polish) followed the reading and specified that: a) "a bloody dressing is not alarming"; b) "the patient is nevertheless welcome to contact their GP to make sure there is nothing to worry about"; c) "it's time to be alarmed and go to the ER the minute the dressing becomes yellowish".

Each participant was asked to assess, on a 7-point Likert scale, the degree of:

- Content coherence
- Clarity of message
- Lexical accuracy
- Stylistic accuracy
- Syntactic accuracy
- The degree to which the translated text sounds natural for a specialist in oncological and palliative care
- The degree to which the translated text keeps the addresser's intentions
- The degree to which a text may lead to the misunderstanding of the addresser's intention
- Subjectively perceived text quality

Debriefings were validated by five independent experts. Finally, the participants were free to leave comments in an open-ended question window.

4.1.1 Results of Quantitative Analysis

Figure 6.1 shows medians for lexical, stylistic, and syntactic accuracy, as well as text coherence, in 12 different translations.

Figure 6.2 shows the degree to which the translated text sounds natural for a specialist in oncological and palliative care, the degree to which the translated text keeps the addresser's intentions, the degree to which a text may lead to the misunderstanding of the addresser's intentions, and subjectively perceived text quality.

These data were subsequently subject to statistical analysis to verify which factors shown in Figure 6.1 affect the dependent variables shown in Figure 6.2. The statistical analysis was conducted by means of the IBM SPSS Statistics and R software. The Shapiro–Wilk test served to verify the normality of data distribution. Following data normalisation, a logistic regression was performed to test how subjectively perceived text quality was affected by lexical, stylistic, and syntactic accuracy, text coherence, text type, the degree to which the translated

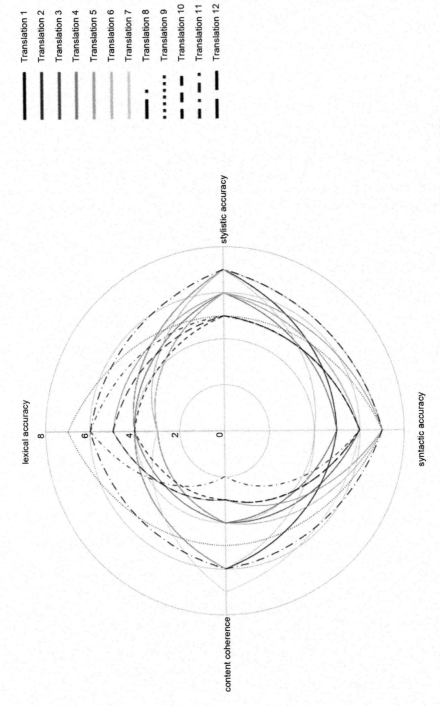

FIGURE 6.1 Medians for lexical, stylistic, and syntactic accuracy, as well as text coherence in 12 different translations

Community Translation for Oncological and Palliative Care **153**

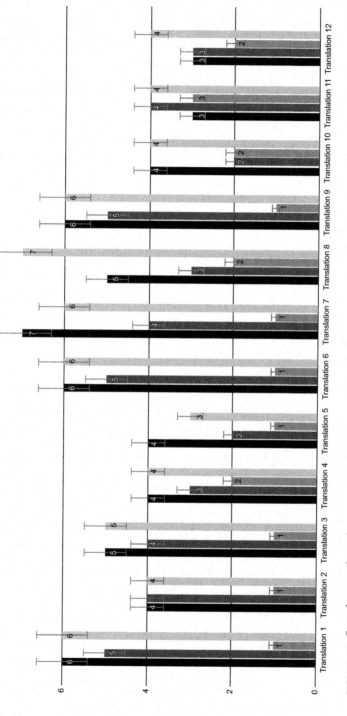

FIGURE 6.2 Sounds natural, retains source text intention, and text quality

text sounds natural for a specialist in oncological and palliative care, and the degree to which the translated text keeps the addresser's intentions. To verify the significance and predictive potential of the studied correlations, a K-fold cross-validation procedure was applied. In addition, a non-parametric Friedman test and Wilcoxon signed-rank test with a Bonferroni correction were conducted for means' differences. Significance was confirmed at p-value < .05.

The logistic regression model was statistically significant, $\chi^2(7) = 29.006$, $p < .05$. The model explained 27.1% (Nagelkerke R2) of the variance in subjectively perceived quality and correctly classified 91.12% of cases. In general, following data normalisation, the effect reached statistical significance in the case of three predictors (see Table 6.1).

4.1.2 Participants' Comments

Sixteen out of 110 participants commented on text characteristics and quality. To give an example, one of the participants commented on a patient's will and the statement of goals for the future, in palliative care. The translation went as follows: "Chciałbym znów być zdrowy i spędzić Święta w domu [I would like to be healthy again and spend Christmas at home]". The mentioned respondent observed that it seems impossible that the patient wanted to be cured while being a palliative care patient. Indeed, the equivalent

TABLE 6.1 Predictors of Subjectively Perceived Quality

	Dependent Variable	Subjectively Perceived Text Quality		
Predictor		B	SE	OR
Content coherence		1.24*	.02	2.16
Clarity of message		.16**	.05	.28
The degree to which the translated text keeps the addresser's intentions		.35*	.01	2.519
Text type	Guidelines	.12**	.05	3.14
	Questionnaire	.42**	.02	5.141
	Patient's will	.51**	.01	5.121
	Discharge documents	.11*	.03	.028

** = p < .001
* = p < .05

sentence in the original document went as follows: "I would like to be better again and spend Christmas at home". In general, three negative comments were made in reference to the patient's will, eight about the translation of guidelines, and five about questionnaires.

The results of Study 1 showed that the translated text coherence, clarity, and accordance with the addresser's intent constitute the key factors affecting subjectively perceived translation quality. This does not indicate that lexical and syntactic accuracy, as well as other target text characteristics should be overlooked in the translation assessment. Instead, the results of Study 1 point to the fact that more attention should be devoted to coherence and clarity, and to training translators and student translators to focus on those aspects of the text that express the addresser's intent and can potentially affect text reception by the target reader. A large number of the translations received relatively poor results when it came to keeping the speaker's intent and sounding natural for a health care practitioner, which points out to those areas of ensuring translation quality that call for improvement in Poland. It seems alarming that five translations were assessed as potentially misleading the reader.

These results also highlight the need to appropriately brief translators about the target readership so that they can better understand how to express the addresser's intent, as that intent directly affects the reader's reaction to the text. In health care, correctly expressed intent can affect patient compliance and medical professionals' responses to the patient's will. In fact, adequate translator briefing is among those elements of the translation process that Taibi (2018) considers essential for translation quality.

At the same time, the results of Study 1 indicate the need to further train community translators in the specificity of oncological and palliative care, with special focus on the latter type of care. The results of the qualitative analysis showed that some translators failed to take the palliative context into consideration, especially when it comes to concepts such as death versus dying, nutritional support prior to death versus nutrition in general, and symptomatic versus causative treatment. This might be due to the fact that in Poland, both community translation in health care and medical translation are unregulated professions. Though courses exist, most translators self-train in a given medical specialisation. This means that expertise is built not in the course of professional training, but rather by gaining hands-on experience, which leaves room for high individual variation in the level of knowledge and competence. In addition, Study 1 points to those text types that may be particularly problematic in community translation for health care. While the text effect was observed in the case of all the texts, it was the strongest in the case of questionnaires and patients' wills, possibly indicating that these types of medical texts could pose problems in translation.

4.2 Study 2: Translation Can Affect Patients' Responses

The second study was based on earlier research conducted by Stachowiak-Szymczak and Stachowiak (2022) on the self-reported degree of patient honesty and disclosure towards different members of medical staff in cancer care. The aim of the original experiment was to investigate the frequency and possible reasons for non-disclosure and misinformation behaviour of patients towards health care professionals in cancer care. The goal was also to identify what type of information is withheld or altered when patients communicate with health care professionals and which health care professionals patients misinform and/or withhold information from. Based on these goals, we formulated the following research questions.

1. Do cancer care patients resort to non-disclosure and/or misinformation when communicating with health care professionals?
2. What type of information is withheld or altered when patients communicate with health care professionals in cancer care?
3. Which health care professionals do patients misinform and/or withhold information from?
4. What factors contribute to – and what are the reasons for – non-disclosure and/or misinformation when patients communicate with health care professionals in cancer care?

We first developed a questionnaire composed of 14 closed and 16 open-ended questions. The questionnaire was split into two parts: one on misinformation, and the other on non-disclosure. Apart from data on age, gender, education, place of living, and type of treatment facility, the questionnaire was designed to ask specifically whether the patient has (ever) misinformed or lied to a medical staff member regarding:

1. The occurrence of symptoms of cancer
2. The duration of symptoms of cancer
3. The process of previous cancer treatment
4. Alternative cancer treatment methods
5. Cancer care-related drug intake
6. Lifestyle and nutritional habits

If yes, the questionnaire asked which medical staff member was lied to and/or misinformed:

1. Leading physician
2. Another physician
3. Anaesthesiologist
4. Nurse
5. Medical rescuer
6. Psychologist
7. Other

These two types of information were collected by means of multiple-choice, closed questions. Every question was followed by an open-ended question asking for the reasons of misinformation or non-disclosure. The questionnaire was validated. Split-half reliability was calculated using the Spearman–Brown formula. Content validity of individual items (I-CVI) and content validity of the overall questionnaire (S-CVI) were calculated based on the ratings of 20 experts.

The results of quantitative and qualitative analyses showed that misinformation and non-disclosure are relatively rare yet present, especially when reporting symptom occurrence and duration to leading physicians. Non-disclosure and/or misinformation were associated with gender (and was more prevalent in females), type of cancer (breast cancer, cervical cancer, and melanoma were contributing factors), and education (people with higher education lied more frequently). This is described and discussed in Stachowiak-Szymczak and Stachowiak (2022).

For the purpose of the present chapter, we conducted a pilot study on the translation of the previously described questionnaire into English. The aim was to test the patients' responses to the translated questionnaire and verify whether the type of translation affects these responses. Although we only report on the translation into MEFL here, the overarching aim of the project is to investigate translations in five different languages: Spanish, German, Vietnamese, Ukrainian, and MEFL.

The translation was carried out by five different translators. Translation was preceded by a briefing which specified the purpose of the translation and the target readership being MEFL users and members of language minorities in Poland. Those translations were subsequently subject to rating, conducted each time by three different experts, based on the EU MQM. Next, three translations with the highest scores were selected and subject to validation. In the validation process, split-half reliability was calculated again using the Spearman–Brown formula. I-CVI and S-CVI were calculated based on the ratings of 20 experts, as they were when we validated the original version.

Next, we presented three validated versions of the questionnaire to 18 patients diagnosed with cancer. The study's sample included 11 females and seven males, aged from 41–65 years. All the patients were native Romani speakers and MEFL users. All the patients were informed about their anonymity and data securing process, and each gave their informed consent. They were also informed that they can resign from the study at any time, without giving a reason for doing so. Subsequently, the patients filled in the questionnaires. The patients were divided into three groups. Each group received a different version of the translation.

4.2.1 Differences in the Translated Texts

Table 6.2 shows the basic characteristics of the original and translated texts. The translated versions of the questionnaire were compared by three judges whose role was to determine the main lexical and structural differences among the translated texts (see Table 6.2).

4.2.2 Patients' Responses

The average age of women who participated in the study was 59.16 (SD = 16.9), while the average age of men was 68.25 (SD = 15.62). Residence types were almost evenly distributed across the study population. Figure 6.3 shows the number of patients in each group of translation readers who reported non-disclosure. Most cases of non-disclosure were reported in reference to the occurrence of new symptom(s) and symptom duration, followed by withholding information on

TABLE 6.2 Differences Among the Translated Texts

Original	Translation 1	Translation 2	Translation 3
Czy kiedykolwiek zataiłeś/-aś informacje dot... [Have you ever withheld information on...]	Have you ever not disclosed information regarding...	Have you ever withheld information regarding...	Have you ever not shared information on...
Czy kiedykolwiek powiedziałeś/-aś nieprawdę na temat... [Have you ever told untruth about...]	Have you ever not told the truth regarding...	Have you ever told untruth regarding...	Have you ever lied about...
leczenia na własną rękę/metodami alternatywnymi? [...self-treatment/alternative treatment methods?]	...self-treatment/using alternative treatment methods?	...self-treatment/using alternative treatment methods?	...using home remedies or alternative treatment methods?
...przyjmowania leków zapisanych przez lekarza prowadzącego? [...taking drugs prescribed by the leading physician?]	...taking the drugs prescribed by the leading physician?	...taking drugs prescribed by your doctor?	...taking drugs your doctor prescribed you?
...nawyków żywieniowych i stylu życia? [...nutritional habits and lifestyle?]	...nutritional habits and lifestyle?	...your eating habits and lifestyle?	...your lifestyle and nutritional habits?

lifestyle. The target readers of Translation 3 reported non-disclosure more frequently than other target readers (which is however unsupported by statistical analysis) when it comes to treatment with alternative/home methods.

Figure 6.4 shows the number of patients in each group of translation readers who reported misinformation. Relatively few patients reported misinformation, with only a few admitting misinformation related to symptom duration. The target readers of Translation 3 reported misinformation more frequently than other target readers (which is, however, unsupported by statistical analysis) when it comes to treatment with alternative/home methods and lifestyle.

Community Translation for Oncological and Palliative Care 159

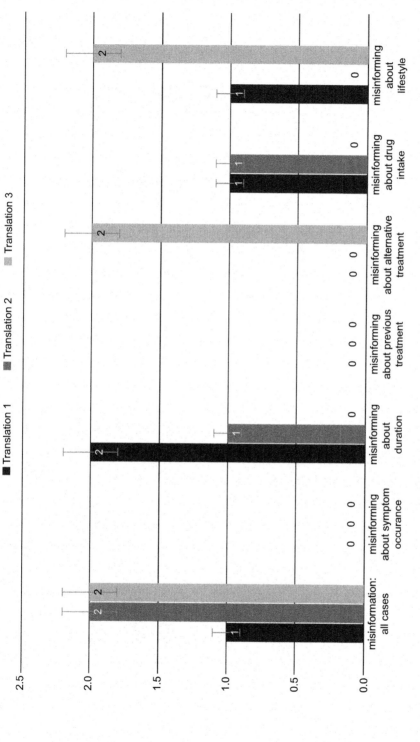

FIGURE 6.3 Non-disclosure in general and depending on the type of information that was not disclosed, in three groups that each received a different translated text

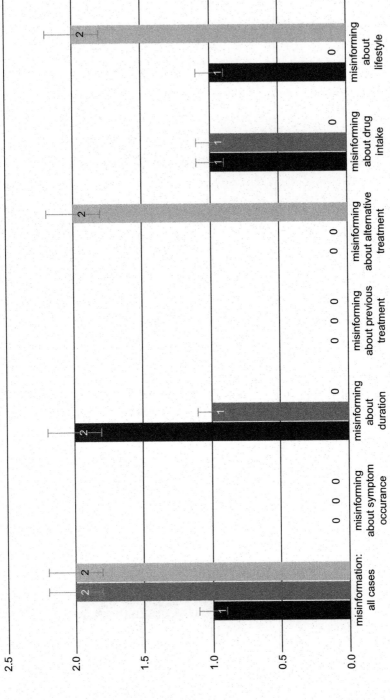

FIGURE 6.4 Misinformation in general, and depending on the type of information that was not disclosed, in three groups that each received a different translated text

Most patients reported non-disclosure towards the main (leading) physician, followed by the nurse and the anaesthesiologist (see Figure 6.5).

Most patients reported misinformation towards the main (leading) physician. Misinforming other physicians, nurses, and anaesthesiologists was less frequent, yet observable (see Figure 6.6).

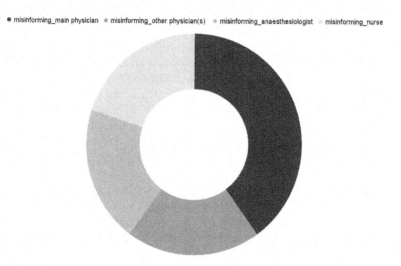

FIGURE 6.5 Non-disclosure depending on the type of information that was not disclosed and type of medical professional

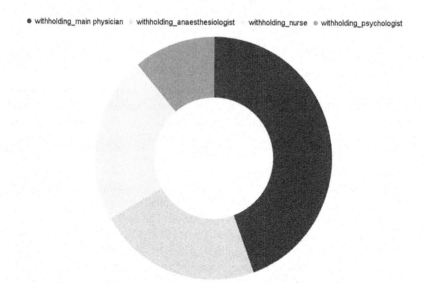

FIGURE 6.6 Misinformation depending on the type of information that was not disclosed and type of medical professional

Due to the small size of the study sample, we did not conduct any statistical analysis in this pilot study.

This study showed that standard re-validation of a translated questionnaire in the target language (see Griffee, 2001) may not be a sufficient measure of translation accuracy.

Study 2 also pointed out the importance of properly briefing the translator on who the target reader is and on the aim of the text. This is because differences in the degree to which the participants reported non-disclosure and/or misinformation depending on translation manifested themselves mainly in those questions which related to lifestyle and alternative treatment methods.

In addition, different approaches to alternative treatment methods and home remedies have been observed in other studies. For instance, Grzywacz et al. (2006) observe that there are substantial ethnic differences in elders' use of home remedies which are not largely attributed to social inequalities. Guido et al. (2020) explain that medicinal cannabis, which has been used as a home remedy for centuries in Latin America, is perceived very differently by other populations where it is either demonised or simply associated with illegal actions. Similar observations were made, for example, by Marssid (2009), albeit in reference to Romani populations, where "home" remedies are frequently used and do not bear the same meaning as "alternative" medicine. For this reason, putting non-official or self-treatment as "home" instead of "alternative" might have accounted for more patients declaring using them when "home" was the word of choice.

In general, Study 2 showed that translators should have extensive knowledge of the sociocultural background of the target readership they translate for. They also should be properly briefed for translation, to ensure they can apply a reader-oriented approach to their work.

5 General Comments

This chapter showed that current measures used to ensure the quality of translation in oncological and palliative care in Poland are not satisfactory. It also illustrated both the need to enhance these measures and the need to further train community translators in the narrow field of translating for oncological and palliative care. The results of the studies presented here indicate the following:

1   Translated target texts need to be evaluated based on criteria that take into account both the health care context and the sociocultural context. In fact, attempts to find parameters of adequate translation and its assessment for health care have been made. For instance, Lin and Ji (2019) propose a patient-oriented and culturally appropriate (POCA) model to evaluate translation in health care, on the example of English-to-Chinese translation. In a study on diabetic patients, they observed that the use of certain linguistic features, such as the imperative or commanding expressions in the target text, discourage patients from reading. Similarly, Teng (2019) discusses the contextual values in health translation whose presence determines func-

tional equivalence. Both of these types of criteria should be used to ensure that target texts are adequate for a given readership in oncological and palliative care.

2   Translator recruitment should be based on criteria that take into account their specialisation and/or expertise in oncological and palliative care. Community translation for health care is frequently outsourced by health care facilities, local authorities, and other institutions to third parties following a public procurement. Recently, attempts have been made to include expertise criteria in the procurement process, albeit in conference interpreting. Namely, the Polish Association of Conference Interpreters (PSTK) has been advocating in favour of greater focus on the evaluation of interpreter expertise (as opposed to cost, for example) in the procurement process (PSTK, n.d.). The PSTK also launched an educational campaign for clients, teaching how to verify that interpreters who are listed in the bidding process are in fact given the assignment. Similar attempts should be made in the field of health care translation, and more specifically, translation for oncological and palliative care.

3   There is still a strong need to train, test, and certify translators in health care translation, and even more specifically, in translation for oncological and palliative care. The results of both studies showed that translated texts are not satisfactory in terms of keeping the speaker's intent (which was then associated with the generally perceived translation quality). While Polish universities usually have health care translation courses in their curricula, there are no full specialisations offered in health care or oncological care. In addition, most of these courses last one or two semesters, touching upon a spectrum of medical specialisations. At the same time, the development of translation specialisations should go along with the development of the medical ones.

4   When it comes to teaching, there is an ongoing need to train students in how to analyse the source text, along with the text's cultural and social aspect(s). In reference to those aspects, Mekheimer and Al-Dosari (2012) point out the importance of training-based or culturally laden texts in community translation. On a similar note, albeit in reference to the emotional aspect of translation, Hubscher-Davidson (2013) discusses the use and development of emotional intelligence in translation, suggesting that there is a strong need to continue research on emotional intelligence in translators and interpreters. This shows that there is still a strong need to focus on those aspects of translation that go beyond lexical and grammatical accuracy.

5   Briefing should constitute an inseparable part of the translation assignment process in community translation. To ensure good quality translation for oncological and palliative care, a translation brief should contain a set of instructions clarifying a concrete medical specialisation, translation purpose and the target audience, defined in terms of their level of health literacy (see e.g., Crezee, 2015), ethnicity, sociocultural background, etc. to ensure the successful rendition of the source text into a given language.

References

Askari, M., & Rahim, M. S. (2015). Evaluation of House's model of quality assessment. *Journal of Social Science Research*, 7(3), 1420–1428.

Bager, L., Elsbernd, A., Nissen, A., Daugaard, G., & Pappot, H. (2018). Danish translation and pilot testing of the European Organization for Research and Treatment of Cancer QLQ-TC 26 (EORTC QLQ-TC26) questionnaire to assess health-related quality of life in patients with testicular cancer. *Health and Quality of Life Outcomes*, 16, Article 128, 1–6. https://doi.org/10.1186/s12955-018-0954-3

Bahrami, M., Parker, S., & Blackman, I. (2008). Patients' quality of life: A comparison of patient and nurse perceptions. *Contemporary Nurse*, 29(1), 67–79. https://doi.org/10.5172/conu.673.29.1.67

Bischoff, A., Perneger, T. V., Bovier, P. A., Loutan, L., & Stalder, H. (2003). Improving communication between physicians and patients who speak a foreign language. *The British Journal of General Practice*, 53(492), 541–546.

California Department of Education. (2006). *Quality indicators for translation and interpretation in kindergarten through grade twelve educational settings: Guidelines and resources for educators.* www.seq.org/documents/Programs/English%20Learners/Translations%20and%20Interpretations/CA%20Dept.%20of%20Ed.%20Quality%20Indicators%20for%20Translation%20and%20Interpretation.pdf

Carl, M., & Buch-Kromann, M. (2010). *Correlating translation product and translation process: Data of professional and student translators* [Paper presentation]. Proceedings of the 14th Annual Conference of the European Association for Machine Translation, EAMT, Saint-Raphaël, France. https://aclanthology.org/2010.eamt-1.14.pdf

Crezee, I. (2015). Introduction to healthcare for interpreters and translators. *The International Journal of Translation and Interpreting Research*, 7(2), 98–100.

de Moissac, D., & Bowen, S. (2019). Impact of language barriers on quality of care and patient safety for official language minority francophones in Canada. *Journal of Patient Experience*, 6(1), 24–32.

Gouadec, D. (2007). *Translation as a profession.* John Benjamins Publishing Company.

Griffee, D. T. (2001, January). Bare bones validation: A guide for teacher consumers of questionnaire research. *Applied Linguistics Forum: Official Newsletter of the TESOL Applied Linguistics Interest Section.*

Grzywacz, J. G., Arcury, T. A., Bell, R. A., Lang, W., Suerken, C. K., Smith, S. L., & Quandt, S. A. (2006). Ethnic differences in elders' home remedy use: Sociostructural explanations. *American Journal of Health Behavior*, 30(1), 39–50. https://doi.org/10.5555/ajhb.2006.30.1.39

Guido, P., Riva, N., Calle, G., Dell'Orso, M., Gatto, M., Sberna, N., & Schaiquevich, P. (2020). Medicinal cannabis in Latin America: History, current state of regulation, and the role of the pharmacist in a new clinical experience with cannabidiol oil. *Journal of the American Pharmacists Association*, 60(1), 212–215. https://doi.org/10.1016/j.japh.2019.09.012

House, J. (1997). *Translation quality assessment: A model revisited.* Gunter Narr.

House, J. (2001). Translation quality assessment: Linguistic description versus social evaluation. *Meta*, 46(2), 243–257. https://doi.org/10.7202/003141ar

House, J. (2009). *Translation.* Oxford University Press.

House, J. (2013). Quality in translation studies. In C. Millan, F. Bartrina, *The Routledge handbook of translation studies* (pp. 534–547). Routledge.

Hubscher-Davidson, S. (2013). Emotional intelligence and translation studies: A new bridge. *Meta*, 58(2), 324–346. https://doi.org/10.7202/1024177ar

Kalfoss, M. (2019). Translation and adaption of questionnaires: A nursing challenge. *SAGE Open Nursing*, 5, 1–13. https://doi.org/10.1177/2377960818816810

Koby, G. S., Fields, P., Hague, D., Lommel, A., & Melby, A. (2014). Defining translation quality. *Revista Tradumàtica: Tecnologies de la Traducció*, 12, 413–420.

Lin, S., & Ji, M. (2019). Assessing linguistic comprehensibility of healthcare translation using the POCA model. In M. Ji, M. Taibi, & I. H. M. Crezee (Eds.), *Multicultural health translation, interpreting and communication* (pp. 69–84). Routledge.

Marssid, N. (2009). *Cultural beliefs and health behaviours of Roma patients in Finland.* [Unpublished bachelor's thesis]. Pirkanmaa University of Applied Sciences. https://core.ac.uk/download/pdf/37988929.pdf

Martin, G. S. (2015). "Sorry can you speak it in English with me?" Managing routines in lingua franca doctor – patient consultations in a diabetes clinic. *Multilingua*, 34(1), 1–32. https://doi.org/10.1515/multi-2013-0053

Meier, E. A., Gallegos, J. V., Montross-Thomas, L. P, Depp, C. A., Irwin, S. A., & Jeste, D. V. (2016). Defining a good death (successful dying): Literature review and a call for research and public dialogue. *American Journal of Geriatric Psychiatry*, 24(4), 261–271. https://doi.org/10.1016/j.jagp.2016.01.135

Mekheimer, M. A., & Al-Dosari, H. (2012). Use of culture-laden texts to enhance culture-specific translation skills from English into Arabic. *Arab World English Journal*, 3(1), 128–146.

Multicultural Health Communication Service. (2014). Guidelines for the production of multilingual resources. *NSW Government*. www.mhcs.health.nsw.gov.au/about-us/services/translation/pdf/updateguidelines.pdf

National Accreditation Authority for Translators and Interpreters. (n.d.). *Certification tests.* www.naati.com.au/become-certified/certification/

Niska, H. (2002). Community interpreter training: Past, present, future. In G. Garzone & M. Viezzi (Eds.), *Interpreting in the 21st century: Challenges and opportunities. Selected papers from the 1st Forlì conference on interpreting studies, 9–11 November 2000* (pp. 133–144). John Benjamins Publishing Company.

Nord, C. (1997). *Translating as a purposeful activity: Functionalist approaches explained.* St. Jerome.

O'Hagan, M. (2011). Community translation: Translation as a social activity and its possible consequences in the advent of Web 2.0 and beyond. *Linguistica Antverpiensia*, 10, 11–23.

Oliveira, S. E. S., & Bandeira, D. R. (2011). Linguistic and cultural adaptation of the Inventory of Personality Organization (IPO) for the Brazilian culture. *Journal of Depression and Anxiety*, 1(1), 1–9.

Ozolins, U. (2009). Back translation as a means of giving translators a voice. *The International Journal for Translation & Interpreting Research*, 1(2), 1–13.

Polish Association of Conference Interpreters (PSTK). (n.d.). *About.* https://pstk.org.pl/o-nas/

Przepiórkowska, D. (2016). Translation of questionnaires in cross-national social surveys: A niche with its own theoretical framework and methodology. *Między Oryginałem a Przekładem*, 31, 121–135.

Redelinghuys, K. (2016). Levelling-out and register variation in the translations of experienced and inexperienced translators: A corpus-based study. *Stellenbosch Papers in Linguistics Plus*, 45, 189–220.

Reiss, K., & Vermeer, H. J. (2014). *Towards a general theory of translational action: Skopos theory explained* (C. Nord, Trans.). Routledge (Original work published 1984).

Rothe-Neves, R. (2007). Notes on the concept of "translator's competence". *Quaderns: Revista de Traducció, 14*, 125–138.

Stachowiak-Szymczak, K., & Stachowiak, K. (2022). *Patients in oncological care resort to misinformation and nondisclosure* [Manuscript submitted for publication].

Taibi, M. (2011). Public service translation. In K. Malmkjær & K. Windle (Eds.), *The Oxford handbook of translation studies* (pp. 214–227). Oxford University Press. https://doi-org.ezproxy.lib.rmit.edu.au/10.1093/oxfordhb/9780199239306.001.0001

Taibi, M. (Ed.). (2018). *Translating for the community*. Multilingual Matters. https://doi.org/10.21832/TAIBI9139

Taibi, M., & Ozolins, U. (2016). *Community translation*. Bloomsbury Academic.

Taibi, M., & Ozolins, U. (2022). *Quality and integrity in the translation of official documents: Perspectives*. https://doi.org/10.1080/0907676X.2022.2053176

Teng, W. (2019). When pragmatic equivalence fails: Assessing a New Zealand English to Chinese health translation from a functional perspective. In M. Ji, M. Taibi, & I. H. M. Crezee (Eds.), *Multicultural health translation, interpreting and communication* (pp. 85–122). Routledge. https://doi.org/10.4324/9781351000390

Yamamoto, K. (2011). Quality assessment of community translation in Japanese context: Functionalist approaches. *Journal of Language and Culture, 30*(1), 99–122.

7
CHALLENGES AND CONSTRAINTS IN THE TRANSLATION OF WIRETAPPING IN SPAIN

Mohamed El-Madkouri Maataoui and Beatriz Soto Aranda

1 Legal Framework for the Translation of Wiretaps in Spain

We consider the translation of wiretaps a form of community translation, as legal interpreting (including court and police) is viewed as a form of community interpreting. This translation specialisation would fall within public service interpreting and translation (PSIT), which is how community interpreting and translation are labelled in Spain. Although the end users of these translations are not the community per se, the translation of this type of material involves the community in the role of victims or criminals. The translation of wiretap materials has the ultimate aim of bringing criminals to justice in order to protect the community and to enable the fair administration of justice.

One of the responsibilities legally conferred to the Spanish state security forces is to monitor in real time anything that could threaten public security and be prepared to identify any action that may be classified as criminal or, more generally, that appears to be contrary to laws and regulations. Therefore, as telephone communications are a means widely used by people for the transfer and exchange of information, wiretapping is used in criminal investigations.

Judicial control is a priori guaranteed over wiretapping in Spain as criminal investigation police must obtain judicial authorisation to carry out telephone follow-ups of citizens or residents and renew such approval monthly if the criminal investigation lasts longer (Ron Romero, 2011). In addition, the agents involved in monitoring and acquiring information must always be meticulous and rigorous when gathering, arranging, and presenting evidence.

The judicial system, as guarantor of citizen justice and fairness for all those living on Spanish territory, ensures that all actions of the judicial police follow the law, in line with the preamble of Act 36/2015, of 28 September, which understands security as:

> The action of the State aimed at protecting the freedom and well-being of its citizens, guaranteeing the defence of Spain and its constitutional principles

DOI: 10.4324/9781003247333-8

and values, as well as contributing together with our partners and allies to international security in the fulfilment of the commitments undertaken.
(Jefatura del Estado, 2015a)

Furthermore, it should be noted that the Spanish Constitution expressly recognises the fundamental right to secrecy of communications (Art. 183.3; Cortes Generales, 1978), and therefore, the rule of law must protect it.

However, neither wiretapping nor the transcription and translation of recordings were adequately regulated in the Spanish legal system until 2015. Due to this poor situation, the European Court of Human Rights warned the Spanish government that there were no adequate legal guarantees for the authorisation of wiretapping in the criminal jurisdiction. The Constitutional Court applied this doctrine in ruling 49/1999 (Tribunal Constitucional de España, 1999) of 5 April when reviewing the conviction of defendants accused of drug smuggling. The Constitutional Court acquitted them on the grounds that there had been insufficient judicial control over the recording, transcription, translation, and selection of the conversations used as evidence against them, and therefore the fundamental right to the confidentiality of communications had also been violated.

In 2015, Spain adopted the Organic Act 13/2015 of 5 April (hereinafter LECrim; Jefatura del Estado, 2015b) amending both the Criminal Procedure Act (Ministerio de Gracia y Justicia, 1882) and Organic Law 6/1985 of 1 July 1985 (Jefatura del Estado, 1985). Under this Act, two European directives were introduced into Spanish law:

1 Directive 2010/64/EU on the right to interpretation and translation in criminal proceedings, with the aim of "seeking to facilitate its implementation in practice, ensuring free and adequate language assistance, enabling the right to defence and safeguarding the fairness of the judicial process". It also provides for the possibility of appealing against the judgement if the translation and interpretation service has not been performed with due guarantees and quality.
2 Directive 2012/13/EU, of 22 May, on the right to information in criminal proceedings of suspects or accused persons, relating to their rights in criminal proceedings and to the accusation against them.

Thus, in the context of criminal proceedings, the quality of legal translation and court interpreting is a crucial issue due to the exercise of the rights to information, hearing, defence, and contestation, to the extent that the judge's decision depends on these. Hence, "the absence of proper interpretation, or an inaccurate interpretation, already since the beginning of the investigation of the procedure may contaminate judicial procedure and does not adequately protect the accused" (de Hoyos Sancho, 2017, p. 15). This conception of court interpreting as a guarantor of equality and fairness in access to a fair trial is based on various international standards (Stern, 2011), including the UN International Covenant on Civil and Political Rights (United Nations, 1966), and the European Convention for the Protection of Human Rights and Fundamental Freedoms (European Court of Human Rights, 1950), to which the EU acceded in Article 6 (2) of the Treaty of

Lisbon (European Union, 2007). Generally, the translation of wiretaps follows the same regulations as court interpreting.

According to Circular 2/2019 (Ministerio Fiscal, 2019), of March 6, of the General State Attorney, on Interception of Telephone and Telematic Communications, wiretapping has a dual nature in criminal proceedings: (1) as a source of investigation of offences by police; (2) as a proof of charge. The authorisation to carry out wiretaps can only be granted in the following cases: (1) intentional crimes punishable by a maximum limit of at least three years in prison; (2) crimes committed by a criminal group or organisation; (3) crimes of terrorism, always observing the weighting criteria of the seriousness of the case, its social significance, the intensity of the existing evidence, and the likelihood of the result proportionate to the restriction of the suspect's right.

The police must deliver a complete copy of the recordings to the judge, ensuring their security. However, the police are not required to present a transcription and full translation of all the recordings, but only those parts that the police consider relevant to the investigation or an incriminating summary, as established in the Supreme Court ruling 307/2016, of 13 April (Tribunal Supremo, Sala de lo Penal, Sección 1, 2016), regarding the accurate translation and interpretation of wiretaps in Igbo (from southeastern Nigeria) into Spanish, related to a crime against public health.

The transcriptions of the recording in the original language, which are subsequently translated, are not available at any time. If the judge considers the translation as proof of charge against the defendant, the judge will request that the translator confirm the translation proposed in the courtroom by the police and may request a review of the translation by another translator. The reviewing translator is usually recruited through a temporary agency, as both the judicial and police translation services have, since 2008, been outsourced, and the positions of official in-house translators are limited.

In a trial, both the defence and the prosecution have the right to listen to the recordings. If there is a disagreement with the translation, they can propose that a new translation be made by an expert – normally a sworn translator – or, if they consider it appropriate, they can request the court to listen to the problematic fragments again and, if necessary, to translate them (El-Madkouri Maataoui, 2019; Ortega Herráez & Hernández Cebrián, 2019).

In 2020, the Spanish government approved the Regulation of the Language Interpretation Office of the Ministry of Foreign Affairs, European Union, and Cooperation 2020 by Royal Decree 724/2020, of 4 August. This decree-law entails, on the one hand, the creation of the two distinct titles of sworn translator and sworn interpreter, abolishing the current title of a sworn translator/interpreter; and, on the other hand, the creation of an Official Registry of Translators and Interpreters acting in court proceedings, and thus qualified to translate wiretaps. Although provision was made in the LECrim for the Registry, it has not yet been created.

Despite its achievements, LECrim has several shortcomings. For example, Art. 124 of the Criminal Procedure Act (1882) states that:

> The court translator or interpreter will be appointed from amongst those included on the lists drawn up by the competent Administration. Exceptionally,

in such cases as require the urgent presence of a translator or interpreter and it not possible for a court translator or interpreter to appear who is registered on the lists drawn up by the Administration, as appropriate, in accordance with the provisions of paragraph 5 of the previous article, another person who is familiar with the language used who is deemed to have the capacity to perform such a task may be used as the eventual interpreter or translator.

(Ministerio de Gracia y Justicia, 1882)

In turn, Art. 441 of the LECrim states that the interpreter will be chosen from "amongst those qualified as such if there are any in the town. In default, a teacher of the relevant language will be appointed and, if there is none, any person with knowledge of it".

In addition to this general legal framework, the work of wiretap translators is governed by the terms of the contracts set by the Police Wiretap Transcription and Translation Service, which has been outsourced to private companies since 2008. The Service has been criticised for its lack of quality and the lack of qualification and training of some of its translators, as several news reports in recent years have pointed out: "A company sends translators with criminal records to the national police force" (Fernández, 2008), or "Translation in court, between intrusiveness and job insecurity" (EFE, 2017). In 2017, two years after the approval of the LECrim, the newspaper Economía Digital reported that:

Judicial and police translations have recently been controversial in Spain. SeproTec, the largest low-cost translation company, hired translators without checking their knowledge in the language that they claimed to command . . . in an investigation that demonstrated the limited skills of translators hired by that company, a Digital Economy journalist was accepted as an Arabic translator without speaking a word of that language.

(Placer, 2017)

This company had even assigned the journalist to interpret in the trial for minor offences 105/2016 in the court of instruction number 5 of Plaza de Castilla, in Madrid (Placer, 2016).

These events prompted the Spanish Professional Association of Court and Sworn Interpreters and Translators to lodge a complaint, on 9 September 2016, about the standard of translation and interpreting services in courts and police stations (Asociación Profesional de Traductores e Intérpretes Judiciales y Jurados [APTIJ], 2016). Currently, these services are, for the most part, outsourced. The lack of control by the administration, together with the precarious employment of the translators and interpreters who provide services to these companies, has meant that many do not have the necessary qualifications to perform their duties and has even allowed people with criminal records to carry out these tasks. This lack of qualifications threatens victims' access to justice and undermines defendants' rights of defence, translation, and interpretation, thus violating the right to a fair trial (APTIJ, 2016).

This reality has led to a gradual change in the technical specifications of the last tenders for translation and interpretation from the Ministry of the Interior (Ministerio del Interior, 2020). While the 2019 tender documents stated that the contractor shall provide initial theoretical and practical training to workers, relating to the functioning of the Administration of Justice, the judicial language and the textual typology of the judicial system (Ministerio del Interior, 2019), those of 2020 included new information stating that the contractor, on behalf of all persons providing these services under its direction, undertakes to reproduce faithfully and in full the content of the oral statements to be interpreted, and that the interlocutor shall, in particular, ensure that the personnel appearing in the relationship are the person actually providing the services in the judicial organs (Ministerio del Interior, 2020).

In 2020, the public procurement tender included the implementation of two training programmes worth 30 points out of a total of 100 for the award of the contract. The courses were to have a minimum duration of 20 hours, and their subject matter would be: (1) translation as evidence in criminal proceedings (20 points); (2) trafficking in human beings (10 points) (Ministerio del Interior, 2020, p. 7). According to the information offered by interpreters who have attended the course, the temporary agency that won the tender only gave two manuals to the participants and a multiple-choice test that they could answer at home. The manual on court interpreting only provided general information on the organisation of the judicial system, but did not say anything about interpreting techniques, professional ethics, or how to deal with stressful situations caused by the content of the recordings, which is usually related to issues such as drug trafficking, human trafficking, money laundering, working conditions, sexual crimes, terrorism, and advocacy of terrorism, among others.

2 Academic and Professional Experience Requirements for Working as a Wiretap Translator

In Spain, the academic and professional experience requirements to work as a court interpreter or wiretap translator vary according to the working language (see Table 7.1).

It is important to note that, as indicated in the technical procurement documents, for languages B and C, the administration may carry out a knowledge test in place of the corresponding C1 and C2 accreditations to accredit the competence level of the person designated to carry out work at this professional level (Ministerio del Interior. Dirección General de la Policía, 2020). Therefore, in practice, any person with a certain degree of proficiency in languages included in categories B or C and Spanish can be recruited to translate wiretaps under the "service needs" excuse (Blasco Mayor, 2020). The case of Arabic, the language for which the Ministry of the Interior tendered the most translator positions, is striking because in the contracting offer for court interpreting services, it is included in Group A, while in the wiretapping translation service, Arabic appears in Group C.

To be an Arabic–Spanish court interpreter, applicants are required to have a bachelor degree in translation and interpreting, a postgraduate degree in translation and interpreting, be a sworn translator, or in the case of another degree, have

TABLE 7.1 Ministry of the Interior Wiretaps Translators.

Classification of Languages in Outsourced Translation Services in the Ministry of the Interior	Academic and Experience Requirements
A. English, French, and German	• Bachelor in translation and interpreting or a bachelor degree in any other speciality, or a sworn translator–interpreter qualification. At least one year's professional experience for graduates in translation and interpreting, for graduates in another field with a postgraduate degree in translation and interpreting, and for sworn translators. • Minimum professional experience of two years for graduates in a different speciality who do not have a postgraduate degree in translation and/or interpreting.
B. Chinese, Japanese, Russian, Portuguese, Italian, Polish, and Dutch	• The requirements indicated for **A.**, or failing that, academic certification of level C2 (Common European Framework of Reference – CEFR) in the working languages. • At least one year's professional experience for graduates in translation and interpreting, for graduates in another field with a postgraduate degree in translation and interpreting, and for sworn translators. • A minimum of two years' professional experience for bachelors in any other field who do not have a postgraduate degree in interpreting and/or translation, and for those who hold an academic certificate attesting to level C2.
C. Arabic dialects, other languages, and dialects	• The requirements indicated for **A.**, or failing that, academic certification of level C1 (CEFR) in the working languages. • A minimum of two years' professional experience for bachelors in any other field who do not have a postgraduate degree in interpreting and/or translation, and for those who hold an academic certificate attesting to level C1. • At least one year's professional experience for all other cases.

two years of experience (Soto Aranda & Allouchi, 2021). However, in the case of wiretap translators of Arabic, many of them face the task of translating highly sensitive matters with judicial repercussions without any academic training, not even a bachelor degree. The different academic requirements for the two roles could be explained by the fact that court interpreting involves written documents that require training in Modern Standard Arabic, while wiretap translators work mostly with spoken dialects. However, not only do both court interpreters and wiretap translators need bilingual proficiency in Modern Standard Arabic and dialects, but they also need to recognise when code-switching occurs with other languages used in the suspect's cultural context of origin, such as Tamazight, Urdu, Kurdish, or Ethiopian – and even French or Dutch, among other languages. Furthermore, together with the differences between Arabic dialects and their sociocultural and register implications, wiretap translators must be capable of dealing with challenges such as identifying criminal jargon, differentiating between the literal meaning of an expression and its pragmatic meaning in each context, the treatment of cultural and religious references, or the evaluation of discursive silences – challenges which are difficult to address without proper training.

In the Arabic–Spanish combination, there are two well-known cases in which the translation of wiretap recordings was shown to condition the judicial rulings. In the first case, the al-Jazeera correspondent Taysir Aloni was accused of belonging to al-Qaeda after securing the first and only interview with Osama bin Laden. According to Taibi and Martin (2012), the translation mistakes found in the wiretap translations were possibly due to "(i) dialectal differences between the translators and the defendants, (ii) their approach to translation as a word-for-word transfer, or (iii) instructions by their police officer employers to adopt a specific translation approach" (p. 78). Taibi and Martin (2012) argue that "in any case, a more professional approach would undoubtedly have guaranteed higher quality translations, presumably less susceptible to manipulation" (p. 78).

The second case was the first trial of an al-Qaeda–inspired attack on European soil. The proceedings took place between 15 March 2007 and 2 July 2007. One of the most striking issues in this trial was the challenge of the quality of the translations used by the Italian authorities to indict Rabei Osman el Sayed. The translations were reviewed by interpreters who were engaged as expert witnesses in the trials held in Spain. The expert advice led to the release of the accused. Martin and Ortega Herráez (2013) point out that one of the problems was the verbatim translation of telephone conversations, in which there were historical references to Islam, without considering the context in which the defendant pronounced them or their pragmatic implications. By not understanding the reference to the Califa al-Mu'tasim (10th century), used as an example to criticise current politicians, translators interpreted this as a reference to current women martyrs. Another issue was the translation of the word "jihad" as "Holy War", while the interpreters at the trial, acting as court experts, considered that the correct thing to do was to transliterate the word jihad, as it is a known word in the target context, and leave it to the readers to decide. Valero-Garcés and Abkari (2010) observe that the errors occurred due to the Italian translators' lack of knowledge of the Qur'an and of classical Arabic and its cultural references.

These cases illustrate that without adequate specialised training, translators are more likely to make mistakes that invalidate police investigations.

3   Challenges and Constraints in Improving Professionalism of Wiretapping Translators

Considering the aforementioned legal issues and training requirements, wiretap translators face a number of challenges in their work. First, the work of translators for security forces – as well as for interpreters in court settings – is not autonomous and independent, and ensuring quality does not solely depend on their translating skills and their command of the subject or the material translated and interpreted. On the contrary, the guarantee of quality depends on negotiating with the agents involved in the process who supervise this work: the police officers and the court personnel. In the offices of the security forces, the police officer is officially the captain of the keyboard and computer. Therefore, it falls to the translator to develop skills beyond their expertise in particular domains to create a climate of empathy, cordiality, and trust with the officer. The goal of these efforts is to guarantee a translation free of orthographic, stylistic, or content errors. Despite this, the quality of translation is – in legal terms – a matter pertaining to the translator alone. The translator is the one who is accountable for it in front of the judge and who deals with possible criticism that could arise during the judicial process. Therefore, rather than equivalence between isolated words, terms, and expressions, an effort is made to negotiate correspondence between the translation and its original at the textual level (Scott, 2019, p. 32).

In Spain, there is no official translator code of ethics as there are in other countries (Kalina, 2015), nor any professional college for translators and interpreters. Furthermore, the concept of legal equivalence is not reflected upon; instead, it is customary for the judge to request a verbatim translation (Ortega Herráez, 2006). Therefore, language is usually considered as static and not influenced by the context, ambiguity, or polysemy (Vigier Moreno, 2017). This view makes the work of wiretap translators more difficult, as the utterances of intercepted discourse say one thing (locutionary act), but usually have a different meaning (illocutionary act) which is not easily detectable in the words that make up their statement. The following example illustrates this point. In a criminal investigation, one of the authors of this chapter – in his capacity as a sworn translator and linguistic expert – was asked by the police to translate the recordings of the tracking of a criminal gang. In the recording, the following could be heard in Moroccan Arabic "quedamos donde el pan, al lado de la guitarra" [let's meet at the bread, beside the guitar]. In Spain, we are used to bread in a baguette form, while, in many other countries, bread is usually round. The term *pan* (bread) referred, in fact, to a *plaza* while *guitarra* (guitar) referred to the logo of a wine brand, still found in some places. The cultural competence on the part of the translator allowed the police to locate where the drug delivery would take place. In this context, it is a complicated task to distinguish between a semantically innocuous segment and another segment loaded with symbolism, semantic switching, and referents. Only the context – in its discursive, environmental, and physical dimensions – along with the help of the police agent, can overcome the issue of determining what is meant in the intercepted communication.

Nevertheless, it is very common to hear a judge ask a translator to make a translation as literal as possible. The judge is interested in knowing exactly what has been said and in what terms. Verbatim translations present a problem when translating expressions such as insults that can have different meanings depending on the tone in which they are said, and different semiotic, pragmatic, or emotional values in two different contexts. One of the references that cause most problems for translators is the expression "hijo de puta" [son of a bitch]. In Spanish culture, one can even say "Qué hijo de puta eres" [what a son of a bitch you are] with a type of affection. However, in other cultures, a person may react with aggression when hearing it. Therefore, it is paramount that translators have a certain knowledge of non-verbal communication that allows them to distinguish the voices heard and be aware of the importance of the tone of the speakers, since when working as wiretap translators they do not have access to the speaker's gestures. This skill is fundamental to determine whether the sentence in question should be translated verbatim or, on the contrary, if a set of implicatures should be presumed, which could only be disambiguated and correctly interpreted with adequate sociocultural competence. Thus, if there is one area in translation and interpreting that requires an in-depth knowledge of applied linguistics and a capacity for meta-discourse, it is the area of wiretap translation. Coding and discourse understanding allow for the capture of extra-conventional meaning, and the pragmatic implications of the discourse(s) of wiretapping. In this regard, for example, Salaets and Balogh (2018) have proposed a new term, "Forensic-Linguistic Tap Expert" or "FoLiTex", to bring together the knowledge and tasks performed by a specialist in this field.

Nevertheless, not all linguistic constructions mean something different from what is being said. In fact, due to stressful working conditions, insufficient time to review recordings, and pressure from police officers for evidence, translators can make errors of over-interpreting. At other times, the translator has difficulty understanding what the recording says, either because the quality of the recording is not optimal or because there is a lot of noise that interferes with the correct hearing of the speech. What is important in these cases is that, on the one hand, Spanish law allows the defence to request a new translation, and, on the other hand, the translator must ratify his or her translation before the judge. Ruling 000047/2021 of the Provincial Court of Huesca is an example of this:

> We must clarify that the name "Carmelo" which appears in the first transcripts of the Guardia Civil was not said by the defendants in the hearings heard at the trial and must have been a translation error on the part of the interpreter [***], who at the trial only heard a similar expression in Romanian, ending with an "el" (something like "be careful with him").

It should be considered that working on such sensitive subjects can often affect both the translator's understanding of what is heard in the recordings and the translator's own health. First, it is recommended that more experienced translators review the translations or that, in case of doubt, a translator consults other colleagues before deciding on the correct translation of a conversational fragment. In a case that occurred when translating terrorism-related eavesdropping, at one point in the recording, a person who was suspected to be a terrorist mentioned that they were going to Soria (a city in the north of Spain). The interpreter deduced that it was Syria, considering that the suspect had mispronounced the name of the place. As a result, the interpreter resorted to the technique of amplification, adding terms such as "die" and "martyrdom" that did not appear in the original recording.

Second, as in other areas of translation and interpreting in the public service, translators work under immense pressure, frequently working long hours against the clock (particularly when an investigation is being closed), in environments with little space and light. They deal with traumatic issues such as drug trafficking, human trafficking, smuggling, sexual crimes, terrorism, glorification of terrorist acts, among other issues (Lai & Costello, 2020; Lai & Heydon, 2015). In some cases, interpreters and translators cannot help but empathise with the victims and take on their pain. Translators sometimes also share the same ethnic or religious background as suspects, which can affect them psychologically and lead them to question their beliefs or take a stand for or against the accused before they have been charged and tried. We would suggest that wiretap translators work in pairs so that they can have mutual support and can provide feedback to each other. Moreover, we suggest that psychological assistance is facilitated, and special training is offered regarding stress and anxiety management. Also, it is worth noting that if the translators are working on a rotational basis covering after hours and night shifts, longer breaks are offered to allow for recovery.

4 Conclusions

Twelve years after the approval of the European Directive 2010/64/EU, translation is still not a regulated profession in Spain. The Official Registry of Translators and Interpreters has not been created, nor is there an official code of ethics to guide good practice. The outsourcing of wiretapping transcription makes the working conditions of translators even more precarious, which has led to poor quality service denounced by newspapers, professional associations such as the APTIJ, and the judiciary. This is due to the lack of qualified translators, especially in languages classified in Groups B and C for which, in practice, no training is required, and a "lack of awareness of the consequences of their interpreting choices, lack of time to think of the best alternatives, or lack of linguistic resources" (Hale, 2004, p. 211). In addition, translators must deal with stressful situations for which they are not psychologically trained, due to the subject matter or – at times – having the same ethnic background as the suspects or the same religion. Despite the importance of wiretap translations for both state security and fair trial guarantees, not to mention the seriousness of the subjects under investigation, quality is still a serious concern in the field of wiretap translation in Spain. To address these issues, greater collaboration between the judiciary, educational institutions, and professional translator associations should be fostered to introduce more rigorous pre-service training, professional development, and interprofessional dialogue in wiretap translation.

References

Asociación Profesional de Traductores e Intérpretes Judiciales y Jurados [APTIJ]. (2016). *Queja ante el Defensor del Pueblo sobre el servicio de traducción e interpretación en juzgados y comisarías* [Complaint issued to the ombudsman regarding translation and interpreting services in courts and police stations]. www.aptij.es/img/not/docs/Queja_web.pdf

Audiencia Provincial de Huesca (2021, March). *Sentencia* [Judgment] (No. 000047/2021). Consejo General del Poder Judicial. Centro de Documentación Judicial. www.poderjudicial.es/search/documento/AN/9582431/robo/20210628

Blasco Mayor, M. J. (2020). Legal translator and interpreter training in languages of lesser diffusion in Spain: A case study about participants' perceptions. In E. Ng & I. Crezee (Eds.), *Interpreting in legal and healthcare settings: Perspectives on research and training* (pp. 133–164). John Benjamins Publishing Company. https://doi.org/10.1075/btl.151.06bla

Cortes Generales (1978, December). *Constitución Española* [Spanish Constitution]. Boletín Oficial del Estado, 311. www.boe.es/buscar/act.php?id=BOE-A-1978-31229

de Hoyos Sancho, M. (2017). Sobre la necesidad de armonizar las garantías procesales en los enjuiciamientos de personas jurídicas en el ámbito de la Unión Europea. Valoración de la situación actual y algunas propuestas [On the need of harmonisation of procedural safeguards of legal persons on trial within the European Union. Assessment of the current situation and some proposals]. *Revista General de Derecho Procesal*, *43*, 1–67. https://redpe.files.wordpress.com/2017/11/garantc3adas-procesales-personas-jurc3addicas-rgdp-43-2017-m-de-hoyos.pdf

EFE (2017, November 4). *La traducción en juicios, entre el "intrusismo" y la "precariedad laboral"* [Translation in trials: Juggle between "intrusiveness" and "precarious working conditions"]. 20minutos. www.20minutos.es/noticia/3178498/0/traduccion-juicios-intrusismo-precariedad-laboral/

El-Madkouri Maataoui, M. (2019). La precisión conceptual y terminológica en el ámbito policial y judicial: traducción y transcripción de escuchas telefónicas [Conceptual and terminological precision in the policing and judicial field: Translation and transcription of wiretapping]. *Entreculturas*, *10*, 119–128. https://revistas.uma.es/index.php/revtracom/article/view/9606/9480

European Court of Human Rights. (1950). *European convention on human rights*. Council of Europe. www.echr.coe.int/documents/convention_eng.pdf

The European Parliament and the Council of the European Union. (2010, October). *Directive 2010/64/EU of the European Parliament and of the Council CIL of 20 October 2010 on the right to interpretation and translation in criminal proceedings*. Official Journal of the European Union, L 280/1. https://eur-lex.europa.eu/eli/dir/2010/64/oj

The European Parliament and the Council of the European Union. (2012, May). *The European Parliament and the Council of the European Union*. Official Journal of the European Union, L 142/1. https://eur-lex.europa.eu/eli/dir/2012/13/oj

European Union. (2007, December). Treaty of Lisbon amending the Treaty on European Union and the Treaty establishing the European Community, signed at Lisbon, 13 December 2007. *Official Journal of the European Union*, C 306/1. https://eur-lex.europa.eu/eli/treaty/lis/sign

Fernández, D. (2008, May 30). *Una empresa envía a la Policía Nacional traductores con antecedentes* [A company sends translators with criminal records to the national police force]. 20minutos. www.20minutos.es/noticia/384035/0/antecedentes/traductores/policia/

Hale, S. (2004). *The discourse of court interpreting: Discourse practices of the law, the witness, and the interpreter.* John Benjamins Publishing Company.

Jefatura del Estado. (1985, July). *Ley Orgánica 6/1985, de 1 de julio, del Poder Judicial* [Organic Law 6/1985 of 1 July 1985 pertaining to the Judicial Power]. Boletín Oficial del Estado, 157. www.boe.es/buscar/act.php?id=BOE-A-1985-12666

Jefatura del Estado. (2015a, September). *Ley 36/2015, de 28 de septiembre, de Seguridad Nacional* [National Security Act 36/2015 of 28 September 2015]. Boletín Oficial del Estado, 233. www.boe.es/diario_boe/txt.php?id=BOE-A-2015-10389

Jefatura del Estado. (2015b, October). *Ley Orgánica 13/2015, de 5 de octubre, de modificación de la Ley de Enjuiciamiento Criminal para el fortalecimiento de las garantías procesales y la regulación de las medidas de investigación tecnológica* [Organic Law 13/2015 of 5 October 2015 to amend the Criminal Procedure Act in order to strengthen procedural safeguards and regulate technological investigation measures]. Boletín Oficial del Estado, 239. www.boe.es/diario_boe/txt.php?id=BOE-A-2015-10725

Kalina, S. (2015). Ethical challenges in different interpreting settings. *MonTI. Monographs in Translation and Interpreting*, Special Issue 2, 63–86. https://doi.org/10.6035/MonTI.2015.ne2.2

Lai, M., & Costello, S. (2020). Professional interpreters and vicarious trauma: An Australian perspective. *Qualitative Health Research*, *31*(1), 70–85. https://doi.org/10.1177/1049732320951962

Lai, M., & Heydon, G. (2015). Vicarious trauma among interpreters. *International Journal of Interpreter Education*, *7*(1), 3–22. https://tigerprints.clemson.edu/ijie/vol7/iss1/3

Martin, A., & Ortega Herráez, J. M. (2013). From invisible machines to visible experts: Views on interpreter role and performance during the Madrid train bomb trial. In C. Schäffner, K. Kredens, & Y. Fowler (Eds.), *Interpreting in a changing landscape: Selected paper from Critical Link 6* (pp. 101–114). John Benjamins Publishing Company.

Ministerio de Asuntos Exteriores, Unión Europea y Cooperación. (2020, August). *Real Decreto 724/2020, de 4 de agosto, por el que se aprueba el Reglamento de la Oficina de Interpretación de Lenguas del Ministerio de Asuntos Exteriores, Unión Europea y Cooperación* [Royal Decree 724/2020 of 4 August 2020 to approve the Regulation of the Language Interpretation Office of the Ministry of Foreign Affairs, European Union and Cooperation]. Boletín Oficial del Estado, 212. www.boe.es/eli/es/rd/2020/08/04/724

Ministerio de Gracia y Justicia. (1882, September). *Real Decreto de 14 de septiembre de 1882 por el que se aprueba la Ley de Enjuiciamiento Criminal* [Royal Decree of 14 September 1882 approving the Criminal Procedure Act]. Gaceta de Madrid – Boletín Oficial del Estado, 270. www.boe.es/eli/es/rd/1882/09/14/(1)/con

Ministerio del Interior. Dirección General de la Policía. (2019). *Pliego de prescripciones técnicas para la contratación del servicio de traducción de escuchas telefónicas y transcripción de cintas grabadas en el marco de las actuaciones del Cuerpo Nacional de Policía* [Terms of technical reference for the engagement of translation services aimed at telephone tapping and transcription of recorded tapes in the framework of the National Police Force] (*Expediente 001/19c0/05*). https://mnhlicitaciones.com/wp-content/uploads/2019/01/DOC20181227142610PPT.pdf

Ministerio del Interior. Dirección General de la Policía. (2020). *Servicio de traducción de escuchas telefónicas y transcripción de cintas de audio u otros soportes informáticos grabados en idiomas distintos del castellano, en el marco de las actuaciones policiales (Expediente Z20CO007/050). ANEXO 1: Cuadro de características del pliego de cláusulas administrativas particulares* [Translation services for wiretap translations and transcriptions of audio tapes or materials in other electronic formats that have been recorded in languages other than Spanish in the framework of police work (File

Z20CO007/050). ANNEX 1: Features of the specific administrative terms] https://contrataciondelestado.es/wps/wcm/connect/c0e82407-16fb-4eb3-9425-1ac337bb7f5b/DOC20200729103916PCAP_Completo_fdo.pdf?MOD=AJPERES

Ministerio Fiscal. (2019, March). *Circular 2/2019, de 6 de marzo, de la Fiscalía General del Estado, sobre interceptación de comunicaciones telefónicas y telemáticas* [Office of the Attorney General, Circular 2/2019 of 6 March 2019 on interception of telephone and telematic communications]. Boletín Oficial del Estado, 70. www.boe.es/diario_boe/txt.php?id=BOE-A-2019-4241

Ortega Herráez, J. M. (2006). *Análisis de la práctica de la interpretación judicial en España: el intérprete frente a su papel profesional* [Analysis of judicial interpreting practice in Spain: the interpreter's professional role] [Master's thesis, Universidad de Granada]. DIGIBUG: Repositorio Institucional de la Universidad de Granada. https://digibug.ugr.es/handle/10481/977

Ortega Herráez, J. M., & Hernández Cebrián, N. (2019). Instrumentos y medidas para transponer al ordenamiento jurídico interno el mandato de calidad de la traducción e interpretación de la Directiva 2010/64/UE: El caso de España a través de un análisis comparativo transnacional [Tools and measures to implement the quality mandate of Directive 2010/64/UE regarding translation and interpreting into the national legal system: Analysis of Spain as a case study through a transnational comparison]. *Revista de Estudios Europeos*, *1*, 97–117. https://rua.ua.es/dspace/bitstream/10045/98233/1/2019_Ortega_Hernandez_RevEstEuro.pdf

Placer, D. (2016, May 14). *Los juzgados me contrataron como traductor de árabe, aunque no sé ni una palabra* [The courts engaged me as an Arabic interpreter despite not speaking a single word of Arabic]. Economía Digital. www.economiadigital.es/politica/los-juzgados-me-contrataron-como-traductor-de-arabe-aunque-no-se-ni-una-palabra_183818_102.html

Placer, D. (2017, November 30). *Más degradación en las traducciones judiciales: "Él me entiende, yo no."* [Further decline in the quality of legal translations: "he understands me, I don't"] Economía Digital. www.economiadigital.es/empresas/mas-degradacion-en-las-traducciones-judiciales-el-me-entiende-yo-no_523187_102.html

Ron Romero, J. (2011). Derecho al secreto de las comunicaciones telefónicas. Un reto para la buena administración [Right to secrecy in telephone communications. A challenge for good administration]. *Anuario Da Facultade de Dereito Da Universidade Da Coruña*, 101–126. https://core.ac.uk/download/pdf/61906631.pdf.

Salaets, H., & Balogh, K. (2018, March 16–17). *Forensic linguistic tap expert: The FoLiT* [Paper presentation]. EULITA Conference 2018, Sofia, Bulgaria.

Scott, J. R. (2019). *Legal translation outsourced*. Oxford University Press.

Soto Aranda, B., & Allouchi, O. (2021). La interpretación judicial en la combinación lingüística árabe-español: las cuatro primeras sesiones del juicio por los atentados del 17A como caso de estudio [Legal interpreting in Arabic-Spanish: A case study of the first four sessions of the trials for the 17A terrorist attacks] *TRANS. Revista de Traductología*, *25*, 433–457. https://doi.org/10.24310/trans.2021.v1i25.12362

Stern, L. (2011). Court interpreting. In K. Malmkjær & K. Windle (Eds.), *The Oxford handbook of translation studies* (pp. 221–231). Oxford University Press.

Taibi, M., & Martin, A. (2012). Court translation and interpreting in times of the "war on terror": The case of Taysir Alony. *Translation & Interpreting*, *4*(1), 77–98. www.trans-int.org/index.php/transint/article/view/194

Tribunal Constitucional de España. (1999, April). *SENTENCIA 49/1999, de 5 de abril.* [Judgment 49/1999 of 5 April 1999] Boletín Oficial del Estado, 100. http://hj.tribunalconstitucional.es/es-ES/Resolucion/Show/3791

Tribunal Supremo, Sala de lo Penal, Sección 1. (2016, April). *Sentencia penal* (No. 307/2016) [Criminal judgment]. Consejo General del Poder Judicial. Centro de Documentación Judicial. www.poderjudicial.es/search/AN/openCDocument/9212199cb330 76a4ddaedeee43551672deb4a70fbad231f0

United Nations. (1966). *International covenant on civil and political rights*. www.unodc.org/ji/resdb/data/1966/_220_/international_covenant_on_civil_and_political_rights.html?lng=en

Valero-Garcés, C., & Abkari, A. (2010). Learning from practice: Interpreting at the 11M terrorist attack trial. *The International Journal of Translation and Interpreting Research*, 2(2), 44–46.

Vigier Moreno, F. (2017). ¿Cómo es la interpretación que se presta realmente en los procedimientos penales en España? [What is the interpreting provided in Spanish criminal proceedings really like?] In T. Barceló Martínez & I. Delgado Pugés (Eds.), *De la traducción jurídica y socioeconómica e interpretación para servicios públicos* (pp. 277–289). Comares.

8

LIFE STORIES IN TRANSLATION

Community Translators as Cultural Mediators

Marija Todorova

1 Introduction

In the past decade, community translation, also referred to as public service translation, has developed as an independent research area within translation studies (see Taibi, 2011). Community translation generally refers to translation from a country's dominant language into the language(s) of communities whose command of the dominant language is insufficient and who could otherwise not access public services. It is defined as the "written translation of mainly informative texts, addressed by the authorities or institutions to people who do not understand texts in the language of the text producer" (Niska, 2002, p. 135). Community translation is used by authorities to "ensure communication with all citizens and permit their participation and, therefore, empowerment" (Taibi, 2011, p. 215). With increasing numbers of people driven from their homes by war and conflict to seek asylum in other countries, community translation now often involves providing and improving information flow about immigration policies and refugee services.

However, in addition to this predominant understanding of the discipline as the translation of state policies and services towards citizens, community translation encompasses a broad range of translation practices within community settings. As Taibi (2011) observes, translating from the language of authorities into the languages of migrants is not the only type of community translation. For example, Townsley (2018) reports an increase in the number of translations for regional police forces in the UK of witness statements and forensic evidence (in written form) from other languages, including Latvian and Lithuanian, into English. Another example of translating languages of immigrant communities into the dominant national language is the translation of official documents such as birth and marriage certificates, divorce decrees, and death certificates (Mayoral Asensio, 2003; Taibi & Ozolins, 2016).

DOI: 10.4324/9781003247333-9

This chapter suggests yet another variety of community translation that involves translation from languages of immigrants and asylum seekers into the dominant language(s) of the host country. This type of translation is related to the work of organisations and activists that facilitate cultural exchange between asylum seekers and the local population. It includes the translation of stories bearing witness to individual histories and violent refugee journeys. Storytelling is closely related to the lives of refugees. For asylum seekers, it is essential to narrate one's story to obtain refugee status and receive necessary legal and humanitarian protections and assistance. However, creative storytelling as part of the integration process – or as a way to counter mainstream media narratives and enable empathy among the local population – remains a topic which is seldom researched within translation studies. This type of translation enables community integration (Pokorn & Mikolič Južnič, 2020).

Focusing on the Hong Kong community, this chapter examines two types of writing that (re)tell asylum seekers' life stories through translation. The first text is a cookbook published in Hong Kong by the charity organisation RUN Hong Kong, including translated food recipes and short personal narratives from 11 asylum seekers now residing in Hong Kong. The second text is a graphic novel about the life and journey of a Somali child refugee published in English in the United States by Dial Books for young readers and introduced as part of an education activity in Hong Kong. The goal of both texts is to promote and disseminate asylum seekers' life stories to the local population in Hong Kong, thereby fostering empathy and emphasising community integration. This chapter shows how *reverse community translation*, or the translation from a minority language into a majority language, fulfils a social role for speakers of the official language(s) in host societies. Reverse community translation aims to rehumanise the crisis of refugees and asylum seekers through the translation of their personal narratives.

In these two cases of reverse community translation, the experiences took place in the first language of the authors, who then translated them themselves into their second language for the host community. The translators as voice-givers put into words the experiences of asylum seekers and refugees. In these cases, translators act in a capacity that exceeds the role typically assigned to them and must be equipped with a nuanced understanding of the refugee's specific situation and culture-specific terminology.

2 Justifying the Need for Reverse Community Translation

People everywhere tell stories about a part of their lives to friends and strangers. Stories can confirm, valorise, and support our experience within social frameworks. Stories help us understand our differences, but also our similarities and relationships with others. However, refugee lives are often narrated in the media in a depersonalised way. In most news coverage, the individual stories of migrants and refugees, "their lives and cultures; thus, information about who these people are", are very often absent (Georgiou & Zaborowski, 2017, p. 3). In Europe, journalistic narratives "continue to represent asylum, and the asylum system in particular, as a problem" (Gross et al., 2007, p. 115). These narratives do not discuss "the causes of the displacement or the needs in terms of reception and accommodation but only [rely] on imagery in which the migrant and the refugee are a burden" (Federici, 2020, p. 254). The negative response to the refugee crisis in Europe is often used by local media to frame asylum seekers and refugees within a discourse of fake claimants that are misusing the system or are involved in criminal activities. Asylum seekers in Hong Kong, although much fewer in number than in Europe, face increasing hostility that is similarly instigated by the local Chinese-language media (Ng et al., 2018).

Amid this negative public representation of refugees, migrants, and asylum seekers in the news media, many non-governmental organisations and advocacy projects, as well as journalists and artists, have attempted to counter the predominantly depersonalised accounts by using alternative means. Operating within the "cultural apparatus of human rights" (Nayar, 2011), individuals and groups have started organising cultural representations of refugees "in art galleries, museums or plays . . . . [to] compete with hostile media scares over bogus asylum seekers scrounging welfare benefits" (Pupavac, 2008, p. 270). Situated in opposition to the dominant news media discourse, personal life stories – due to their reportage mode and realistic illustrations – have been seen by many as a valuable tool in reinstating individuality and evoking empathy towards refugees and migrants. Creating these narratives relies on becoming acquainted with the refugee's life story, translating it from the refugee's language into the host country's language, and presenting it to the host population. Empathising with the refugee is an essential skill for everyone involved in these processes to maximise the impact of such stories (Todorova, 2020; Todorova & Poposki, 2022).

In the early 1990s, discursive constructions tended to represent refugees as helpless and lacking agency; as an "ahistorical, universal humanitarian subject" (Malkki, 1996, p. 378). Since then, stories of refugees have been written and translated around the world to empower refugees by providing accounts of their individual experiences. These narratives do not intend to represent all refugee experiences, but to grant agency and a voice to individuals. Most of these narratives are written by refugee writers and translated into English. There are several examples of reverse community translation that showcase and validate the experiences of refugees and asylum seekers. The Iraqi writer Najem Wali (2003) explores themes of memory and loss in his story, "Homeland as Exile, Exile as Homeland", translated from Arabic by Jennifer Kaplan. The poem "I Am a Refugee" by Mohamed Raouf Bachir (2014) was translated from Arabic by Thomas Aplin. Iranian cartoonist Mana Neyestani (2015/2016) wrote and drew "The Short Guide for Being a Perfect Political Refugee", which was translated from Persian into English by Ghazal Mosadeq. More recently, European refugee crises have resulted in many examples of refugee personal stories translated by both professional and non-professional translators. In Greece, three Syrian men living in the Idomeni refugee camp handwrote in Arabic the accounts of their journeys to safety. Their stories, published in a collection titled "Refugee Stories: Idomeni Greece" (2016), were translated into English by Karen Emmerich, Martin Trabalik, and Jonathan Wright – volunteers during the refugee crisis in Greece and the Balkans. These examples represent an attempt to use life stories to create greater understanding for refugees internationally and within host communities. This chapter identifies similar representations of refugee life stories used in the context of Hong Kong. As Hong Kong has two official languages, English and Chinese, the chapter also considers the need to present the life stories in both English and Chinese translation.

3 Stories of Asylum Seekers and Refugees in Hong Kong Through Translation

Hong Kong has a history of accepting asylum seekers, especially from China and Vietnam (Todorova, 2021). However, since 2000 and the closure of the last Vietnamese refugee camp, Hong Kong has become "one of the regions of the world with the slowest pace of [non-refoulment] claims processing and one of the lowest degrees of acceptance of claims" (Lau & Gheorghiu, 2017, p. 21), with only about 300 claims substantiated out of 38,650 (Immigration Department, n.d.). At present, most of the claimants are from Indonesia, Vietnam, and the Philippines, followed by Bangladeshi, Pakistani and Indian nationals. Most of the substantiated claimants are from Yemen and Pakistan, while other groups include Rwandan, Somali, Sri Lankan, Egyptian, Bangladeshi, Congolese, and Cameroonian nationals. The procedure of processing a non-refoulement claim by the Hong Kong government can last several years. During this time, non-refoulement claimants are not allowed to work in Hong Kong and are provided with limited government support. Thus, these non-refoulement claimants mainly depend on support from charities and have little to no interaction with the local population in the host country, leading to an increasingly negative public image.

RUN Hong Kong is a charity that supports asylum seekers and refugees in Hong Kong. It was established in 2015 by Virginie Goethals and Brenda Sawyer. It aims to help asylum seekers in Hong Kong overcome trauma and fight depression by spending time outdoors and to "show, particularly women, in Hong Kong that they can get out of the house and hike in the hills without having any expense except transport and feel better about themselves through exercise" (B. Sawyer, personal communication, November 1, 2021). However, "participants often arrive at the sports activities on empty stomachs, especially near the end of the month when their government food coupons are used up, and there is not enough left for three meals a day" (B. Sawyer, personal communication, November 1, 2021). For this reason, RUN Hong Kong introduced a food programme, which included a healthy breakfast and lunch for the participants in RUN activities. Besides providing nutritional food supplements for the asylum seekers and refugees, the programme also allowed for community food sharing events "as people of different cultures came together, refugees, asylum seekers and volunteers alike, established a community, and enjoyed eating as a community, so they soon wanted to share their home dishes with everyone else in this community" (B. Sawyer, personal communication, November 1, 2021). Asylum seekers were given funds to source ingredients and were allowed to use the office kitchen to prepare dishes from their home countries. The recipes for the food they prepared have been documented in a cookbook, *The RUN Cookbook: Stories and Recipes from Refugees in Hong Kong* (Lampard, 2019), by volunteers who wrote the recipes and the life stories of each asylum seeker cook. The recipes are accompanied by photos illustrating the dishes, which can be understood as a form of intersemiotic translation.

The Hong Kong cookbook is not an isolated example, as similar publications have been produced in both Hong Kong (Todorova, 2022) and other parts of the world. For example, *Cooking a Home: A Collection of the Recipes and Stories of Syrian Refugees* by Pilar Puig Cortada (2015) is a collection of recipes and stories shared with the author by Syrians seeking asylum in Jordan. Another example is *Between Meals* by Dani Fisher and Lauren Markham (2014), a cookbook project by Refugee Transitions which documents traditional recipes of refugees from around the world who have found a new home in California, United States.

The RUN Hong Kong cookbook, in addition to the recipes, includes a short personal story of each cook. The aim of the cookbook is for refugees and asylum seekers to tell their stories while sharing their food culture. This cookbook seeks to empower and give people pride and ownership in their work while raising awareness about the daily lives of refugees in Hong Kong. The cookbook includes 11 interviews conducted by RUN volunteers with asylum seekers. The asylum seekers included in the book originate from Burundi, Cameroon, Egypt, India, Kenya, Pakistan, Rwanda, Somalia, Sri Lanka, and Yemen. Their personal stories and recipes are written in English, in the first person. This means that the authors translate the stories and recipes mentally and transfer them into paper in their second language.

A more direct way of telling a personal story is through a longer biographical or autobiographical narrative, and that is the reason why this chapter also analyses such genres from the angle of community translation. Besides translations of autobiographical war diaries (Todorova, 2017), publishers and advocacy organisations have noticed the potential in using graphic novels to represent the human face of the immigration and refugee crisis, as they are "well placed to counter the tendencies of news media and policy debates that render the individual experiences of refugees invisible" (Mickwitz, 2020, p. 278). Graphic novels are "book-length comic books that are meant to be read as one story" (Weiner, 2012, p. xi). Graphic novels such as Art Spiegelman's Pulitzer Prize-winning *Maus* (Spiegelman, 1987) and *Persepolis* by Marjane Satrapi (2000) present personal accounts of war, trauma, and exile. Karrie Fransman's *Over Under Sideways Down* (Fransman 2014), commissioned by the British Red Cross, recounts the true-life story of Ebrahim Esmail, and *L'Odyssée D'Hakim* by Fabien Toulmé (2018), depicts the story of Syrian refugee Hakim Kabdi in French. Both graphic novels were created as the author documented the refugee story using interviews mediated by an interpreter.

When Stars Are Scattered (Jamieson & Mohamed, 2020) is a graphic novel aimed at middle-grade readers. It was published in English in the United States and was written and illustrated by award-winning author Victoria Jamieson, in collaboration with Somali refugee Omar Mohamed. The graphic novel presents the reality of the refugee's journey through compelling narratives told in the first person by the main child protagonist. Although the story does not exist in the form of a physical book or a text in the source language, it is based on the real-life events of Omar Mohamed, a refugee who is native in Somali and is writing in English as his second language, enabling the story to reach English-speaking target readers. The protagonists in this story communicate in a language different from English. In this context, the authors themselves take up the role of translators of the refugee story, Mohamed writing in his second language, while Jamieson acts as a collaborating editor of the English language text and as the illustrator. The illustrations transform the refugees' narratives into visual representations, allowing us to examine the process of intersemiotic translation involved.

This graphic novel was one of the 20 books selected for the annual Hong Kong Battle of the Books interschool competition in 2021. The schools that participate are primarily international schools that use English as a medium of education. In 2009, the competition was expanded to include local schools using Chinese as a medium of instruction. A special, modified, and shortened list of English-language books is used in these schools. Unfortunately, *When Stars Are Scattered* has not been included on the modified list. Although English-language bookstores in Hong Kong distribute all the books that are part of the competition, including *When Stars Are Scattered*, these are often too expensive and difficult to access for students attending local schools using Chinese as a medium of instruction. The book has not yet been translated into Chinese.

In both examples presented in this chapter, translation is understood in its broad meaning of interlingual but also intersemiotic practice whereby culture-related items play a significant part. The process of these reverse community translations is primarily examined through the text, illustrations, and paratext. Given the social role reverse community translation fulfils in society, the textual analysis of the cookbook and graphic novel is supplemented with structured and semi-structured interviews conducted online with Brenda Sawyer and Pristine Lampard from RUN Hong Kong and Victoria Jamieson and Omar Mohammed, authors of *When Stars Are Scattered*. The next section summarises the information extracted from the textual analyses and the interviews.

4 Translation Process

4.1 The Cookbook

A significant aspect of the lives of asylum seekers and refugees is related to the provision of food. In a context of displacement and limited resources, food can, on the one hand, help maintain social and cultural links to the home country, but, on the other hand, it becomes an expression of restriction and control. Images of food lines in camps (Luckhurst, 2021; Dinham, 2017) or the prohibition of meals to stop migrants from setting up a new camp (Kroet, 2017) are just some examples covered in the news media.

In the RUN Hong Kong cookbook, the recipes are first presented as oral narratives by participants in the organisation's programme. The interviews are conducted in English – the participants' second language – and are transcribed with the help of volunteers. Volunteers act as collaborating translators and editors in recording traditional recipes with refugee women from different parts of the world, along with corresponding personal histories, foodways, and experiences about adapting their food cultures to their new homes. In this process, the asylum seekers provide a translation of the culture specific food items. The recipes included in this book are not just journeys into food diversity but are accompanied by stories bearing witness to violent histories. The stories that are part of the recipes convert the culinary narratives into a form of witness and testimony of injustice and violence. The goal of the cookbook is to give voice to the refugee women by documenting their recipes and stories but also to present their culinary knowledge in a professional manner using professional photographs. Finally, it creates a community among refugees from different backgrounds, as well as with local and international readers.

As a communication system that can be used to exchange knowledge, promote social values, and reaffirm personal and ethnic identities, food inevitably relates to translation. Ciribuco (2020) maintains that food is translated, as it is

> carried across both physically and in terms of discourse, to the point that the food that is consumed in the target culture is rarely the same as the food that the migrant tastes "back home" – changes may occur in taste, but most importantly in meaning.
>
> (p. 102)

Understanding food "as a system of communication that brings to light differences between cultures, and as a reflection of the values held by different societies" (Vidal Claramonte & Faber, 2017, p. 191) gives the translator the possibility to become a point of transmission of food knowledge and how it is transformed through displacement (Desjardins et al., 2015). The translator, in such instances, may be the one writing the food narrative in a cookbook as heard from the asylum seeker. However, most frequently, it is the cook who is very often bilingual or multilingual and provides a self-translation of the cultural and social practices accompanying the making and consumption of food, as it was the case with the cookbook analysed in this chapter.

Although not necessarily translated from a source text, as they were written and published in English, the recipes and stories in the cookbook represent a translation of the asylum seekers' and refugees' culinary knowledge into their new host country's language. The cookbook is created in the form of notes that volunteers took while observing an asylum seeker cook the dish. It involved discussion between the cook and the writer, clarification of ingredients and measures, as well as negotiation of names and words used to describe a cooking procedure, tool, or technique. Most of these discussions with the asylum seekers were conducted in English, with some help from other speakers of the same language or dialect.

Analysing the cookbook, we can identify two possible instances where translation is visible in the presentation of the recipes and serves as a cultural mediator offering explanations and cultural substitutions. First, translation occurs in terms of how the names of the dishes are written. Second, translation occurs in the listing of the ingredients. For the names of some dishes, an English descriptive translation is used (e.g., "Beans with Tomatoes", "Watermelon and Lemon Juice", "Lentil Soup"). However, for most dishes, the name provided is the one used by the cook to describe the dish. This means the name in the original language is preserved, possibly transcribed, or transliterated (e.g., "Sukuma Wiki"). Frequently, to make the dish more familiar to the target reader, the original name is followed by a description in English (e.g., "Ikibonde [Smoked Fish]").

Moreover, some of the ingredients presented in the cookbook are described using English substitute word(s) in conjunction with the original name. For example, one ingredient often present in Togolese and Nigerian cuisines is egusi, frequently used in West Africa as a thickening agent in different dishes. The recipe that requires the use of 5–6 egusi seeds is accompanied by the word "melon" in parentheses. On the other hand, the preparation of Sukuma Wiki, a traditional Kenyan dish, calls for bok choy, Chinese kale, or collard greens. This dish's main ingredient is referred to in Swahili as *sukuma*, a plant belonging to the same family as the colewort. However, this ingredient is not easily found in Hong Kong, whereas bok choy is a ubiquitous and inexpensive staple.

Another notable aspect of the cookbook is the illustrations that accompany the recipes: "close-up photographic images that capture the individual colours, forms and preparation processes of dishes have a potentially valuable function in terms of attracting and informing" (Li, 2019, p. 11).

The cookbook fills a gap for information in English, as one of the official languages of Hong Kong, about food from other cultures, particularly those of asylum seekers from African countries offering dishes that are less familiar to the local community.

4.2 The Graphic Novel

Many graphic novels for young adults centred on refugees' lives use first-person narratives. However, only a small portion of these stories are told by the refugees themselves. The graphic novel presented in this chapter reflects the childhood of Omar Mohamed and his younger brother Hassan, who spent 15 years in Dadaab refugee camp in Kenya before being resettled to the United States. The two young boys from Mareerey lost their father and were separated from their mother during the civil war in Somalia. Most of the novel's events happen while the two boys are in the Dadaab refugee camp. However, we also learn about their plight and the journey to Kenya from Omar's recollection of the events.

When Stars Are Scattered is written in English. However, English appears to be a foreign language for Omar, thus allowing us to conclude that the rest of the dialogues in the book between Omar and the other refugees in the camp are conducted in a language other than English, presumably Somali. When interviewed, Jamieson stated that she "wanted to convey that although the book is written in English, this was not the language commonly spoken in the refugee camp" (personal communication, February 17, 2021). The need to learn English and access education is one of the central issues in *When Stars Are Scattered*. Omar soon realises that most school classes in Dadaab, apart from some Arabic and

Kiswahili (Swahili), are conducted in English and that his education depends on his willingness and aptitude to learn English. Education in the refugee camp is in English because the child refugees in the camp come from many different countries, such as Ethiopia, Sudan, Somalia, etc., and "English is something everyone can understand" (Jamieson & Mohamed, 2020, p. 48). At first, Omar is frustrated, as "everything in school is in English, so I barely understand anything . . . maybe I should just give up" (Jamieson & Mohamed, 2020, p. 57), but learning English has helped Omar settle in the United States, find a job, and graduate from college.

If we look at writing in a second language as a process of translation, "where the writer translates both language and self" (Evangelista, 2013, p. 178), then the autobiographical narrative is intrinsically linked to the concept of self-translation (auto-translation) as the author is involved in telling their story in their second language. Evangelista (2013) defines self-translation as a "translation process occurring when a bilingual writer chooses to write in a second or acquired language, translation thereby forming an integral part of the 'original' creative writing process" (p. 178). In *When Stars Are Scattered*, self-translation allows the author to use his own voice when speaking to his audiences (Hokenson & Munson, 2007). Mohamed takes up a double role as the author and the translator simultaneously, whereas his co-author and illustrator Jamieson takes up, among other roles, that of the editor.

The self-translator also acts as a cultural mediator, explaining the refugee's culture – in this case, in the form of religious practice interwoven throughout the novel. We listen to a call for prayer announced over loudspeakers; Omar studies the Quran and observes Ramadan, participating in the refugee camp's "big Eid prayer" (Jamieson & Mohamed, 2020, p. 149). The religious activities are explained to the readers who may not be familiar with Islam. Furthermore, the reader encounters some Somali words throughout the text. Often those are greetings. One of the most important Somali words at the story's centre is *hooyo*. This is the only word pronounced by Hassan, Omar's younger brother who stays by his side throughout the whole journey and is otherwise non-verbal. Although the reader can make a good guess based on the illustrations, we learn that *hooyo* means "mum" in Somali at the end of the story.

Additionally, the use of italics to signal non-English words is not adopted in this novel, signifying that the Somali words are not different from the rest of the dialogue. Omar also uses Somali to tell the story of his traumatic refugee experience in an interview with a UNHCR (United Nations High Commissioner for Refugees) officer conducted in English through an interpreter, Salat. Here we gain a glimpse of how an interpreted encounter works (Jamieson & Mohamed, 2020). We also see both languages on the page during the interpreted exchange between Somali and English.

In terms of translating the refugee narrative into visuals, Jamieson stated that she was guided by the fact she was creating this for young readers. Thus, she decided to keep the illustrations simple to read and follow, avoiding more complex layouts that may be distracting to younger audiences. Her primary goal was to communicate the story to the young readers clearly. Like in many other graphic novels, in *When Stars Are Scattered*, we find instances of intersemiotic translation, as Jamieson relied on photographs as source material and inspiration that she transcoded into drawings. She found these images online while doing her research, as Mohamed did not have any photos of his childhood days. As Jamieson explains, the process of creating the illustrations was collaborative, with Mohamed giving feedback on every illustration to ensure its accurateness:

> For example, some of the photos I used for reference were taken more recently and did not match what the refugee camp looked like when Omar was a boy. Omar would also draw maps or diagrams when needed, like the layout of his block in the camp or specific tools made and used by the people in the camp.
> *(Personal communication, February 17, 2021)*

5 Conclusion

Both the cookbook and the graphic novel presented in this chapter are examples of reverse community translation that use self-translation from the language of the asylum seeker and refugee to the dominant language of the country as a tool to present real-life experiences overshadowed by media and government narratives. In doing so, they reconstruct personal journeys, combining snapshots of violent historical events but including feelings and insight into the culture of the refugees and asylum seekers. The narrative relies on self-biography and uses the techniques of cultural mediation whereby the source culture is distinctly preserved, and some of the original words are present in the books.

First-person accounts help weave a tale which challenge the official macro-historical narratives depicted in the media and by government agencies. In these instances, reverse community translation acts as a tool for cultural mediation as well as education and awareness raising (Felman, 1995).

The use of the cookbook and graphic novel to tell refugee life stories involves one more translation mode: transcoding the narrative story into a visual representation. The illustrators rely heavily on using photographs. Furthermore, both case studies are examples of collaborative co-creation and translation. However, the translations into English, as one of the official languages of Hong Kong, means that these stories are mainly available to the Hong Kong expatriate community and young people educated in international English-language schools. Therefore, efforts still need to be made to translate these texts into Chinese, the most widely used official language in Hong Kong, to make them available to the broader Hong Kong population.

Acknowledgement

The research presented in this chapter was partially funded by the HKBU Start-up grant (Tier 1) RCSTARTUP/21–22/25.

References

Bachir, M. R. (2014, October). *I am a refugee* (T. Aplin, Trans.). Words Without Borders. https://wordswithoutborders.org/read/article/2014-10/i-am-a-refugee/

Ciribuco, A. (2020). How do you say *kélén-kélén* in Italian? Migration, landscape and untranslatable food. *Translation Studies, 13*(1), 99–115. https://doi.org/10.1080/14781700.2019.1662837

Cortada, P. P. (2015). *Cooking a home: A collection of the recipes and stories of Syrian refugees*. AuthorHouse; Bloomington.

Desjardins, R., Cooke, N., & Charron, M. (2015). Food and translation on the table: Exploring the relationships between food studies and translation studies in Canada. *The Translator, 21*(3), 257–270. http://dx.doi.org/10.1080/13556509.2015.1103095

Dinham, P. (2017, January 11). *Food queue with echoes of Europe's dark past: Freezing migrants wait for aid in Belgrade today in pictures chillingly similar to those from the Second World War*. Mailonline. www.dailymail.co.uk/news/article-4107102/Belgrade-migrants-wait-food-pictures-similar-Second-World-War.html

Evangelista, E.-M. (2013). Writing in translation: A new self in a second language. In A. Cordingley (Ed.), *Self-translation: Brokering originality in hybrid culture* (pp. 177–188). Bloomsbury Academic. http://dx.doi.org/10.5040/9781472542038.ch-011

Federici, F. M. (2020). Emergenza migranti: From metaphor to policy. In C. Declercq & F. M. Federici (Eds.), *Intercultural crisis communication: Translation, interpreting and languages in local crises* (p. 233–259). Bloomsbury Academic.

Felman, S. (1995). Education and crises, or the vicissitudes of teaching. In C. Caruth (Ed.), *Trauma: Explorations in memory* (pp. 13–60). Johns Hopkins University Press.

Fisher, D., & Markham, L. (2014). *Between meals*. Lulu Press.

Fransman, K. (2014). *Over under sideways down*. The British Red Cross Society.

Georgiou, M., & Zaborowski, R. (2017). *Council of Europe report: Media coverage of the "refugee crisis": A cross-European perspective*. Council of Europe. https://edoc.coe.int/en/refugees/7367-media-coverage-of-the-refugee-crisis-a-cross-european-perspective.html#

Gross, B., Moore, K., & Threadgold, T. R. (2007). *Broadcast news coverage of asylum April to October 2006: Caught between human rights and public safety*. Cardiff School of Journalism, Media and Cultural Studies. https://orca.cardiff.ac.uk/id/eprint/53007/1/BroadcastNewsCoverageofAsylum.pdf

Hokenson, J. W., & Munson, M. (2007). *The bilingual text: History and theory of literary self-translation*. St Jerome.

Immigration Department. (n.d.) *Statistics on non-refoulement claim*. The Government of the Hong Kong Special Administrative Region of the People's Republic of China. www.immd.gov.hk/eng/facts/enforcement.html

Jamieson, V., & Mohamed, O. (2020). *When stars are scattered*. Dial Books.

Kroet, C. (2017, March 2). *Calais mayor bans distribution of food to migrants*. Politico. www.politico.eu/article/calais-mayor-bans-food-distribution-migrants-refugee-camp

Lampard, P. (2019). *The RUN cookbook: Stories and recipes from refugees in Hong Kong*. RUN Hong Kong.

Lau, P., & Gheorghiu, I. (2017). Vanishing selves under Hong Kong's unified screening mechanism. *Cultural Diversity in China, 31*(1), 21–35. https://doi.org/10.1515/cdc-2018-0003

Li, S. (2019). A corpus-based multimodal approach to the translation of restaurant menus. *Perspectives, 27*(1), 1–19. https://doi.org/10.1080/0907676X.2018.1483408

Luckhurst, T. (2021, November 28). Calais activists: Migrants call us from boats asking for help. *BBC News*. www.bbc.com/news/world-europe-59444335

Malkki, L. H. (1996). Speechless emissaries: Refugees, humanitarianism, and dehistoricization. *Cultural Anthropology*, *11*(3), 377–404.

Mayoral Asensio, R. (2003). *Translating official documents*. St Jerome.

Mickwitz, N. (2020). Comics telling refugee stories. In D. Davies & C. Rifkind (Eds.), *Documenting trauma in comics: Traumatic pasts, embodied histories, and graphic reportage* (pp. 277–296). Palgrave Macmillan. https://doi.org/10.1007/978-3-030-37998-8

Nayar, P. K. (2011). Subalternity and translation: The cultural apparatus of human rights. *Economic and Political Weekly*, *46*(9), 23–26.

Neyestani, M. (2016). *A short guide to being the perfect political refugee* (G. Mosadeq, Trans.). Words Without Borders Campus (Original work published 2015). www.wwb-campus.org/literature/a-short-guide-to-being-the-perfect-political-refugee

Ng, I., Choi, S. F., & Chan, A. L. (2018). Framing the issue of asylum seekers and refugees for tougher refugee policy – a study of the media's portrayal in post-colonial Hong Kong. *Journal of International Migration and Integration*, *20*(2), 593–617. https://doi.org/10.1007/s12134-018-0624-7

Niska, H. (2002). Community interpreter training: Past, present, future. In G. Garzone, & M. Viezzi (Eds.), *Interpreting in the 21st century: Challenges and opportunities* (pp. 133–144). John Benjamins Publishing Company.

Pokorn, N. K., & Mikolič Južnič, T. (2020). Community Interpreters versus intercultural mediators. Is it really all about ethics? *Translation and Interpreting Studies*, *15*(1), 80–107.

Pupavac, V. (2008). Refugee advocacy, traumatic representations and political disenchantment. *Government and Opposition*, *43*(2), 270–292. www.jstor.org/stable/44484135

Satrapi, M. (2000). *Persepolis*. Random House.

Spiegelman, A. (1987). *Maus*. Pantheon Books.

Taibi, M. (2011). Public service translation. In K. Malmkjær & K. Windle (Eds.), *The Oxford handbook of translation studies* (pp. 214–227). Oxford University Press. https://doi-org.ezproxy.lib.rmit.edu.au/10.1093/oxfordhb/9780199239306.001.0001

Taibi, M., & Ozolins, U. (2016). *Community translation*. Bloomsbury.

Todorova, M. (2017). Children's voices from war zones: Muted by adult mediation. *Bookbird*, *55*(2), 20–27. https://doi.org/10.1353/bkb.2017.0020

Todorova, M. (2020). Interpreting for refugees: Empathy and activism. In C. Declercq & F. M. Federici (Eds.), *Intercultural crisis communication: Translation, interpreting, and languages in local crises* (p. 153–173). Bloomsbury Academic.

Todorova, M. (2021). Interpreting for refugees in Hong Kong. In M. Todorova & L. Ruiz Rosendo (Eds.), *Interpreting conflict: A comparative framework* (pp. 273–289). Palgrave Macmillan.

Todorova, M. (2022). Translating refugee culinary cultures: Hong Kong's narratives of integration. *Translation and Interpreting Studies*, *17*(1), 88–110. https://doi.org/10.1075/tis.21019.tod

Todorova, M., & Poposki, Z. (2022). Rehumanising the refugee: Personal narratives in graphic novels. In S. O'Brien & F. Federici (Eds.), *Translating crises*. Bloomsbury Academic.

Toulmé, F. (2018). *L'odyssée d'Hakim* [Hakim's odyssey]. Delcourt.

Townsley, B. (2018). Community translation in the UK: An enquiry into practice. In M. Taibi (Ed.), *Translating for the community* (pp. 42–68). Multilingual Matters. https://doi.org/10.21832/TAIBI9139

Vidal Claramonte, M. Á., & Faber, P. (2017). Translation and food: The case of *mestizo* writers. *Journal of Multicultural Discourses*, *12*(3), 189–204.

Weiner, S. (2012). *Faster than a speeding bullet: The rise of the graphic novel* (2nd ed.). NBM Publishing.

Wali, N. (2003, October). *Homeland as exile, exile as homeland* (J. Kaplan, Trans.). Words Without Borders. https://wordswithoutborders.org/read/article/2003-10/homeland-as-exile-exile-as-homeland/

9
THE VOICES OF MIGRANT FAMILIES

(Auto)biography, Testimonio, Service-Learning, and Community Translation

Alicia Rueda-Acedo

1 Introduction

Students enrolled in SPAN 3340 Introduction to Translation at the University of Texas at Arlington (UTA) in the United States have translated 122 stories into English that were originally published in Spanish. The stories were written by parents participating in Stories to Our Children (STOC), a programme sponsored by the Arlington Public Library (APL) in collaboration with the Arlington Independent School District (AISD), to promote literacy and family storytelling among Latino families. The students trained in community translation and service-learning before translating the stories that were then published and catalogued by the APL. Most of the stories are (auto)biographical and testimonial texts from newcomers to Arlington and the United States. The translation of these *testimonios*, or personal narratives, allows the Arlington community to have access to these family life stories, enabling them to better know their immigrant neighbours. These translations are key instruments for fostering dialogue and understanding among community members while providing a feeling of belonging. As part of this service-learning and community translation course, students have also organised and participated in the STOC Final Celebration. This chapter presents the context and characteristics in which the translation and other related activities took place and explores the advantages and benefits of combining community translation and service-learning.

2 Context: Translation Programmes at UTA and the Need for Service-Learning and Community Translation in the Dallas–Fort Worth–Arlington Area

UTA currently offers five programmes in the field of Spanish translation and interpreting: 1) bachelor degree in Spanish translation and interpreting, 2) minor in Spanish translation, 3) minor in Spanish interpreting, 4) certificate in Spanish interpreting, and 5) certificate in Spanish translation.

DOI: 10.4324/9781003247333-10

The Certificate in Spanish Translation was created in 2008 and has been awarded 267 times since its inception. The first SPAN 3340 Introduction to Translation course was offered in 2006, and the first service-learning component was offered in 2011 with the translation into Spanish of the Dallas/Fort Worth Toys for Tots campaign webpage. The certificate programme was created to address the demand for professional translators of Spanish in the Dallas–Fort Worth–Arlington (DFW) area, where 41.5% of Dallas city and 35.1% of Fort Worth city is Hispanic (U.S. Census Bureau, 2021b). The US Census indicates that 40.2% of the population in Texas is Hispanic, while the remainder is 40.3% White, 13.2% Black, and 5.5% Asian (U.S. Census Bureau, 2021b). In the United States, 62.1 million people are Hispanic (U.S. Census Bureau, 2021a) and more than 40 million people speak Spanish (U.S. Census Bureau, 2017). This demographic data was considered in the design, (re)structure, and implementation of the programmes offered at UTA, following Kelly's (2005) model for translation programme building:

> Systematic approaches to curricular design take as their starting point the institutional and social context in which training is to take place, and from there establish their objectives or intended outcomes with input from the professional sector for which students are to be trained, from society at large and from the academic disciplines involved; careful attention is paid to the resources available, and to the profile of the participants involved: students and teaching staff.
>
> *(p. 30)*

Community translation is defined by Taibi (2017) as "the written language service that facilitates communication between the public services and speakers of minority or marginalised languages" (p. 1). Taibi and Ozolins (2016) highlight that "community translation is still in its infancy as a subfield of translation studies and as an area of translation practice" (p. 17). As the authors explain, this is, in part, because "disempowered users of translation such as migrants, refugees and members of ethnic and linguistic minorities have been left out of focus" (Taibi & Ozolins, 2016, pp. 17–18). After reviewing several definitions of community translation, Taibi and Ozolins (2016) point out that a key characteristic of this kind of translation is its "social mission" (p. 11). They also highlight that community translation:

> bridges the communicative gap between public services and those citizens or residents who do not speak the mainstream language, and thereby improves relations and cohabitation between different social groups; facilitates information flow between mainstream/established community members and less powerful, minority or newcomer members; and provides opportunities for the latter to improve their socio-economic position and participate more effectively in their (new) community.
>
> *(Taibi & Ozolins, 2016, p. 11)*

Community translation theory is offered in class, while community translation practice is offered outside of class through service-learning in three courses:

SPAN 3340 Introduction to Translation, SPAN 4341 Business and Legal Translation, and SPAN 4342 Translation in Healthcare Settings. As mentioned before, the demand for translation services in the Metroplex area is immense as speakers of languages other than the official language rely on translation to access public services and "what distinguishes community translation from other types and domains of translation is that its main mission is to empower local communities and give their members voice and access to information, services and participation" (Taibi, 2017, p. 8). The texts translated in the STOC community translation project are generated "by smaller communities (linguistic or ethnic communities within the larger society, local communities, religious groups, etc.)" that become available to a larger community ensuring "communication with all citizens [and residents] and permit[ting] their participation and, therefore, empowerment" (Taibi, 2011, pp. 214–215). Usually, community translation "*into* the mainstream language [is] mostly limited to private documents (driving licences, birth or marriage certificates, academic transcripts, police clearances, etc.) for restricted official use in legal, immigration or residency matters" (García, 2017, p. 99, emphasis in original). In this regard, the STOC community translation project is impactful because it allows the minority community to inform the mainstream community in the majority language about the minority's life experiences.

Community partners that accommodate UTA service-learners include numerous non-profit organisations with limited resources to offer translation services. This situation is relevant to what Taibi (2017) describes: "in situations requiring community translation, public services and translation agencies often find themselves torn between quality standards, on one hand, and, on the other, budgetary considerations and availability of qualified translators in the relevant working languages" (p. 15). Therefore, while student-translators benefit from service-learning projects by acquiring professional experience, they are also an enormous help to non-profit organisations in need of translation services. Also, service-learning impacts participants' lives because it fosters academic learning, community engagement, reflection, and civic responsibility as described by Bringle and Hatcher (1995):

> We consider service-learning to be a course-based, credit-bearing educational experience in which students (a) participate in an organized service activity that meets identified community needs and (b) reflect on the service activity in such a way as to gain further understanding of the course content, a broader appreciation of the discipline, and an enhanced sense of civic responsibility.
>
> *(p. 112)*

Participation in service-learning components represents 20% of students' final grade. Unlike other experiential learning activities, service-learning is weighted in the syllabus: "this is in contrast to co-curricular and extracurricular service, from which learning may occur, but for which there is no formal evaluation and documentation of academic learning" (Bringle & Hatcher, 1995, p. 112).

3 Stories to Our Children: Programme Characteristics

The APL defines STOC as follows:

> Our goal is to enforce the idea that mothers and fathers are the first and most important teachers and role models to their children. Likewise, we seek to create a bond between Arlington families and the library. By being published in the library, families will gain a sense of ownership for the library. Too often, we hear the myth that reading to your child is a middle-class tradition. Families from all backgrounds tell stories to their children. For many families, however, their cultural stories and life experiences are not available on library bookshelves. The goal is to create a special collection of books that are written specifically by Arlington families who have diverse traditions, values and life experiences. By making these unique stories available, we hope to ignite a passion for reading.
> *(Kieffer, 2015, p. 1)*

The APL further explains that through this programme,

> underserved mothers and fathers will be empowered to pen their own children's stories, written from life experiences, imagination and heart. Participants will attend a series of five volunteer-run writing workshops, in which they will write, refine, and illustrate their stories.
> *(Kieffer, 2015, p. 1)*

In turn, their children learn about their family's history and the value of its preservation through literacy. The APL's role in this process also promotes civic understanding of the role of libraries within society as community hubs that offer opportunities for learning, support literacy and education, and preserve cultural heritage.

Several students majoring in Spanish participated in an internship programme called the Latino Outreach Assistants providing many hours of planning, teaching, editing, and copyediting assistance to parents participating in STOC. In sessions led by UTA teaching interns, parents learned how to explore their ideas at deeper levels while getting hands-on experience with the writing process. Parents also worked on their stories at home, putting into practice the reading and writing skills they had learned in these sessions. Some parents shared that their children were inspired to explore the world of books through a new lens and even to write and illustrate their own stories. As described by Rosado et al. (2015), "the program was developed on the premise that sharing stories, in writing or orally, can create a lasting bond between parents and their children, regardless of one's ethnicity, first language, or socioeconomic status" (p. 75).

4 Service-Learning Project Description: STOC Programme Characteristics and Translation into English

SPAN 3340 Introduction to Translation students have translated 122 stories written in Spanish out of a total of 134 stories that were published by the APL in 2013, 2015, 2016, and 2017. Most of the stories are non-fiction autobiographical texts in which family traditions, immigration journeys, motherhood, and childhood are recurring topics. These stories are incredibly relevant as "unfortunately, for many Latina/o families, their cultural traditions and life experiences are not only not available on library bookshelves, but finding literature in their own languages is difficult" (Rosado et al., 2015, p. 75).

SPAN 3340 Introduction to Translation is an introductory course to the theory, methods, techniques, and practice of English–Spanish translation. Students in the course learn how to address translation problems related to culture and language, as well as the fundamentals of translating general material from different fields such as gastronomy and recipes, journalism, advertising, tourism, health, business, etc. Students also acquire basic knowledge of translation theory and history. The main student-learning outcomes are the following:

1   Demonstrate the ability to identify text communicative functions and follow translation assignments.
2   Demonstrate the ability to analyse original texts for translation and examine the conventions of the text and genre.
3   Demonstrate the ability to differentiate types of texts, tools, language, and strategies for general translation.
4   Demonstrate the ability to compare and use parallel texts and reference works (dictionaries, databases, grammars, internet, thesauri, etc.).

In 2015, 2017, and 2018, a service-learning component was incorporated into SPAN 3340 Introduction to Translation with the additional student-learning outcomes:

1   Practice general translation inside and outside of the classroom.
2   Demonstrate the ability to provide professional translations for the APL.
3   Gain professional and work experience translating for the APL.
4   Demonstrate an understanding of the Hispanic immigrant community needs.

Students enrolled in the course could choose between taking an exam or participating in the service-learning component (20% of their final grade). The latter required students to translate one or two stories into English, participate in discussions about the experience throughout the semester, and turn in a reflective essay about their experience with the APL and the Hispanic community. All students presented with the choice opted to take the service-learning component. By participating in the STOC translation project, students not only impacted their immediate community while strengthening their translation skills – they also received the publication of their first translated work that it is catalogued by the APL.

4.1 Methodology and Community Translation Assignment

Before undertaking the STOC translations into English, students analysed the original texts in class. The conventions of the text and genre were examined to identify communicative function and text type (Reiss, 1971/2000). Students evaluated the target audience and the purpose of the translation, and became familiar with *skopos* theory (Vermeer, 1996; Reiss & Vermeer, 1984/2013). Students were also required to follow an assignment or brief in their translation for the APL and its clients, the Arlington community. Nine steps summarise the process students followed to translate the STOC texts:

1. Students were assigned one or two stories to translate.
2. The first draft of the translation had to be completed within four weeks.
3. Translations were turned in anonymously.
4. In their role as student-editors, students were assigned another classmate's translation to review and had to complete an evaluation form based on Way's (2009) Evaluation Sheet.
5. After being reviewed by their assigned editor, students had another two weeks to incorporate the corrections suggested by the editors and turn in a final version of their translation.
6. Each student turned in their final version, together with their first draft and the feedback from their editor.
7. The instructor reviewed translations and gave further feedback and comments to be incorporated into the final version of the translation. Each student was graded on their combined performance in their role as translator and as editor.
8. Translated stories were submitted for publication.
9. Students turned in a reflective essay addressing their role as translator and as editor, detailing their overall experience.

One of the students described this process in their final reflective essay as follows:

> My class partnered with the Arlington Public Library's Stories to Our Children, the service-learning component of the Introduction to Spanish Translation class. I along with a classmate translated a story written by an immigrant parent to their child from Spanish to English. Students were paired and given their own story to translate, and Dr. Rueda-Acedo guided us through the process. The stories were published through the library system making them available for any Arlington resident to read. After six years of learning Spanish, Dr. Rueda-Acedo provided me with my first opportunity to give someone a voice, and I was even provided with a copy of the book to keep as a memory.

Most of the STOC texts translated into English could be categorised as hybrid texts, between testimonio and biographic forms (Senabre, 1998). In the majority of stories, parents share an account of some biographical aspect of their own lives, their family's, or their children's:

> This is a story based on real life. It was during the 60's in a small village ... not even a small village ... just a country house. In a town in San Luis Potosí, a boy named José was born. He was the joy of the family; everyone would spoil him because he was the last born in the family and a very lively and happy boy.
> *(J. G. Ipiña, 2015)*

This biographic form is also reflected in many of the stories' titles, such as, "Vivencias de ayer y hoy"/"Experiences of Yesterday and Today", "Mi familia"/"My Family", "Para mis dos amores"/"For My Two Loves", "Mis recuerdos. Mi tesoro"/"My Memories. My Treasure"; "La historia de un hombre luchador"/"The Story of a Fighting Man"; and "Una pequeña historia"/"A Little Story".

The lives of the authors and their families can be understood as part of what Unamuno (1991) calls *intrahistory*, which is related to *microhistory*, or the social history concept that allows for the lives, ideas, and practices of ordinary people to be known. Their stories provide us with lived testimonies that will be preserved for generations:

> It was a girl that came on a cold night at 3 in the morning on December 7th. I had my baby on me for some time; she wouldn't stop crying.... The doctor came and took my baby and it broke my heart to hear she wouldn't stop crying. Three hours later, I didn't hear my daughter crying, I felt something. There was a silence that I didn't like at all. I felt something was happening. When my husband returned he had such a sadness reflected deeply on his face ... He told me she had died. I couldn't believe it and this news was very hard to hear. My heart was shattered, again, I cried for a long time.
> (P. Ipiña, 2015)

These biographical forms are an expression of the microhistory that tries to construct, from a particular situation, from "the normal-exceptional", the way in which individuals produce the social world (Chartier, 1996, p. 21). They are truly life stories in which, as it happens with oral tradition, the word becomes the transmitter of history, being speech an essential element and the foundation of this new way of approaching history and sociology that is oral history (Chartier et al., 1996, pp. 286–287). In this vein, these stories can be seen as a variant of history, which is properly the narration of the events of a community – a people, a culture, a family – while biography would reduce the broad panorama of history to the strictly individual scope (Senabre, 1998, p. 29).

Most of these stories can be also considered "migrant texts" (King et al., 1995, p. xiii), in which the authors relate their own migratory experience or allude to the family they have left in Mexico and other Latin American countries:

> These are some of my childhood memories. I was happy in my hometown. Now I can come back with my children and re-live some of my past experiences with them. Every time I get a chance, I take them to Juan Aldama for a visit, to spend time with my grandparents, to see the places where I was happy with my family, and where I spent my childhood. I take them to the place where I came from and where they have their origins. The places I will never forget. I want them to create their own memories. Hopefully, one day they will take their own children and they will never forget my lovely town, my Juan Aldama, my San Juan del Mesquital.
> (Fabela, 2015/2018)

These stories illustrate authors' shared experiences of migration and the loss and gain resulting from the experience, the idea of return, of prejudice suffered, of life between two worlds, and of homesickness:

> We came here on October 22, 2017, because my son had to enter Kindergarten. It was something very difficult for me, leaving everything behind, my family and friends, and everything in general. I lived in Mexico for 30 years, and I never thought that this day would arrive . . . "What would San Felipe be like when I am no longer there? What would the streets be like without me?" I would think about all of these things because when the day arrived, I came with conflicted feelings. On the one side, there were so many things left behind, and on the other, it was necessary for my husband and I to be together . . . the three of us as a family.
>
> *(Rodríguez Huerta, 2018)*

Writing within and for the community, as was the case with the STOC programme, "can be a powerful exercise in consensus building and collective knowledge production" (González, 2015, p. 131). When the authors shared their lives and immigration stories, the published stories became living testimonies that share "closely-guarded borderlines with fictional writing and with other forms of auto-biography" (Davies, 2014, p. 174). These texts not only have in common the immigration experience, but they can also be considered hybrid texts between testimonio, (auto)biography, creative non-fiction, and memoir narrative. At the same time, "translation can transform texts into testimonies" (Davies, 2014, p. 171), while "translators and editors of translations negotiate between potentially differing conceptions of testimony in source and target context" (Davies, 2014, p. 172). This aspect was appreciated by students in both their roles as translators and editors. Each translation was reviewed anonymously by a student-editor who corrected content, accuracy, language and style, terminology, and format. Each student-editor proposed corrections and changes, alternative terminology, and discourse and stylistic changes, following the recommendations given by Way (2009) in the Evaluation Sheet presented in "Bringing Professional Practices into Translation Classrooms". This deliberate practice activity allowed students to reinforce their decision-making process when translating. Adopting different roles as translators and as editors helped students develop their ability to assess, revise, and edit their own translation and their peers' (Way, 2009). In one student's own words:

> In this final version of the translations that I did, there weren't very many changes to be made like the editor had mentioned. I did correct the majority of the things the editor advised me to do . . . Now that we have completed these translations I can see where it is helpful to have someone edit your work.

The hybrid form, between orality and writing, of the STOC texts posed another challenge to students as the stories often did not conform to the conventions of written texts, presenting both grammatical and spelling problems, and having a closer resemblance to oral texts. As Davies (2014) points out, a testimonial text:

> poses particular problems for translators, in that decisions have to be made concerning the aspects of the text that are made visible or emphasized in translation. Does one stress the text's linguistic, cultural, or literary historical context(s), or does one ensure that it is legible as belonging to the genre of testimony? When approaching the question of genre, translators are faced with a range of issues that go beyond the formal and linguistic properties of the text.
>
> *(pp. 174–175)*

Student-translators encountered problems such as these, particularly with some stories that were written by mothers and fathers with low literacy levels, as clearly stated in a student reflexive essay: "Although I enjoyed reading and translating these stories, they were a bit of a struggle in some parts. Those stories presented grammar, syntax, culture specifications and in some cases terminology problems". Other students faced similar problems with the translation of culturemes and Mexicanisms as they noted in their reflective essays:

> This story has a lot of Mexican cultural references and I am still wondering how to present them . . . In my opinion translating all the names would take a lot away from the story . . . I consulted two Mexican friends and my editor was Mexican as well and I still do not feel confident that this is the best version of the story. This translation made me realize how hard it can be at times when you are not familiar with a specific culture and their traditions.

After thorough consideration, it was decided in class that translations would not reflect grammatical or syntactical errors so the text could be "accessible or 'relevant' for the target audience" (Davies, 2014, p. 177). As Davies (2014) explains, "by making the text easily accessible, the translator and editors have worked against the assumptions of testimony as a genre. However, it is only the explicit statement that is unusual, not the procedure itself" (p. 178). Students made the original stories accessible when necessary, and they explicitly stated so in their reflections. The reason behind this procedure was not only to make the texts more readable, but also because translating the orality of these texts and reflecting the grammatical, orthographical, and syntactical problems posed a very difficult challenge for novice translators. Nevertheless, student-translators made the effort to be faithful to the spirit of the original texts, navigating the "the negative aura surrounding the translator as a potential cultural traitor" (Polezzi, 2006, p. 169), to ensure that "the translated text embodies the witness and transmits the voice in the same way as the original" (Davies, 2014, p. 183). This was expressed in the following student's reflective essay:

> My goal was to translate as accurate[ly] as possible so that whoever reads this translation, may as well put themselves in the author's shoes and

understand what he or she felt during the time of the events. This was something I felt when I read the stories in Spanish and wanted the reader to have the same feeling with my translation.

The testimonios and (auto)biographic forms present in the STOC texts "speak to the unique experiences they [parents] bring to this country – be it through a different cultural or linguistic lens or through the sharing of stories which would have otherwise gone unheard" (Rosado et al., 2015, p. 73). The translation of these immigration stories into English increases their dissemination, allowing the whole community to have access to them, permitting a dialogue, and giving the authors a feeling of belonging. The authors' voices are thus amplified, while allowing students to improve their translation and editorial competence, and to gain professional experience along with the publication of their first translation book. One student describes the overall experience:

> I really enjoyed working with these short stories . . . Knowing that their stories were real life experiences written by people gave it a whole different meaning to it. It challenged me to do my very best in order to provide a translation as accurate as possible in order for my English reader to understand not only the language but also the message that these writers are wanting to send to the reader. Some of them even touched my heart . . . My packet was just filled with great inspiring stories that people shared for us to read and learn about their lives and how we can learn from them to make a better self out of us.

4.2 Event Planning and Leadership: STOC Final Celebration

At the end of the academic year, students in SPAN 3340 Introduction to Translation and families participating in STOC came together for a celebration of translation, family, and literacy. Student-translators and STOC participating families were invited to UTA to provide everyone with a better understanding of the three organisations that made the project possible: the APL, the AISD, and UTA. For many parents, this was the first time they visited a college campus, and the event provided a great opportunity to talk to their children about college. For student-translators, it was an opportunity to meet the authors and see first-hand the impact of their translations. All participating parents, families, and students received a copy of the published book they had written or translated. This closing event was attended by 150–200 people, and it represented an excellent avenue to culminate the STOC programme and the SPAN 3340 Introduction to Translation subject. A children's author was invited to give a talk, and the attendees also enjoyed the opportunity to share tacos and refreshments in a festive environment.

When implementing a service-learning component into a course, Jenkins and Sheehey (2011) recommend following a checklist which "delineates the four-stage service-learning process: (a) preparation, (b) implementation, (c) assessment/

reflection, and (d) demonstration/celebration" (p. 52). In planning the STOC Final Celebration, the Latino Outreach Assistants were responsible for the following tasks:

1. Identify and invite a children's book author as guest speaker for the event.
2. Create and distribute an invitation to the event for parents and families and student-translators.
3. Reserve, decorate, and set up the space for the event (UTA Central Library or Maverick Activities Center).
4. Contact donors that sponsor children's events to serve light refreshments.
5. Prepare the bilingual script (English/Spanish) for the event and include all participants: APL and AISD staff, UTA faculty and students, parents, and guest author.
6. Welcome parents and families the day of the event.
7. Interpret for non-Spanish speaking parents.
8. Take photos of the event and post them on social media.

The event was a complete success, providing parents and children with the opportunity to interact with UTA faculty and students, APL staff, and the guest authors. It was a real celebration of writing and translation. In the words of one of the student-translators:

> I really think this is an amazing project because this gives the Arlington parents the opportunity to make a difference in their community and their kids' lives. I really enjoyed this service learning for various reasons: 1) I was able to translate their stories into English so other people can read them 2) I felt part of the community and making a difference 3) I was able to put my translation and editing skills into practice.

5 The Advantage of Integrating Community Translation and Service-Learning

Participating in a service-learning component of this kind, which is reinforced by related activities such as the STOC Final Celebration, is rewarding for students from a community engagement perspective, but also from a translation practice standpoint. In the words of one of the students:

> I have greatly enjoyed my experiences with Stories to Our Children. Having the opportunity to read, translate, and edit these parents' stories has been incredible. I loved reading the stories and learning more about some of the families in this program. I feel privileged to have had a glimpse into the most private and intimate details of their lives. I had never truly known the depth of a parent's love until I read what these parents wrote for their children. Not only have I increased my own skills as a translator, but I have helped their stories live on through my work. This has been an amazing

experience, and I am grateful for the chance to use my skills to help these families through Stories to Our Children.

With community translation and service-learning, students are conscious of the impact of their own work. As Taibi (2017) points out, "with community empowerment as a foregrounded goal, community translators demonstrate their awareness of their role as social agents and of the social ramifications of their translatorial actions beyond processing of individual sentences and texts" (p. 19). In this regard, another student pointed out that:

> When I finally decided to begin to translate the stories, I realized that the parents' life was not much different than a lot of minorities in the United States. There are more similarities than differences, from Mexico to the US and from the "Ghetto or Projects" to mainstream America. In each case, there is an underlying factor; a better life for the kids. There is this struggle for the child to have a life different than that of the parents and with each generation it is supposed to get better. I could relate to the stories that I translated because I am older than the parents that wrote them. There is always the struggle and the sacrifice for the betterment of the next generation, for the child or the children. More often than not the gap is not bridged and the parent loses the dream. In the case of the stories I translated, there was this silent resilience that moved the families forward and they made it.

Students agreed that participating in the STOC project improved their translator competence, and specifically, their "ability to transition from a classroom community of practice to a professional community of practice through Situated Learning" (González-Davies & Enríquez-Raído, 2016, p. 2). This situated learning project allowed us to observe that: "translator competence emerges as the result of the collaborative completion of authentic translation work" (Kiraly, 2005, p. 1101). It also demonstrated that:

> by observing translators, both non-professional and professional, in the socially-situated praxis of authentic translation work, we can acquire a privileged view of the nature of the translation process and glean readily applicable insights into how best help students develop their capability to function as professional translators in the real world outside of the academic ivory tower.
> *(Kiraly, 2005, p. 1101).*

Transitioning from the classroom to a professional setting is usually a challenge as students lack translation competence. Different models of translation competence have been proposed to develop objectives and learning outcomes for translation curricula (Way, 2009). Kelly (2002) points out that translation competence is the macro-competence that comprises the different capacities, skills, knowledge and even attitudes that professional translators possess, and which are involved in translation as an expert activity (p. 14). Service-learning has proven to be an excellent curriculum addition to improve the following translation subcompetences described by Kelly (2005):

- "Strategic competence. Organizational and planning skills. Problem identification and problem-solving. Monitoring, self-assessment and revision" (p. 84). Students' comments from reflective essays confirm improvement of this competence: "This project was a new experience I had never had. I became more knowledgeable in understanding the concepts of translating for an author that is not at a professional level, making the translation a challenge"; "the whole process in this service-learning helped me to become a good translator; from translating to revising and editing, to finally doing a final version was amazing".
- "Subject area competence. Basic knowledge of subject areas the future translator will/may work in, to a degree sufficient to allow comprehension of source texts and access to specialized documentation to solve translation problems" (Kelly, 2005, p. 84). Here again, several students identified improvements: "I enjoyed it because it gave me a feel of real-life situations. I encountered problems I didn't think about before"; "This service experience was very rewarding and made me feel that I was gaining real-life insight in the translation process".
- "Attitudinal or psycho-physiological competence. Self-concept, self-confidence, attention/concentration, memory. Initiative" (Kelly, 2005, p. 84). The following testimonials from other students show the impact of service-learning on this sub-competence: "I really enjoyed this class as well as working with service-learning. It was challenging at times, but I know all the effort I put will soon pay off"; "I am grateful for the opportunity to work with the Arlington Public Library through this service learning. It's been a great experience, I feel that I have become a much better translator".
- "Cultural and intercultural competence . . . . Awareness of issues of intercultural communication and translation as a special form thereof" (Kelly, 2005, p. 84).
- "Professional and instrumental competence. Use of documentary resources of all kinds, terminological research, information management" (Kelly, 2005, p. 84). In another student's words:

   This translation project was one of the most difficult, but something very rewarding. I really liked being part of something so significant for the Latino community, especially since I can relate with many of the authors for being an immigrant myself. I think it is a nice way to share our culture and our experiences in a foreign country.

- "Interpersonal competence. Ability to work with other professionals involved in translation process . . . and other actors (clients, initiators, authors, users, subject area experts). Team work. Negotiation skills. Leadership skills" (Kelly, 2005, p. 84). This was observed by different students as follows: "At first, I thought it was going to be really difficult, but once I got started, it wasn't that bad. It also helped having someone edit my translation so that my final product was the best it could be"; "It was a great experience doing this project because it gave me real translating experience outside of the class. It helped me realize the importance of translation in my community and on getting feedback/help from other translators".

In 2017, pre- and post-questionnaires were distributed at the beginning and end of the semester, respectively. There were 13 participants and questionnaire responses were given on a 5-point rating scale (1 = *strongly disagree* to 5 = *strongly agree*). To the statement: "I think I will learn more in this class than if there was no service-learning experience", only 38.46% participants responded affirmatively (4 or 5 on the scale) at the beginning of the semester. At the end of the semester, 84.61% agreed that they learned more with this service-learning experience. All of the participants (100%) also agreed that they gained valuable experience for their résumés, that they contributed to the betterment of the community, and that the texts translated in class helped their translation while collaborating with the APL (92.3%). Students also agreed that their translation competence improved and that they gained professional experience as a translator (100%). In a student's own words: "I think this was a great experience for me because it helped me learn more about the families in my community, helped me become stronger in translating, and also got input from a fellow peer". Surveyed students agreed that the reflective essay helped them understand the translation process and the relevance of their service-learning collaboration (100%). All of them (100%) would recommend this course because of its service-learning component. When asked to check the following reasons for recommending this course because of its service-learning component, all of them checked "yes" as their answer to: "General positive and rewarding experience", "Possibilities for career exploration and networking", "Real world experience added to course content", "Community involvement", "Gaining real work experience", and "Having my first translation published".

6 Conclusions: The Benefits of Combining Community Translation and Service-Learning in Introductory Translation Courses

Service-learning helps students improve their translation competence and their decision-making process. It also reduces their anxiety when translating, and reinforces their motivation, confidence, and self-esteem as translators, as can be observed from students' reflective essays. Not only do students strengthen their skills while affecting their immediate community, but they also have the chance to publish their first translation which is then catalogued by the APL. For translation students seeking to develop their professional experience before graduation, service-learning allows them to develop readiness for the job market and self-confidence, promoting civic responsibility and active citizenship. Combining community translation and service-learning in a project like the STOC translations allows students and community members to better understand the connection between migration, testimonio, and (auto)biography. Service-learning and community translation are extraordinary tools to train future translators, particularly those interested in empowering the members of minority communities.

Although the association between translation and service-learning may seem evident, there is very little literature on the matter, with only a few studies that examine the relationship between the two, such as, Bugel (2013), Faszer-McMahon (2013), Lizardi-Rivera (1999), Nelson and Scott (2008), Shaw and Roberson (2009), Rueda-Acedo (2017, 2021), Tocaimaza-Hatch (2018), and Thompson and Hague (2018). Bugel (2013), emphasises the multiple ramifications of translation and service-learning:

> most aspects of life and interaction between members of different speech communities relate to translation, given the production of intragroup and intergroup meaning. Thus, familiarizing students with translation through service-learning is an endeavor that quite naturally extends beyond the four walls of a classroom or a university campus to reach the community.
> *(p. 371)*

In this regard, Nelson and Scott (2008), Shaw and Roberson (2009), Thompson and Hague (2018), Lizardi-Rivera (1999), and Rueda-Acedo (2017, 2021) highlight the benefits and impacts on students and community members alike. Additionally, Nelson and Scott (2008), Tocaimaza-Hatch (2018), and Fazer-MacMahon (2013) point out that the combination of service-learning and translation supports the development of students' transcultural and translingual skills, and the improvement of their cultural and linguistic competence. Moreover, Nelson and Scott (2008), Rueda-Acedo (2017, 2021), and Martínez-Gómez (2018) agree that service-learning is an extraordinary tool to overcome the lack of practical experience that translation and interpreting students face before graduation.

Community translation and service-learning complement each other and allow the development of multilingual and multicultural projects like STOC. These activities foster communication and partnership between instructors, students, and community partners and members. They provide students with translation experience involving real clients and real needs, replacing the artificiality of classroom instruction. As one student reports:

> Being able to translate the stories that parents who do not speak English wrote for their children gave me a heartwarming feeling because I know the work, effort, and thought came from within deep feelings. I understand that in many cases parents who do not speak the English language may have a tougher time becoming involved with their child's academics because of language barriers, so this opportunity is very fulfilling.

The STOC translation project has been very rewarding for all agents involved: students, faculty, and community members and partners. Thanks to this community translation and service-learning project, the whole Arlington community has been granted access to the (auto)biographical and testimonial texts from newcomers to Arlington. At the same time, these translations afford the authors a sense of inclusion and acceptance in their new community. For students, it was an extraordinary opportunity to gain professional experience before graduation while affecting their surrounding community and receiving their first published translation book.

References

Bringle, R. G., & Hatcher, J. A. (1995). A service-learning curriculum for faculty. *Michigan Journal of Community Service Learning, 2*(1), 112–122. http://hdl.handle.net/2027/spo.3239521.0002.111

Bugel, T. (2013). Translation as a multilingual and multicultural mirror framed by service-learning. *Hispania, 96*(2), 369–382.

Chartier, R. (1996). La historia de hoy en día: dudas, desafíos, propuestas. [History today: Doubts, challenges, proposals]. In I. Olábarri & F. J. Caspistegui (Eds.), *La "nueva" historia cultural: la influencia del postestructuralismo y el auge de la interdisciplinariedad* (pp. 19–34). Editorial Complutense.

Chartier, R., Caspistegui, F. J., & Morales Moya, A. (1996). Las formas de expresión (el habla, la escritura, el gesto) [The forms of expression (speech, writing, gesture)]. In I. Olábarri & F. J. Caspistegui (Eds.), *La "nueva" historia cultural: la influencia del postestructuralismo y el auge de la interdisciplinariedad* (pp. 271–302). Editorial Complutense.

Davies, P. (2014). Testimony and translation. *Translation and Literature, 24*(2), 170–184. https://doi.org/10.3366/tal.2014.0148

Fabela, B. (2018). My lovely town (R. Lallave, Trans.). In *Stories to our children*. Arlington Public Library (Original work published 2015).

Faszer-McMahon, D. (2013). Social networking, microlending, and translation in the Spanish service-learning classroom. *Hispania, 96*(2), 252–263. https://doi.org/10.1353/hpn.2013.0045

García, I. (2017). Volunteers and public service translation. In M. Taibi (Ed.), *Translating for the community* (pp. 98–109). Multilingual Matters. https://doi.org/10.21832/TAIBI9139

González-Davies, M., & Enríquez-Raído, V. (2016). Situated learning in translator and interpreter training: Bridging research and good practice. *The Interpreter and Translator Trainer, 10*(1), 1–11. https://doi.org/10.1080/1750399X.2016.1154339

González, M. E. (2015). "Sobreviviendo": Immigration stories and *testimonio* in song. *Diálogo, 18*(2), 131–138.

Ipiña, J. G. (2015). A little story (P. Gómez, Trans.). In *Stories to our children, 1*. Arlington Public Library (Original work published 2015).

Ipiña, P. (2015). A life (E. Griffin, Trans.). In *Stories to our children, 1*. Arlington Public Library (Original work published 2015).

Jenkins, A., & Sheehey, P. (2011). A checklist for implementing service-learning in higher education. *Journal of Community Engagement and Scholarship, 4*(2), 52–60.

Kelly, D. (2002). Un modelo de competencia traductora: bases para el diseño curricular [A model for translation competence: Foundations for curriculum design]. *Puentes, 1*, 9–29. http://wpd.ugr.es/~greti/revista-puentes/pub1/02-Kelly.pdf

Kelly, D. (2005). *A handbook for translator trainers: A guide to reflective practice*. St. Jerome.

Kieffer, I. (2015). *Stories to our children: Share special stories through your writing!* [Class handout]. Arlington Public Library.

Kiraly, D. (2005). Project-based learning: A case for situated translation. *Meta, 50*(4), 1098–1111. https://doi.org/10.7202/012063ar

King, R., Connell, J., & White, P. (Eds.). (1995). *Writing across worlds: Literature and migration.* Routledge.

Lizardi-Rivera, C. (1999). Learning the basics of Spanish translation: Articulating a balance between theory and practice through community service. In J. Hellebrandt & L. T. Varona (Eds.), *Construyendo puentes (building bridges): Concepts and models for service-learning in Spanish* (pp. 107–121). American Association for Higher Education.

Martínez-Gómez, A. (2018). Experiential learning in court interpreting education: A pilot internship in New York City courts. *Cuadernos de ALDEEU, 33,* 113–142.

Nelson, A. L, & Scott, J. L. (2008). Applied Spanish in the university curriculum: A successful model for community-based service-learning. *Hispania, 91*(2), 446–460. https://doi.org/10.2307/20063729

Polezzi, L. (2006). Translation, travel, migration. *The Translator, 12*(2), 169–188. https://doi.org/10.1080/13556509.2006.10799214

Reiss, K. (2000). *Translation criticism, the potential and limitations: Categories and criteria for translation quality assessment* (E. F. Rhodes, Trans.). St. Jerome (Original work published 1971).

Reiss, K., & Vermeer, H. J. (2013). *Towards a general theory of translational action: Skopos theory explained* (C. Nord, Trans.). St. Jerome (Original Work published 1984).

Rodríguez Huerta, H. (2018). A Life Change (S. Fernandes, Trans.). In *Stories to our children.* Arlington Public Library (Original work published 2018).

Rosado, L., Amaro-Jiménez, C., & Kieffer, I. (2015). Stories to our children: A program aimed at developing authentic and culturally relevant literature for Latina/o children. *School Community Journal, 25*(1), 73–93.

Rueda-Acedo, A. (2017). From the classroom to the job market: Integrating service-learning and community translation in a legal translation course. In M. Taibi (Ed.), *Translating for the community* (pp. 42–68). Multilingual Matters. https://doi.org/10.21832/TAIBI9139

Rueda-Acedo, A. (2021). A successful framework for developing a certificate in Spanish translation through community translation and service-learning. *Hispania, 104*(2), 241–258.

Senabre, R. (1998). Sobre el estatuto genérico de la biografía. [On the genre status of biography]. In J. Romera Castillo & F. Gutiérrez Carbajo (Eds.), *Biografías literarias (1975–1997): Actas del VII seminario internacional del instituto de semiótica literaria, teatral y nuevas tecnologías de la UNED* (pp. 29–38). Visor.

Shaw, S., & Roberson, L. (2009). Service-learning: Recentering the deaf community in interpreter education. *American Annals of the Deaf, 154*(3), 277–283.

Taibi, M. (2011). Public service translation. In K. Malmkjær & K. Windle (Eds.), *The Oxford handbook of translation studies* (pp. 214–227). Oxford University Press. https://doi-org.ezproxy.lib.rmit.edu.au/10.1093/oxfordhb/9780199239306.001.0001

Taibi, M. (2017). Quality assurance in community translation. In M. Taibi (Ed.), *Translating for the community* (pp. 7–25). Multilingual Matters.

Taibi, M., & Ozolins, U. (2016). *Community translation.* Bloomsbury.

Thompson, G. L., & Hague, D. (2018). Using community service learning in the Spanish translation classroom: Challenges and opportunities. *Cuadernos de ALDEEU, 33,* 87–111.

Tocaimaza-Hatch, C. (2018). Linguistic and social affordances in the translation and interpretation course via service-learning. *Cuadernos de ALDEEU, 33*, 53–58.

Unamuno, M. (1991). *En torno al casticismo.* Espasa-Calpe.

U.S. Census Bureau. (2017, August 31). *Facts for features: Hispanic heritage month 2017.* www.census.gov/newsroom/facts-for-features/2017/hispanic-heritage.html

U.S. Census Bureau. (2021a, August 12). *2020 Census statistics highlight local population changes and nation's racial and ethnic diversity.* www.census.gov/newsroom/press-releases/2021/population-changes-nations-diversity.html

U.S. Census Bureau. (2021b, November 19). *Quick facts Texas.* www.census.gov/quickfacts/TX#qf-headnote-b

Way, C. (2009). Bringing professional practices into translation classrooms. In I. Kemble (Ed.), *The changing face of translation: Proceedings of the eighth annual Portsmouth translation conference held on 8 November 2008* (pp. 131–142). University of Portsmouth.

Vermeer, H. J. (1996). *A skopos theory of translation: (Some arguments for and against).* TextconText Verlag.

10
THE MULTILINGUAL COMMUNITY TRANSLATION CLASSROOM

Challenges and Strategies to Train Profession-Ready Graduates

Miranda Lai and Erika Gonzalez

1 Introduction

Australia is a multicultural and multilingual country where more than 250 languages are spoken, including Aboriginal languages and Auslan (Australian Sign Language). According to the census of 2016, Australia is a "fast changing, ever-expanding, culturally diverse nation" (Australian Bureau of Statistics, 2017, para. 1), with nearly half of the population being born overseas or having one or both parents who were born overseas (49%). Moreover, according to the 2021 census, 5.5 million people speak languages other than English at home and nearly 1 million Australians (850,000 out of a total of approximately 25.7 million) stated not being able to speak English well or very well, which justifies the high demand for community interpreting and translation services (Australian Bureau of Statistics, 2022).

Australia is a nation with one of the richest and most ancient Indigenous cultures on the planet and was already a multilingual country before European settlement. Hlavac (2021) discusses the development of community translation and interpreting in Australia, explaining that "interpreting, if not translation, predated the arrival of Europeans in Australia in the eighteenth century. We can infer this because in many Indigenous groups two conditions were present that commonly precipitate linguistic mediation – exogamy and geographical mobility" (p. 65). Indigenous interpreters also played an important role when white settlers arrived:

> The need for effective communication between Europeans and Australian Aboriginal people was evident from the earliest days of European settlement at Sydney in 1788. Arabanoo was the first Aboriginal to be captured so that Europeans could learn Aboriginal language. However, he soon died from smallpox and two more men were captured for the same purpose. One

of these men, Bennelong, made considerable progress in learning English and was soon utilised as a cultural broker and interpreter.

(Cooke, 2009, p. 86)

However, it was not until the arrival of displaced migrants from Europe after World War II that the need for community translation and interpreting was acknowledged: "the Australian 'community interpreter' [and translator] was born out of necessity during post-war immigration in the 1950s" (Hale, 2004, p. 15). A couple of decades later, the Vietnam War and conflicts in other parts of the world attracted more migrants and refugees to Australia (Bell, 1997), producing a "kaleidoscope of diverse peoples" (Richards, 2008, p. 244). Initially, it was believed that the problem with language barriers would cease once migrants learnt English, but the offer of English courses did not provide the expected results (Hale, 2004; Ozolins, 1998), and many still required the assistance of interpreters and translators to communicate. As pointed out by Taibi et al. (2021), "government discourse started to acknowledge the language barriers faced by speakers of languages other than English and the ensuing need for government intervention and assistance to overcome those barriers and work towards a more equitable society" (p. 87).

The first interpreters and translators, however, were ad hoc practitioners, migrants who had a better command of the English language than their peers, or the children of such migrants. Negative communication outcomes due to the engagement of non-professionals consequently prompted a change that led to the inception of professional community translation and interpreting services. Reports with recommendations for best practice were issued throughout the next decade, including: *Migrants and the Legal System: Research Report* (Jakubowicz & Buckley, 1975), "The Galbally Report" (Galbally, 1978), *Evaluation of Post-Arrival Programs and Services* (Australian Institute of Multicultural Affairs, 1982), and *Report on a National Language Policy* (Senate Standing Committee on Education and the Arts, 1984). The outcomes of this extensive research led to the beginning of translation and interpreting services as we know them today (see Hale [2004] for a full discussion on the reports), including the creation of a national accreditation system in 1977 known as the National Accreditation Authority for Translators and Interpreters (NAATI). Within two decades, Australia achieved important milestones in the provision of community-based interpreting and translation services, paving the way for the professionalisation of the discipline: "Australia has developed a comprehensive system of accreditation, service provision and training, and has pioneered many innovations in multilingual communications such as telephone interpreting, training of users of interpreters, etc." (Ozolins, 1995, p. 2).

The profession of translation and interpreting in Australia has been shaped by the migration history of the country, and it can therefore be posited that most translators and interpreters in Australia today work in community settings (Hlavac, 2021; Taibi et al., 2021). It is thus unsurprising that most of the educational programmes around the country have a strong focus on educating future community translators and interpreters.

2 Training and Educating Community Translators

Translator education in Australia was introduced in 1975, at the Royal Melbourne Institute of Technology (RMIT), then a polytechnic (Taibi et al., 2021). The programme we will analyse and describe in this chapter evolved from that pioneering translating and interpreting programme in Australia.

Despite having one of the oldest accreditation/certification systems in the world and a broad offering of training programmes that date back to the 1970s and 1980s, pre-service, compulsory translator education and training were not introduced in Australia until 2018. Prior to that time, there was a dual pathway to enter the profession. The first pathway required candidates to pass a NAATI translation exam, while the second pathway required the successful completion of a course at an approved tertiary education provider, which included universities and Technical and Further Education (TAFE) vocational colleges. Due to this dual entry system into the profession, it can be concluded that there are a significant number of translators who have never received any training in translation. The certification system introduced in 2018 also requires practitioners to undertake professional development (PD) and recertify their NAATI credentials every three years. Those translators who obtained their accreditations before 2007 were given the option to convert their accreditation into a certification. The new system prompted many translators to address knowledge gaps and a lack of solid theoretical foundations with PD (see González [2019] for a full discussion), one of the pre-requisites for recertification. However, many translators decided not to transition. These practitioners have been excluded from community translation projects, as government departments only accept translations completed by certified professionals.

Compulsory pre-testing education was introduced as the result of a national report that put forward a set of recommendations to improve the NAATI testing system and access to the profession in general (Hale et al., 2012). The first recommendation specified that "all candidates complete compulsory education and training in order to be eligible to sit for the accreditation examinations" (Hale et al., 2012, p. 7). It is not surprising that pre-testing and pre-service training was recommended as one of the priorities. Definitions of professionalism stress that professionals are those who have theoretical knowledge and skills derived from education and training. As Mulayim and Lai (2017) state, "the most distinguishing features that define a particular activity as a profession are special skills and knowledge and training" (p. 30). Although some individual and innate qualities may help, it is training and education that define a professional (González, 2013; Mackintosh, 1999). Currently, the main challenge in Australia is to train and certify translators of a broader linguistic background. In the case of those who work with languages not taught at translation faculties and vocational colleges, the society and the industry still rely on their innate abilities and bilingual skills.

2.1 Social Commitment

One of the main issues affecting translation faculties across the globe is that university departments do not have the capacity to cover the languages in demand in our societies. Downing (1998) raised this issue more than two decades ago by stressing that "a major difficulty is the fact that the languages of immigrants and indigenous ethnic groups are often not the languages in which universities have curricula and faculty expertise" (p. 28). Most universities in Australia offer translator training in a limited number of languages, and as with interpreting, "most provide a range of six to ten languages with Chinese being ubiquitous" (Taibi et al., 2021, p. 92).

In 2020, RMIT University introduced a new teaching approach to respond to the increasing societal need to train local community translators at the tertiary level in languages other than those that had been traditionally taught at the institution and at other Australian universities. The Australian tertiary education sector depends heavily on the income generated by international students, and translation programmes have not been immune to this dependency:

> The commoditisation and internationalisation of Australia's education system has been so far-reaching that Australia's economic stability, and the future of higher education institutes, are now largely dependent on the continued enrolment of overseas students into their courses.
>
> *(Debets, 2018, p. 23)*

Historically, the stability of translation programmes has therefore relied heavily on attracting international students for financial reasons. In the case of translation programmes, Chinese students constitute the majority of international enrolments and are the largest language group in most universities. However, this model prevents local capacity building and the development of strategies to address community-specific needs. Academics are pressured to comply with staff–student ratios imposed by university management, which often does not understand translation studies. Large language cohorts, such as the Chinese, fund other smaller language streams. This is a reality which some scholars have already raised:

> In the university level training of translators and interpreters, the field is dominated by students from China and by work on English-Chinese translation, to the extent that translator training in most other languages, could not be profitably offered without fairly high proportions of courses being shared with Chinese-language students.
>
> *(Pym, 2021, p. 297)*

We have found it increasingly difficult to justify small staff–student ratios in the language-specific tutorials or practical classes for groups other than the Chinese. Anecdotal evidence shows that colleagues at other universities face similar challenges. In many cases, universities require a minimum of 20–30 students to offer a course or tutorial. That is an impossible number to achieve for smaller language streams, especially for those languages of new and emerging communities.

2.2. Educating Graduates for the Real World

Upon graduation, the vast majority of translation and interpreting graduates in Australia end up working in community settings. In translation, this is especially the case for those who work from English into other languages. Community translation "covers translation not for readers in different countries, but translations made for readers *within* a country or region" (Taibi & Ozolins, 2016, p. 1, emphasis in original). Community translation includes the translation of official documents, as well as the translation of information that has been produced in the official language(s) of a country, for dissemination purposes into other non-official languages for the benefit of community members who are not fluent in the official language(s). The dissemination of government information in multiple languages regarding the COVID-19 pandemic is a good example of community translation. Given that these translations are produced for a very specific target audience, in a unique socio-political and geographical context, community translators not only require solid foundations in translation theories and skills, but also an in-depth knowledge of the local, political, social, and ethnographic context in which the translations will be disseminated.

In order to be work-ready and profession-ready, community translators need to develop skills and abilities that will allow them to produce high-quality translations. They should also be aware of the conditions surrounding the production and reception of translations, given that the translation process does not happen in a vacuum (Holz-Manttäri, 1984). Moreover, gaining knowledge regarding "translation tradition, historical trends, socio-economic constraints, market conditions, institutional practices, budgetary issues and/or resource availability" (González-Davies & Enríquez Raído, 2016, p. 2) will help graduates become profession-ready. González and Revolta (2021), in reference to Brown et al. (1989), state that "traditional pedagogies have treated knowledge as a self-sufficient area that is theoretically independent regarding the contexts where that knowledge materialises" (p. 154). In the case of community translation, it is paramount that pedagogy is framed in a manner that allows for the development of knowledge as a "product of the activity, context and culture in which it is developed and used" (Brown et al., 1989, p. 32). This concept of experiencing *knowledge-in-action* (Kiraly, 2000) is also closely related to the concept of employability, since the more exposure students have to the conditions they will encounter in the professional world, the more employable they will be. As Bennett (2019) states, "employability is a vital lynchpin in the balancing act between student, community, government and industry expectations of higher education and what the sector can deliver" (p. 35), adding that "all learning should have relevance to possible disciplinary, societal, personal and/or professional futures of students" (p. 46). Knowledge-in-action allows students to experience the subject matter under the same circumstances as in the real world. Knowledge-in-action is also connected to the notion of *authenticity* and the experience of authentic work in the learning journey (Pacheco Aguilar, 2016). Therefore, we believe that the community translation curriculum should offer a balance between the acquisition of the theoretical and philosophical foundations of the discipline and the development of skills and attributes needed to practise the discipline in a real professional setting. Moreover, a balance between commercial languages and languages in demand should be pursued by university programmes, whenever possible, to meet societal needs.

2.3 Work-Ready and Profession-Ready Graduates

In our programme, producing well-rounded community translators who are work-ready and profession-ready requires a scaffolded approach to curriculum design. This means that in the initial stages of their studies, students acquire solid theoretical foundations that will allow them to gain a good understanding of translation as a discipline, the translation process, and translation approaches. In the foundational stages, they are also introduced to professional ethics and the Code of Conduct. In Australia, the introduction of ethics in the translation curriculum is compulsory for NAATI-endorsed educational institutions. Some see this as an imposition (Pym, 2021), but if educators craft the ethics curriculum in a meaningful manner, students learn to apply ethical principles by reflecting on the theoretical contents they have acquired in other subjects. The study of ethics offers an excellent avenue to reflect on the visibility and invisibility of the translator; notions of accuracy, censorship, adaptation, transcreation, etc.; and how these aspects fit with the principles of the Code of Conduct. Students learn that the Code is not a dogmatic instrument, but a guide that only those with deep theoretical knowledge of the discipline can interpret and apply coherently (González, 2013).

Once students gain theoretical knowledge about the discipline and develop acceptable translation skills, they become work-ready, meaning that they have gained the necessary abilities to undertake work and translation assignments. However, to be profession-ready, it is important to allow students to experience knowledge-in-action. The gradual introduction of situated learning components into the curriculum is paramount to achieve such a goal, as it enables the exposure to authenticity and the recreation of environments that are similar to those students will encounter when they graduate. The notion of a gradual curricular transition from work-ready to profession-ready graduates was developed by González and Revolta (2021) in their work on the introduction of situated learning pedagogies in the conference interpreting curriculum. Similarly, Miner and Nicodemus (2021) advocate for a scaffolded approach to situated learning which they call the "Staircase Model" (p. 43). This model requires that interpreting students complete a five-step learning journey before they practise in the real world. First, students acquire "Theoretical Foundations", and then apply the knowledge acquired in this initial stage in the second phase of "Theoretical Application", before they transition to "Situated Community Engagement", whereby they observe and participate in real-life activities (Miner & Nicodemus, 2021, p. 45). In the "Situated Simulated Performance" or fourth stage, students apply their knowledge in the real world but without the actual consumers, and in the last stage or the "Situated Authentic" phase, students practise by completing semi- or fully authentic assignments under the supervision of mentors with participants or consumers present (Miner & Nicodemus, 2021, p. 45). Finally, students would be ready to join what Miner and Nicodemus (2021) describe as the "Community of Practice" (p. 45). The approach followed at RMIT in the community translator education emulates this scaffolded approach to situated learning.

3 Case Study: Community Translation at RMIT

Guided by González and Revolta's (2021) situated learning model and the "Staircase Model" by Miner and Nicodemus (2021), we believe that profession-ready community translators exiting training should: (a) have a suite of theoretically supported translation strategies to deal with linguistic disparities between the source and target languages in the domain of public services; (b) be aware of the asymmetric power relations between the source text producer and the target text reader; and (c) be skilful in their translation practice and able to reflect and justify the decisions they take and the positioning of their role in the process of translation. This will also equip them to sit the national translator certification test administered by NAATI before they can practice as community translators.

3.1 Pedagogical Overview

In RMIT's postgraduate translating and interpreting (T&I) studies, three programme configurations are available for students to choose depending on the length of time they study. They can acquire a graduate certificate after one semester of full-time study, a graduate diploma after two semesters, or a master's degree after four semesters. In theoretical courses, students are taught together in English regardless of their respective language backgrounds. This also extends to the lectures of practical T&I courses or subjects. In addition, students participate in language-specific tutorials for the practical courses, in which experienced instructors are normally engaged via casual employment arrangements. These instructors are usually recruited from the T&I industry and have postgraduate training and are reputable practitioners. It is a pivotal role as students get feedback on their performance into their language other than English (LOTE) in these tutorials and can have discussions and seek advice on questions of a bilingual nature, including transfer difficulties, expression issues, or target text language conventions. For the more established community languages, there are senior practitioners suitable to be recruited to teach the tutorials, who not only have the required standing in the industry but have themselves been through relevant T&I education, so they have better theoretical underpinnings to support their instruction. It is much more challenging to recruit tutors for new and emerging languages, as the pools of practitioners are by nature much smaller to start with due to the more recent arrival and settlement of those communities, as well as the fact that there may not be any suitably qualified candidates who have the preferred level of industry experience as well as relevant prior T&I education due to the lack of opportunities described previously in Section 2.1.

To overcome the challenge of having a programme with student enrolments from new and emerging language backgrounds, and the resulting difficulty of forming a language-specific tutorial group due to low numbers, a multi-pronged approach is taken to ensure the student has the best support and alternative arrangements for their learning. The measures include attempting to recruit at least a pair of students of the same language to facilitate peer learning, locating external practitioner mentors recommended by the industry, providing extra instructions in English in lieu of a LOTE tutorial, focusing on guidance for source text analysis, target text self-reflection, and research skills for parallel texts. In situations when a small tutorial group is formed and a casual tutor is identified but the tutor is new to tertiary teaching and may not have as much practical experience as other tutors of more established languages, a teaching mentor who is normally on staff in the programme team is assigned to support the newly recruited tutor.

The mentorship provided is highly individualised, complementing the new tutor's skill set and needs. Detailed briefing sessions are indispensable, including suggestions on session structure, class activities, and sources to look for materials suitable for adaptation into LOTE or bilingual materials, on top of administrative matters covering university onboarding procedures and setting up self-service portal access, such as to access pay information and use library resources. Respectful and honest discussions must also be had in relation to the tutor's role, role boundaries, and inclusive teaching. Regardless of established or newer language backgrounds, new tutors may come from a different education system and be accustomed to pedagogical styles and interactional dynamics between teachers and students that are different from those of Australian tertiary education settings. It is therefore helpful to cover these topics to ensure the new tutor is aware of the institutional expectations and feel fully supported. Debriefing sessions after each class are also offered for the tutor to seek advice or clarification on queries. These debriefing sessions are usually related to what students ask in class. On some occasions, these queries need to be referred to the programme staff as they are related to study pathways, elective options, etc. On other occasions, questions are related to aspects of T&I theory which the tutor is not clear about, or to practical T&I issues the tutor wants to re-confirm before advising students. It is always emphasised to tutors, new or experienced, that no tutors are expected to know the answer to every question posed in the classroom, and that it is completely acceptable to either defer it to the programme staff or delay the answer. Finally, a team teacher – who may be a programme staff member or an experienced tutor from another language background – is sometimes arranged through mutual agreement with the new tutor to join the tutorial to provide the latter with support and supplement their skill set. Sometimes this type of team-teaching lasts for a few sessions before the new tutor is comfortable to "go solo", while at other times, the arrangement lasts for the whole semester as the new tutor feels more comfortable with support throughout all sessions. Understandably, team-teaching can be an expensive arrangement, particularly for a small student cohort and when the other teacher is not on staff and must also be remunerated from the casual teacher budget. Normally, a case must be made to university management and evidence provided to show potential future demand in the language in question; otherwise, this is not a sustainable arrangement for the programme or the university, for obvious reasons. This reflects the conundrum faced by all university programmes of balancing financial viability with the social responsibility of supporting minority languages that otherwise would not be offered at a higher education level. Kelly (2017) observes the same difficulties, remarking that "it will never be the case that universities can offer all the languages demanded on mainstream translator programmes, and institutions need to look for imaginative and creative ways to cover societal needs in this regard" (p. 36).

Using Miner and Nicodemus's (2021) "Staircase Model", the course designs of the three T&I degrees at RMIT embody the progression from work-ready to profession-ready. Due to our focus on community translation, Table 10.1 shows only the translation stream, although all three degrees offer the flexibility for students

TABLE 10.1 Course Mapping of Core Translation Courses Using the Staircase Model

		Courses (Short Title for Each Course in Bold)	Graduate Certificate	Graduate Diploma	Master's Degree
Work-Ready	(1) Theoretical foundations	**Theoretical Bases** of Translating and Interpreting	x	x	x
		Discourse Studies for Translators and Interpreters	x	x	x
	(2) Theoretical applications	**Advanced Theories** of Translating and Interpreting			x
		Advanced Discourse Studies			x
	(3) Situated community engagement and situated authentic activity where possible	**Translation** Certification Practice	x	x	x
		Translation and Technologies		x	x
Profession-Ready	(4) Work Integrated Learning (WIL)-situated authentic activity	**Ethics** and professional issues (WIL embedded)	x	x	x
	(5) WIL-situated authentic or simulated activity	**Extended Professional Project** (WIL embedded)			x

to specialise in translation or interpreting exclusively, or both. For those doing the graduate diploma and master's degree, additional T&I elective courses are offered to fulfil the required number of credit points before graduation.

3.2 Situated Learning

According to Miner and Nicodemus (2021), situated learning is "a theory that holds as its foundational tenet that individuals learn by engaging in experiences in authentic environments" (p. 23). Learners are, therefore, expected to grapple with real-world problems and the associated social interactions. Four cornerstones that contribute to the authenticity of situated learning include: "(1) real-world context where the students will apply what they have learned, (2) authentic activity, (3) social interactions, and (4) use of tools" (Miner & Nicodemus, 2021, p. 33). In this section, we explore two types of situated learning offered in our programmes.

3.2.1 Work Integrated Learning

Work Integrated Learning (WIL) broadly refers to "on-campus and workplace learning activities and experiences which integrate theory with practice in academic learning programs" (Jackson, 2013, p. 99). It has become an important element in higher education institutions in Australia and abroad due to increased attention on preparing students for transition into the workforce, as well as governments seeking direct links between employability and higher education in return for their funding (Zegwaard et al., 2021). WIL activities can take shape in many forms to respond to different disciplinary needs and organisational contexts. They can range from the more traditional format of full-time immersion in the workplace, such as work placements and internships, to other forms of engagement with an external stakeholder on campus such as work-related projects, student consultation projects, or an external stakeholder as a client (Zegwaard et al., 2021). Most importantly, WIL is "an educational partnership between industry, professions or community, university and their students" (Trede, 2021, p. xii), and it is underpinned by "principles of the involvement of external stakeholders, the learning activity as an intentional component within the curriculum, and the tasks students undertake being authentic and meaningful practices of work" (Zegwaard et al., 2021, p. 6). After its development and accompanying scholarly attention over recent decades, WIL is now widely accepted as augmenting graduate employability in a number of ways: (a) building student confidence in their capabilities in professional practice; (b) fostering student appreciation of the importance of employability skills; (c) introducing students to the workplace, enhancing their understanding of workplace values and culture, and developing professionalism; and (d) improving future employment opportunities (Jackson, 2013).

As shown in Table 10.1, WIL is embedded in the course Ethics and Professional Issues for the graduate certificate and the graduate diploma, with the master's degree entailing the additional course Extended Professional Project (EPP) to offer further WIL experience. At RMIT, WIL is formally assessed for credit towards the qualification. In the EPP course, for example, which is normally taken in the last semester before a student graduates, WIL takes the format of either an authentic or a simulated translation project of a substantial text (or combination of a few) of at least 6,000 English words or equivalent. Most students undertake community translation projects, although there are a few who are interested in literary translation and are also fully supported. Students must provide a quote for their "translation service"; nominate a delivery date; undergo peer checking arranged by the translation commissioner, as per industry practice (in this case, organised by the course coordinator); undertake revision in response to the peer checking received; and submit a final translation by the due date. Holz-Mänttäri's (1984) "Translatorial Action Model" is used to guide students' practice in this project, as it is most applicable to real-world, commercial, non-literary translation and focuses on producing a target text that is functionally communicative for the target audience (Munday, 2012). This model regards translation as a communicative process involving different players and is therefore ideal for students to gain an appreciation of the various roles involved in the translation commission, as well as the stakes of each role. In addition to the translation component, this course also entails a 4,000-word essay in which students analyse their translation issues and use T&I theories to justify their translation decisions – an important competency to demonstrate before they complete the master's degree. In the essay, students are required to explicate their translation commission using the Translatorial Action Model; this is designed to reinforce their ability to apply the analysis framework to their future community translation practice.

3.3.2 Work Experience

Another form of situated learning closely related to WIL – but clearly delineated by the university as work experience – relates to activities which do not form part of assessment of a course or contribute to credit towards their qualification. Although the programme is constantly on the lookout for authentic translation projects to facilitate situated learning, projects sometimes become available when all EPP students have already identified and started their own project. In such cases, these opportunities are offered as work experience to students doing the Translation Certification Practice course who are still in the work-ready stage of their learning trajectory. For example, an authentic translation project of a convention on fishery resources in the South Pacific Ocean was undertaken by a team of volunteer students when they were studying the Translation Certification Practice course in the second semester of 2020. The students were given a full briefing on the project, contextual information about the convention, translation protocols, and translation feedback which was provided by the organisation offering this opportunity. A project such as this fulfils the four cornerstones of situated learning experience, with authentic translation activity in a real-world context, so students must use tools (i.e., the resources they have) to respond to project demands, whereby social interactions were facilitated among students in the project team as well as between students and the offering organisation. Another example, in the same semester, was an authentic text for children on how to deal with COVID-19, written by a well-established children's book writer. It was translated into other languages (some of which were minority languages) to add to the collection of languages the author was able to source translators for. The languages for this project included Indonesian, Korean, Mongolian, Thai, and Vietnamese. The author collated all the translations onto a free-access website as a public service. Our programme also partnered with RMIT's Centre for Urban Research in a project designed to elicit input from multicultural and multilingual communities in the suburb of Sunshine North, Melbourne, regarding the transformation of the suburb. Students who had completed the Translation and/or EPP course(s) and were from Burmese, Chinese, Italian, and Vietnamese backgrounds were offered a work experience opportunity to translate all community-facing documents into their LOTE, including participant information sheets, consent forms, recruitment advertisements, etc. Students then received feedback on their translated work from their respective language tutors and undertook a revision exercise to finalise the translated materials.

When organising WIL of work experience activities, it is important to bear in mind that the centrality of such activities is the pedagogical and experiential value students gain from them in order to prepare for their future professional practice. Therefore, it is extremely important to have clear guidance and supervision from the course coordinator and input throughout the activity by the offering organisation, such as briefing on the project and the organisation, work protocols, relevant industry standards, and feedback for work completed. The activities should not be used as a way for the industry partner to save money for the work which they would otherwise have to pay professional translators to deliver. Both the course and the industry partner must commit to nurturing and supporting students, and making the students' experience positive, so that their contribution is in turn meaningful and rigorous (Zegwaard et al., 2021)

3.3 Reflective Practice

In addition to assessments which are translation proper and which are paramount to evaluate the technical competence of the translation student, reflective writing is built into the assessment of various courses such as Translation, Ethics, and Advanced Discourse to encourage ongoing thinking processes to bridge theory and practice (Ono & Ichii, 2019). This form of learning is particularly fitting for a practice profession such as translation. According to Schön (1987), reflection for professionals can take place during an experience or an event – *reflection in action* – and afterwards – *reflection on action*. The reflective entry writing can capture both forms of reflection, and thus foster the student's capacity to think and make sense of their learning (Cisero, 2006; Morrison, 1996; O'Connell & Dyment, 2011). We use the DIEP strategy adapted from Boud et al. (1985) to guide students' reflection. This approach requires each student to structure their reflection in four steps: to **D**escribe an insight or new understanding, to **I**nterpret the insight, to **E**valuate what has been learnt, and finally, to **P**lan how this learning will be applied in future practice (Boud et al., 1985). This strategy is similar to Rolfe et al.'s (2001) three questions asked of the so-called "helping professions" (i.e., nurses, counsellors, and social workers): *What? So what? Now what?* In a similar vein, students reflect on *what* the problem or difficulty that they encountered was, what their role was in the situation, what was good or bad about the experience, etc.; they then consider *so what* does this experience tell me or mean to me and to others, what is my new understanding of the situation, what are the broader issues arising from this situation; and lastly, they ask: *now what* do I need to do in order to make things better or to improve my practice, and what may be the consequences of this action?

Writing reflections is significantly different from other more traditional genres of academic writing such as essays, reports, or literature reviews, which postgraduate students in the programme are generally more used to. However, the experience of the programme has been that reflective assessments are well received by students, and most are able to demonstrate deep learning (Moon, 1999) through their writing, with the assistance of a few exemplars from past students posted on the learning platform. It is posited that through situated learning embedded in the work-ready stage of the Translation course, all students – regardless of having prior real-world translation experience or not – are able to experience near-authentic translation practice through which they can reflect upon, both *in action* and *on action*. This makes their reflective writing significantly more meaningful and purposeful. In Ono and Ichii's (2019) study, research participants reported difficulties in reflective writing, as this was required in one course only, rather than across a few. Their study showed that conducting reflective practice in only one course did not provide participants with the opportunity to develop their reflexivity and to articulate it through writing. Therefore, this form of assessment has been introduced in multiple courses in our programmes, which has strengthened students' reflective practice and reinforced their appreciation of the utility of such practice. Moreover, reflective practice journals allow educators to track each student's progress and implement remedial measures in the curriculum if the need for additional support is identified.

3.4 Student-Led Learning

There is no consistent definition of *student-led learning* in the literature. What can be confirmed is that it originated in experiential learning (Kolb, 2015), which is based on students' ability to experience – and therefore learn – and in the concept of active learning techniques (Bernot & Metzler, 2014; Prince, 2004), which is to engage students in the learning process and to defer the instructional role to the student rather than the teacher. For the purposes of this chapter, we opt for the term *student-led learning* since it is more self-explanatory. Such pedagogical design is an inherently learner-centric way of learning which focuses on students' autonomous control over the learning process. It allows students to come to a decision on what to learn and how to learn, through which students develop learning skills in addition to knowledge (Bernot & Metzler, 2014), while internalising the individual learning experiences at cognitive, emotional, perceptive, and behavioural levels (Bordia, 2019).

An example of student-led learning is implemented in the Discourse Studies course (see Table 10.1), whereby regular weekly lectures as well as weekly student-led learning sessions are scheduled. Moreover, a *flipped classroom* design is adopted for this course, the idea of which is squarely student-led learning and pre-class preparation. Before students attend each weekly lecture, they must have read the required texts, supplemented by a five-question quiz to bolster understanding. The teacher-led lecture is highly interactive, interspersed with active learning techniques such as problem solving, questioning, brainstorming, and audience response (Steinert & Snell, 1999). For example, the week when the lecture content covers Searle's (1969) three speech acts – locutionary, illocutionary, and perlocutionary acts – students are put in small groups to choose a speech act – for example, a favour or a complaint – and to:

- Discuss how it is performed in English and in their LOTE.
- Discuss cross-cultural differences: how it is performed, how it is responded to, and why.
- Discuss whether what people say is influenced by different views of social behaviour or different views of social relationships.
- Role-play with their group.

The student-led sessions are structured around the specific topics related to the lecture and prescribed readings of the week. For example, in the week when ideological issues are covered in the lecture, the following statement is provided in the student-led session: "Given that 'translation, simply because of its existence, has always been ideological'" (Fawcett, 1997, p. 107), and students are asked to discuss their thoughts on the following questions:

- What are the different ways a professional translator might encounter discourse considerations relating to ideology in their work?
- What are the different ways in which ideology might affect professional translation practice?
- In which ways can the translator–commissioner relationship influence a translator's professional decision-making?
- Think of a situation in which a translator might ignore an author's intent or worldview in translating a document. In other words, how might we justify in discourse terms ignoring a document's author?
- What approaches might be available to a professional translator when disagreeing with opinions contained in a document they are required to translate?
- In which ways might an agency, publisher, or other commissioning party to a translation assignment influence the work of a professional translator?

In the curriculum, topical and related newspaper articles are added to the materials for students to relate to the topic in discussion and link theory to practice. After each student-led session, each student is also required to make a discussion board contribution on the learning platform, which accounts for one mark per week as an incentive for them to document their learning and reflection, as well as to encourage peer learning.

Another example of student-led learning is designed into one of the assessment tasks for Advanced Discourse, when students are to write an essay analysing a written text for translation by considering text type, genre, and thematic contents of the source text and target text in their cultural and linguistic environments. Rather than assigning a set text for all students, the assessment asks students to look for a text of their own choice, which can be from one of the areas covered in the course, such as tourism, technical, advertising, legal, and medical translation. This design allows autonomy for students to encourage engagement and to choose a topic that is most relevant to their language combination and future professional translation environment.

4. Challenges and Future Insights

This chapter outlined the nature of Australia's multicultural and multilingual society whereby demands for community translation arise. Facilitating access to information for community members who are not proficient in English is the responsibility of community translators. Attending a university T&I programme prepares aspiring translators to be equipped with the required skills and knowledge to pass the NAATI certification test and enter the profession. With the huge range of languages spoken by community members in Australia, university T&I programmes have been faced with the dilemma of fulfilling their social responsibility to provide education in minority languages for small numbers of students or opting for languages that can achieve a reasonable class number to ensure programme viability. In recent years, T&I programmes at RMIT have been admitting small numbers of students in a broad range of minority languages. For the more theoretical courses, using reflective and student-led pedagogical designs provides students with enriched and autonomous learning experiences, while for the practical translation course, innovative methods of both non–language-specific and language-specific pedagogy have been used. The challenge is always in giving all students – even if they are from minority language backgrounds – the best possible learning experience within a budget.

References

Australian Bureau of Statistics. (2017). *Census reveals a fast changing, culturally diverse nation*. www.abs.gov.au/ausstats/abs@.nsf/lookup/media%20release3

Australian Bureau of Statistics. (2022). *2021 census*. www.abs.gov.au

Australian Institute of Multicultural Affairs. (1982). *Evaluation of post-arrival programs and services*. Australian Institute of Multicultural Affairs.

Bell, S. (1997). The challenges of setting and monitoring the standards of community interpreting: An Australian perspective. In S. E. Carr, R. P. Roberts, A. Dufour, & D. Steyn, *The Critical Link: Interpreters in the community* (pp. 93–108). John Benjamins Publishing Company.

Bennett, D. (2019). Meeting society's expectations of graduates: Education for the public good. In J. Higgs, G. Crisp, & W. Letts (Eds.), *Education for employability: The employability agenda, Volume 1* (pp. 35–48). Brill. https://doi.org/10.1163/9789004400832_003

Bernot, M. J, & Metzler, J. (2014). A comparative study of instructor- and student-led learning in a large nonmajors biology course: Student performance and perceptions. *Journal of College Science Teaching, 44*(1), 48–55. https://doi.org/10.2505/4/jcst14_044_01_48

Bordia, S. (2019). Experiential learning through student-led assessments: The noodle bar strategy. In M. A. Gonzalez-Perez, K. Lynden, & V. Tara (Eds.), *The Palgrave handbook of learning and teaching international business and management* (pp. 359–380). Palgrave Macmillan. https://doi.org/10.1007/978-3-030-20415-0_17

Brown, J. S., Collins, A., & Duguid, P. (1989). Situated cognition and the culture of learning. *Educational Researcher, 18*(1), 32–42. https://doi.org/10.3102/0013189X018001032

Boud, D. J., Keogh, R., & Walker, D. (Eds.). (1985). *Reflection: Turning experience into learning*. Kogan Page.

Cisero, C. A. (2006). Does reflective journal writing improve course performance? *College Teaching, 54*(2), 231–236. https://doi.org/10.3200/CTCH.54.2.231-236

Cooke, M. S. (2009). Interpreter ethics versus customary law: Quality and compromise in Aboriginal languages interpreting. In S. E. Carr, A. Dufour, & D. Steyn (Eds.), *The Critical Link 5: Quality in interpreting – a shared responsibility* (pp. 85–97). John Benjamins Publishing Company. https://doi.org/10.1075/btl.87.08coo

Debets, J. (2018). The internationalisation of Australia's higher education system: Trading away human rights. *Griffith Journal of Law and Dignity, 6*(1), 23–64.

Downing, B. T. (1998). Community interpreting and translation in the USA context. In C. Valero-Garcés & I. de la Cruz (Eds.), *Nuevas Tendencias y Aplicaciones de la Traducción* (pp. 15–33). Universidad de Alcalá de Henares.

Fawcett, P. (1997). *Translation and language: Linguistic theories explained*. St. Jerome.

Galbally, F. (1978). *Migrant services and programs: Report of the review of post-arrival programs and services for migrants*. Australian Government Publishing Service.

González, E. (2013). *Intérpretes comunitarios formados y no formados, y el significado del término "profesional"* [Trained and untrained community interpreters and the meaning of "professional"]. [Unpublished doctoral dissertation]. University of New South Wales.

González, E. (2019). Professional development as a vehicle on the road towards professionalism: The AUSIT experience. *Intralinea, 21*, 1–10.

González, E., & Revolta, A. (2021). A pedagogical approach to work integrated learning in conference interpreting. In R. Porlán Moreno & C. Arnedo Villaescusa (Eds.), *Interpreting in the classroom: Tools for teaching* (pp. 153–171). UCO Press.

González-Davies, M., & Enríquez-Raído, V. (2016). Situated learning in translator and interpreter training: Bridging research and good practice. *The Interpreter and Translator Trainer, 10*(1), 1–11. https://doi.org/10.1080/1750399X.2016.1154339

Hale, S. (2004). *The discourse of court interpreting: Discourse practices of the law, the witness and the interpreter*. John Benjamins Publishing Company. https://doi.org/10.1075/btl.52

Hale, S., García, I., Hlavac, J., Kim, M., Lai, M., Turner, B., & Slatyer, H. (2012). *Improvements to NAATI testing. Development of a conceptual overview for a new model for NAATI standards, testing and assessment*. University of New South Wales. www.naati.com.au/wp-content/uploads/2020/01/Improvements-to-NAATI-Testing.pdf

Hlavac, J. (2021). The development of community translation and interpreting in Australia. In J. Wakabayashi & M. O'Hagan (Eds.), *Translating and interpreting in Australia and New Zealand* (pp. 65–85). Routledge. https://doi.org/10.4324/9781003150770

Holz-Manttäri, J. (1984). *Translatorisches Handeln. Theorie und Methode* [Translational action. Theory and method]. Suomalainen Tiedeakatemia.

Jackson, D. (2013). The contribution of work-integrated learning to undergraduate employability skill outcomes. *Asia-Pacific Journal of Cooperative Education*, *14*(2), 99–115.

Jakubowicz, A., & Buckley, B. (1975). *Migrants and the legal system: Research report*. Australian Government Publishing Service.

Kelly, D. (2017). Education for community translation: Thirteen key ideas. In M. Taibi (Ed.), *Translating for the community* (pp. 26–41). Multilingual Matters.

Kiraly, D. (2000). *A social constructivist approach to translator education: Empowerment from theory to practice*. St Jerome.

Kolb, D. A. (2015). *Experiential learning: Experience as the source of learning and development* (2nd ed.). Pearson Education.

Mackintosh, J. (1999). Interpreters are made not born. *Interpreting*, *4*(1), 67–80. https://doi.org/10.1075/intp.4.1.08mac

Miner, A., & Nicodemus, B. (2021). *Situated learning in interpreter education: From the classroom to the community*. Palgrave Macmillan.

Moon, J. A. (1999). *Reflection in learning & professional development: Theory & practice*. Kogan Page.

Morrison, K. (1996). Developing reflective practice in higher degree students through a learning journal. *Studies in Higher Education*, *21*(3), 317–332. https://doi.org/10.1080/03075079612331381241

Mulayim, S., & Lai, M. (2017). *Ethics for police translators and interpreters*. CRC Press.

Munday, J. (2012). *Introducing translation studies: Theories and applications* (3rd ed.). Routledge.

O'Connell, T. S., & Dyment, J. E. (2011). The case of reflective journals: Is the jury still out? *Reflective Practice*, *12*(1), 47–59. https://doi.org/10.1080/14623943.2011.541093

Ono, A., & Ichii, R. (2019). Business students' reflection on reflective writing assessments. *Journal of International Education in Business*, *12*(2), 247–260. https://doi.org/10.1108/JIEB-08-2018-0036

Ozolins, U. (1995). *Research project: Interpreting and translating in Australia: An international response to communication needs in multilingual settings*. Centre for Research and Development in Interpreting and Translating, Deakin University.

Ozolins, U. (1998). *Interpreting and translating in Australia: Current issues and international comparisons*. Language Australia.

Pacheco Aguilar, R. (2016). The question of authenticity in translator education. In D. Kiraly et al. (Eds.), *Toward authentic experiential learning in translator education* (pp. 13–32). Mainz University Press.

Prince, M. (2004). Does active learning work? A review of the research. *Journal of Engineering Education (Washington, D.C.)*, *93*(3), 223–231. https://doi.org/10.1002/j.2168-9830.2004.tb00809.x

Pym, A. (2021). Contours of translation studies in Australia. In J. Wakabayashi & M. O'Hagan (Eds.), *Translating and interpreting in Australia and New Zealand* (pp. 291–309). Routledge. https://doi.org/10.4324/9781003150770

Richards, E. (2008). *Destination Australia: Migration to Australia since 1901* (Illustrated ed.). University of New South Wales Press.

Rolfe, G., Freshwater, D., & Jasper, M. (2001). *Critical reflection for nursing and the helping professions: A user's guide*. Palgrave Macmillan.

Schön, D. A. (1987). *Educating the reflective practitioner*. Jossey-Bass.

Searle, J. R. (1969). *Speech acts: An essay in the philosophy of language*. Cambridge University Press.

Senate Standing Committee on Education and the Arts. (1984). *Report on a national language policy*. Australian Government Publishing Service.

Steinert, Y., & Snell, L. S. (1999). Interactive lecturing: Strategies for increasing participation in large group presentations. *Medical Teacher*, *21*(1), 37–42. https://doi.org/10.1080/01421599980011

Taibi, M., & Ozolins, U. (2016). *Community translation*. Bloomsbury Academic.

Taibi, M., Ozolins, U., & Maximous, A. (2021). Interpreter education in Australia: Community settings, generic skills. In J. Wakabayashi & M. O'Hagan (Eds.), *Translating and interpreting in Australia and New Zealand* (pp. 86–104). Routledge. https://doi.org/10.4324/9781003150770

Trede, F. (2021). Foreword. In S. J. Ferns, A. D. Rowe, & K. E. Zegwaard (Eds.), *Advances in research, theory and practice in work-integrated learning: Enhancing employability for a sustainable future* (p. xii). Routledge. https://doi.org/10.4324/9781003021049

Zegwaard, K. E., Ferns, S. J., & Rowe, A. D. (2021). Contemporary insights into the practice of work-integrated learning in Australia. In S. J. Ferns, A. D. Rowe, & K. E. Zegwaard (Eds.), *Advances in research, theory and practice in work-integrated learning: Enhancing employability for a sustainable future* (pp. 1–14). Routledge. https://doi.org/10.4324/9781003021049

INDEX

Note: Page numbers in *italics* indicate figures.

Abdel-Latif, M. M. M. 104
Abkari, A. 173
Aboriginal languages, Australia 212–213
Adem, Ali 119
Advocacy 27–31; AUSIT Code of Ethics 56; as component of role image 45; constraints on 30–31; Lesch's argument for 42
Al-Dosari, H. 163
Aloni, Taysir 173
Amanatidou, Despina 2
Angelelli, C. V. 44, 46
Aotearoa New Zealand: community translation of health texts 104–5; community translation with visuals and voice-overs 121–123; conventions of written Samoan 137; misleading translation choices 131; misunderstandings of medical concepts 109–112, 127–130; overview 101–103, 123–125; Samoan translations of health texts 105–118; Talking Cards project 118–121
Aplin, Thomas 183
Arabic language 17–18; Arabic-Spanish translation 171–173
Askari, M. 144
assertiveness 35, 36
asylum seekers 27–28; and life stories 181–190; *see also* migration flows
Auckland, Aotearoa NZ 102

Australia: COVID-19 outbreaks 68; NAATI certification system 145; overview 212–213; 2021 survey of LSPs *10*, 10–18, *11*, *13*; *see also* English-Japanese translators case study
Australian Institute of Interpreters and Translators (AUSIT) 1, 6; Code of Ethics 42–43, 51, 56; community translation protocols 19

Bachir, Mohamed Raouf 183
back translation 80, 88, 150; English/Samoan in Aotearoa New Zealand 106–117, 126–127, 129–135
Bager, L. 149–150
Balogh, K. 175
Bandeira, D. R. 149
Barsky, R. F. 28
Bateson, Gregory 32
Bennett, D. 216
Between Meals (Fisher & Markham) 185
Blackledge, A. 28
Bloom, B. S. 34
Bloom's taxonomies 34
Boud, D. J. 223
briefing sessions 19, 146, 155, 157, 162, 163, 219
Bringle, R. G. 196
Brown, J. S. 216
Buch-Kromann, M. 147
Bugel, T. 208
Burns, A. 77

Index

CALD (culturally and linguistically diverse) communities 5–6, 8–9, 18
California Department of Education quality indicators 145
Cantonese language 102, 120
Carl, M. 147
Carney, T. R. 29
certification systems 143, 214; Australia (NAATI) 2, 6, 145
challenging languages *13*, 17–18
children's books 222–223
Chinese language *see* Cantonese language; English-Chinese health care translation study
Chung, L. 15
Ciribuco, A. 187
Çoban, F. 34
co-design approach 7–9
collaboration (co-design approach) 7–9
community checkers/readers 12, 17–18
community engagement 8–9, 104, 196, 204
community feedback 18
community translation: background and overview 1–2, 23–26, 103, 142–144, 181, 195–196; integrated with service-learning 204–209; professionalisation of 2, 143; *see also* translators
competence: cultural competence 174–175; education for 146–147, 205, 207; types of competence 205–206; *see also* quality assurance; soft skills
computer-assisted translation (CAT) tools 12, 17
contextual issues: ideational and interpersonal meanings 76–77; meanings 69–70, *70*; and quality assurance 8–9; values, 162–163; for wiretap translators 174–175
cookbooks, translation of 184–185, 186–188
Cooking a Home (Cortada) 185
Cortada, Pilar Puig 185
COVID-19 pandemic 2, 216; Australian study on community/government collaboration 8; and increased volume of translation work 15; response in Australia 8–9
creare approach 23
Creese, A. 28
Crezee, Ineke 3, 77, 102, 118–123
criminal investigations 167, 169; *see also* wiretaps in Spain, translation of
Critical Link Conference 7

Crots, E. 53, 57
cultural mediation 45, 190; *see also* intercultural mediation
Cultus (Katan & Spinzi) 30

Darwish, A. 30
Davies, P. 202
debriefing sessions 151, 219
detachment, professional 44; *see also* impartiality
Devakumar, D. 6
DIEP strategy (Boud) 223
Discourse Studies course, RMIT 225
Downing, B. T. 214–215
Dut, G. M. 7
Dutt, R. 36
dynamic equivalence (Nida) 72

education for translators 146–147; *see also* training programmes
El-Madkouri Maataoui, Mohamed 3
Emmerich, Karen 183
emotional intelligence (EI) 32, 34–35, 163; *see also* interpersonal skills
emotional quotient (EQ) 34
empathy 35–36, 182
EMT (European Master's in Translation) group 31–32
English-Chinese health care translation study: assessment results 77–87; and contextual meanings 89–92; data 97–98; linguistic analysis 87–89; methodology 70–76; sample texts 93–96; semantic meanings 76–77
English-Japanese translators case study: conclusions and implications 56–59; data 60–65; methodology 45–47; qualitative analysis 53–56; quantitative analysis 47–53
errors, translation 2
Esmail, Ebrahim 185
ethics: professional contrasted with personal 57–58; in training curricula 217
Ethics and Professional Issues course (RMIT) 221–222
European Court of Human Rights 168
European Master's in Translation (EMT) group 31–32
Evaluation of Post-Arrival Programs and Services 213
Evangelista, E.-M. 189
exclusion, linguistic, dangers of 5–6
Extended Professional Project (EPP) at RMIT 221–222

Index

family storytelling 182, 194
Farsi language 17–18
Faszer-McMahon, D. 208
Federation of Ethnic Communities of Australia (FECCA) 18, 19
Fisher, Dani 185
Fishman, J. A. 123
Fleary, S. A. 103
flipped classroom design 225
Forensic-Linguistic Tap Expert (FoLiTex) 175
Fransman, Karrie 185
Fukuno, Maho 2–3
functional equivalence and contextual values 162–163
functionalist translation theories 7, 27

"Galbally Report, The" 213
Gardner's model of multiple intelligences 34–35
Geldenhuys, N. 29
German language 157, 172
Goethals, Virginie 184
González, Erika 2, 4, 10, 18, 216, 217, 218
Göpferich, S. 31
Gouadec, D. 142, 143
graphic novels, translation of 188–190
Grey, A. 5, 18
Griffee, D. T. 149
Grzywacz, J. G. 162
Guido, P. 162

Hague, D. 208
Hall, E. T. 34
Hall's Triad of Culture 32–34, *33*
Hatcher, J. A. 196
health care translation: community level 69; community translation 104–105; health literacy 2, 103–104, 123–124; health vocabulary 107–109; medical concepts, misunderstandings of 109–112; pragmatic equivalence 69; Talking Cards 118–121; *see also* oncological and palliative care settings
heritage languages 103, 123, 125
hermeneutic model 58
Hill-Madsen, Aage 29
Hindi language 13, 102, 123
Hlavac, J. 212
Holz-Mänttäri, J. 7–8, 222
"Homeland as Exile, Exile as Homeland" (Wali) 183
Hong Kong 181–190
House, J. 144

Hubscher-Davidson, S. 32, 34, 163
human rights 168, 183; *see also* advocacy
Hymes, D. 34

"I Am a Refugee" (Bachir) 183
Iceberg/Logical Levels model 32–34, 36–37
Ichii, R. 224
ideational meanings 76–77
immigration and life stories 181–190; *see also* migrants
impartiality: as component of role image 44–45; in English-Japanese translators case study 50–51; as ethical principle 42–43; and professional backgrounds of translators 52
Indigenous languages, Australia 212–213
intercultural mediation 2; *see also* cultural mediation
International Community Translation Research Group (ICTRG) 1
International Conference on Community Translation 1
interpersonal skills 31–35, 76–77, 206–207
Interpreter's Interpersonal Role Inventory (IPRI) 46
Interpreting and Translating for Perinatal and End-of-Life Care project 150
intersemiotic translation 186, 190
intrahistory 200
invisibility of translator 44–45
ISO 9000 standard 145

Jamieson, Victoria 185–186, 188–190
Japan; *see* English-Japanese translators case study
Japan Association for Interpreting and Translation Studies 47
Japan Association of Translators (JAT) 47
Jenkins, A. 203–204
Ji, M. 162
Judd, J. 5

Kabdi, Hakim 185
Kalfoss, M. 149
Kaplan, Jennifer 183
Katan, David 2, 31; survey methodology 23–26, *25*
Kautz, T. 32
Kelly, D. 1, 31, 205, 206, 219–220
knowledge-in-action 216, 217
Koby, G. S. 144
Kruger, H. 52, 57

Lai, Miranda 4, 18, 214
Lambert, J. 43
Lampard, Pristine 186
latere approach 23, 27, 36
Leanza, Y. 36
LECrim (Spain, Organic Act 13/2015) 168–170
legal translation 168, 196
Lesch, H. 6, 42
Lin, S. 162
Lizardi-Rivera, C. 208
L'Odyssée D'Hakim (Toulmé) 185
Logical Levels/Iceberg model 32–34, 36–37

machine translation (MT) 12, 17
Mandarin language 17, 28, 69, 71–72, 102, 119–120
Markham, Lauren 185
Marssid, N. 162
Martin, A. 173
Martin, G. S. 149
Martínez-Gómez, A. 208
Matthiessen, C. 70
Maus (Spiegelman) 185
Mayer, J. 34
Medical English as Lingua Franca (MEFL) 149, 157
Mekheimer, M. A. 163
Microhistory 200
migrants: in Aotearoa New Zealand 102; migrant texts 200–201; and translation demands 17
Migrants and the Legal System: Research Report 213
migration flows 17, 23, 24, 213; *see also* asylum seekers
Mind (mental health charity, UK) 28
Miner, A. 217, 218, 220, 221
minority languages 1, 149
Mohamed, Omar 185–186, 188–190
Morón, M. 27
Mosadeq, Ghazal 183
Mulayim, S. 214
Multidimensional Quality Metrics (MQM) 145, 157
multiple intelligences, model of (Gardner) 34–35

National Accreditation Authority for Translators and Interpreters (NAATI) 2, 6; Code of Ethics 43; formation of 213; role perception 51–53, 58–59; testing system 18, 214

National Association of Judiciary Interpreters and Translators (NAJIT) 27
navigator role in hospitals 119–121
Nelson, A. L. 208
neutrality *see* impartiality
New Zealand *see* Aotearoa New Zealand; English-Chinese health care translation study
New Zealand Ministry of Health (MoH) 121
New Zealand Society of Translators and Interpreters (NZSTI) 72
Neyestani, Mana 183
Nicodemus, B. 217, 218, 220, 221
Nida, Eugene 72
Niska, H. 142
non-cognitive competencies *see* soft skills
non-verbal communication 175
Nord, C. 144
Nutbeam, D. 103–104

O'Hagan, M. 143
Oliveira, S. E. S. 149
omissions and additions of information 113–117, 132–136
omissions of articles, prepositions, and particles in target text 126–127
oncological and palliative care settings: overview 147–150; quality assurance 162–163; study on accuracy of translations 150–155; study on patient response to translations 155–162
Ono, A. 224
operative texts 27
Ortega Herráez, J. M. 173
Over Under Sideways Down (Fransman) 185
Ozolins, U. 10, 42, 143, 144, 146, 195

PACTE project 31
palliative care settings *see* oncological and palliative care settings
pandemic *see* COVID-19 pandemic
participatory action research (PAR) 105
Persepolis (Satrapi) 185
Piller, Ingrid 6
POCA (patient-oriented and culturally appropriate) model 162
Polaron Language Services 8
Polish Association of Conference Interpreters (PSTK) 163
Polish-English translations 150–155
pragmatic equivalence: contextual meanings 69–70, *70*; health care translation 69; maximum equivalence

70; and methodology in English-Chinese study 72–76, *73*, *74*, *75*; and quality of service 68
pragmatism 57
process-oriented approaches 104
product-oriented approaches 104
professionalisation of translation 2, 143
profession-ready training 212–220
Promoting Intercultural Competence in Translators (PICT) 31
Prunč, E. 44
public messages 6–7
public service translation *see* community translation
Punjabi language 13, 17, 102
"pure" community contrasted with non-community translators 24–26
Pym, A. 26, 35

quality assurance 7–9, 16, 19, 144–147; study on accuracy of translations 150–155; for wiretap translators 174

Rahim, M. S. 144
reader-oriented approaches 23
reader reaction 24–25
reception studies 104–105
Redelinghuys, K. 147
reflective practice as component of training 199, 202–203, 207, 223–224
refugee journeys and life stories 181–190
refugees 17
"Refugee Stories: Idomeni Greece" 183
Reiss, K. 27, 144, 146
Report on a National Language Policy 213
requirements for wiretap translators 171–174
research questionnaires, translation of 149–150
reverse community translation 182–190; need for 182–184
revision of materials 16
Revolta, A. 216, 217, 218
Roberson, L. 208
roles of translators 44–45, 48–49, 51–53
Rolfe, G. 223–224
Rosado, L. 197
Routledge Handbook of Translation and Activism, The (Gould & Tahmasebian) 30
Rowan, Dr. Janet 119
Royal Melbourne Institute of Technology (RMIT) 1, 4, 214, 215; case study of translation programme 218–226
Rueda-Acedo, Alicia 3–4, 208
Ruiz-Cortés, E. 29

RUN Cookbook, The (Lampard) 184–185; translation process, 186–188
RUN Hong Kong 184–185
Russell, Bertrand 32

Salaets, H. 175
Salovey, P. 34
Samoan language: conventions of written Samoan 137; Samoan/English translation 101–102; translations of health texts 105–118
Satrapi, Marjane 185
Sawyer, Brenda 184, 186
Schön, D. A. 223
Scott, J. L. 208
Searle, J. R. 225
Seattle Children's Hospital, Center for Diversity and Health Equity 118–119
self-translation (auto-translation) 189, 190
semantic meanings 76–77
service learning 196, 197–198, 204–209
Severin, A. A. 5
Sewell, P. 26
Shaw, S. 208
Sheehey, P. 203–204
"Short Guide for Being a Perfect Political Refugee, The" (Neyestani) 183
Simeoni, D. 26, 44
Sin, K. F. 88
situated learning: RMIT case study 221–223; Situated Learning model 205, 217, 218
skopos theory 7, 57, 144, 199
Smith, J. A. 5
Social Care Institute for Excellence (SCIE) 28
social mission *see* advocacy
soft skills: training in 35–36; and translation competence 31–35
Somali-speaking families 119
Soto-Aranda, Beatriz 3
Spain, translation of wiretaps 167–176
Spanish language 157; Spanish-speaking immigrants U.S. 26–27
speech act theory (Searle) 225
Spiegelman, Art 185
Spinzi, Cinzia 2
Stachowiak, Karolina 3, 155–162
Stachowiak-Szymczak, Katarzyna 3, 155–162
Staircase Model (Miner & Nicodemus) 217, 218, 220
Stories to Our Children (STOC) programme 194, 197; final celebration

203–204; process 198–203; translation into English 197–198
student-led learning 224–226
style guides 18
systemic functional linguistics (SFL) 70

Taibi, M. 5–6, 8, 18, 24, 42, 103, 104, 142, 143, 144, 145–146, 155, 173, 181, 195, 196, 205, 213
Takimoto, M. 53, 57
Talking Cards project (Crezee) 118–121
Teng, Wei 3, 104, 162
testimonios and testimonial texts 194, 202, 203, 209
text-centred contrasted with reader-oriented approaches 23
Theory of Logical Levels 32
Thompson, G. L. 208
Tocaimaza-Hatch, C. 208
Todorova, Marija 3
Tongan language 13, 102, 123
Toulmé, Fabien 185
Townsley, B. 24, 181
Trabalik, Martin 183
training programmes: approaches to 26–27; in Australia 214–217; curriculum design 217; real world knowledge 215–216; and service-learning 196, 197–198, 204–209; and soft skills 35–36; at University of Texas at Arlington (UTA) 194–196; for wiretap translators 171
transcreation 26–27
Translation Automation User Society Dynamic Quality Framework (DQF) 145
translation studies, community translation as subfield 23–24
Translatorial Action (Holz-Mänttäri) 7
"Translatorial Action Model" (Holz-Mänttäri) 222

translators: competencies 206–207; concern for reader 24–26, *25*; as cultural mediators 189; misunderstandings of medical concepts 109–112, 127–130; and pay-scaling 19; profession development (PD) for 19; recruitment of 19, 163; reflection on choices 112–113; roles 44–45, 48–49, 51–53; and soft skills 31–35; training initiatives 20
Translators and Interpreters Australia (TIA) 6

Ukrainian language 157
Unamuno, M. 200
uncertainty avoidance 35
University of Salento 26–27
University of Texas at Arlington (UTA) translation course 194; STOC programme 197–204

Valero-Garcés, C. 173
Venuti, L. 44
verbatim translations 175
Vermeer, H. J. 7, 27, 144, 146
Vietnamese language 157

Wali, Najem 183
Way Evaluation Sheet 199, 201
When Stars Are Scattered (Jamieson & Mohamed) 185–186; translation process 188–190
wiretaps in Spain, translation of 167–176
Wong Soon, Hoy Neng 3, 101–102, 104, 105–118, 125
work experience during training 222–223
Work Integrated Learning (WIL) 221–222
work-ready to profession-ready training 220
Wright, Jonathan 183

Yamamoto, K. 146
Yu, A. 26

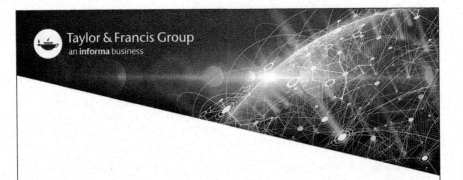